Investing in Information

Andy Bytheway

Investing in Information

The Information Management Body of Knowledge

Springer

Andy Bytheway
Department of Computer Science
University of the Western Cape
Bellville
South Africa

ISBN 978-3-319-11908-3   ISBN 978-3-319-11909-0 (eBook)
DOI 10.1007/978-3-319-11909-0

Library of Congress Control Number: 2014951687

Springer Cham Heidelberg New York Dordrecht London

Printed on acid-free paper

Springer is part of Springer Science+Business Media (www.springer.com)

This book is dedicated to all those amazing people who have overcome the endless challenges of science, and research, and even management, in bringing new technologies into the world.

It especially celebrates and acknowledges the work of Charlie Kao, who gave us fibre optics.

In the time between his seminal publication in 1966 and the Nobel Prize in 2009 Charlie was derided by some of his peers and periodically ignored by management. Those of us who have been privileged to know him are in awe of his scientific achievement and amazed by his passion for business, education and society at large. What a difference he has made.

Thank you, Charlie.

Foreword

At the outset I must declare that I am a long-time believer in (and teacher of) the IMBOK, in my opinion it is the nearest thing to a comprehensive framework of information technology and systems in business. In an elegantly simple way it explains how information and communications technology links with and contributes to business strategy, and how business strategy drives investment in information technology. More importantly, to me as a teacher of business information systems it provides a useful framework for understanding the difference between technology and systems and how they fit within a typical business structure. It is a model that is easily understood by both business and IT professionals.

In this book Andy has extended the IMBOK to highlight Business Information as a counterpart to the Business Process domain. This is a very important addition, as in many modern organisations the main entity being transacted or processed is information. In this new feature of the IMBOK we are offered two interesting insights: first the 64 characteristics of information, and second the Information Portfolio which is based on the internal/external and structured/unstructured dichotomies.

Other important features of this book are:

- It takes a reflective rather than a prescriptive approach, making the book easier to read and a better basis for discussion. The models and techniques covered are offered as important and potentially helpful ideas, not as some kind of absolute truth.
- In keeping with the IMBOK itself, the book presents quite complicated ideas in a simple structure; it includes at least one important new model (the Information Portfolio) and a rationalisation of several existing well-known models.
- There are short summary chapters towards the end of the book that give useful advice: first to practitioners and second to academic researchers.
- There are 61 figures that illustrate and consolidate the ideas that are presented.
- Finally, there is an extensive index that provides useful backup to the otherwise easy structure of the book.

I would recommend this book to ICT practitioners who are lost in the functional decomposition that is taking place in the ICT industry at the moment, and who want to get an understanding of the "big picture" and how they fit into it. Also to managers in both business and technology roles, who need to have a working framework for linking business to technology opportunities and a framework that can facilitate conversation between technical and non-technical managers at all levels. Finally, I would recommend the IMBOK to academics as a model rich with application and explanatory power that really deserves further investigation. I for one, will make it recommended reading for management students on my courses.

Namibia, September 2014

Prof. Grafton Whyte
Director—Harold Pupkewitz Graduate
School of Business

Preface

This text is a guide to established and current thinking about how to get the best out of information technology and information systems investments. It relies on actual experience as well as research outputs from universities and business schools, but strives to be practical in the way the material is presented. It is intended for working professionals, in all disciplines that involve the management of information, as well as for students. It differs from other books because it deals with a complex domain in a reflective rather than a descriptive way, and it organises the approach to information management in six stages, from simple consideration of information *technology* right through to issues of organisational *strategy*. These six stages exactly parallel six areas of management competency required to reliably deliver value.

Information Management Is Everyone's Business

Many professional people (from all disciplines) have come to understand the importance of information in their work. Lawyers, teachers, journalists and logisticians are all heavily dependent on information for professional success, and yet these generally very capable people are still battling to get the best out of technology. Some choose to undertake part-time postgraduate studies in order to understand more about the impact of information technology; some choose to undertake short-term management education about management information systems; some choose to struggle on, regardless. The problem is that the breadth of issues associated with information management practice is potentially vast, extending from an understanding of the base technologies that are used, right through to questions of organisational strategy and how it can accommodate the potential benefits of information technology. Hence, the central problem today for many people is the wide scope of the issues that need to be understood and the fact that so many different kinds of people are involved.

Information Management Is Complex but it Can Be Dealt with

This text is based on an easily understood framework that deals with the complexity, relates organisational needs to new information technology opportunities in a simple way, and makes clear the competencies that an organisation needs if it is to make good with information management.

The framework presented here, the "Information Management Body of Knowledge" (or just "IMBOK") allows us to locate problems and opportunities and to move our ideas more easily from one stage in information value-adding to another—from consideration of raw technologies through to issues of practice, performance management and strategy. It also provides us a means to organise the literature about the subject and it is hoped that the fruits of present and future research will accumulate within and around the IMBOK framework. Using it, students, professionals and managers now have easier access to the diagnostic tools and management techniques that they need; further, researchers will have the means to position their research ideas and to share them with others more effectively than would otherwise have been possible.

Benefits and Limitations of the Approach Taken

Of course, organising the issues in such a simplistic way might be misleading. Real life is not simple, and the tendency of "IT people" to try and deal with complexity in a hierarchical or reductionist way masks many of the unexpected connections that might exist outside the structured view that is presented here. For example, if in a successful business the chief executive decides that it is necessary to move to "cloud services", for reasons that are not entirely clear, then it is probable that the workforce at all levels will set about achieving exactly that, whatever their misgivings about cloud services. The origins of strategic thinking are many and various, and not always based on rational strategic analysis.

It is also true that the scope of strategic thinking, especially about information technology, is also broadening. In recent years there has been a move to look much more seriously at the soft issues: the attitudes that people adopt, their emotional reactions to the introduction of new technologies, and the cultural factors that colour everything that goes on in a organisation, especially the relationships (between people) that so often override pure logic. It is now common to hear culture discussed in the context of information systems research and practice, and to acknowledge that if an organisation has no cultural bias to embrace and adopt change, then investments related to change are doomed to difficulty and even outright failure. An appropriate culture that allows change is axiomatic to success, despite what managers might think; it is just as important to understand what the workforce thinks as what the management thinks.

This work takes an international view of information management. The examples that are used to illustrate the narrative are not confined to Europe and North America. Working in South Africa for more than 16 years has caused me to take on an even more careful view of culture, and the differences that exist in organisations, and while much of what is written in this text is predicated on experience in Europe and North America, occasionally we will look elsewhere.

We Can Now See Issues that Are Timeless

Turning an investment in new information technology and information systems into improved organisational performance has proved to be a tortuously difficult thing. Despite occasional successes, initiatives of one kind or another seem to have failed to deliver the hoped-for results. Of course there are reasons for this, and because of the time that has passed we can now see and deal with problems in ways that are proving to be *timeless*. Despite the turmoil of endless technology-driven change, there are management tools and techniques that will be good for many decades to come, not just for next year or next week. I hope that the tools and techniques presented here will prove to be useful and timeless for you.

The Audience for This Book

This book is intended to provide a reference for all those who are concerned to understand or even to bridge the "divide" (actual or perceived) that sits between information technology "specialists" and non-technological "generalists". So, this text should be useful for…

- Secondary and tertiary teachers and lecturers, who are looking for a way to design courses in business management that deal effectively with information technology and information systems.
- Senior students and junior researchers who are looking for a simple contextual framework within which to organise their ideas, when what they are hearing and reading becomes too complex or too overwhelming.
- IS researchers who need to position their work in a management context.
- Managers who wish to identify and understand appropriate management tools that will help them in their work.

In the hope that the book will be read by senior students (and in case others are interested), at the end of each chapter there are pointers to selected research papers, with comments. There is also a full list of references and a bibliography.

Provenance of the Work

This book has been developed from a working text that has been available as the "Information Management Body of Knowledge", that has circulated internationally for 10 years and has been adopted as a standard course text in South Africa, Europe and the Americas. For this new version, "properly" published at last, shortcomings in the original text have been dealt with, the examples have been extended, updated and improved, substantial additional material has been added, and accumulated experience with the IMBOK has made possible a more careful and more complete treatment of the issues.

Acknowledgments

The IMBOK originally emerged from a research project at the University of the Western Cape in Cape Town, South Africa, funded by the Carnegie Corporation of New York, to whom we express our appreciation. I wish to acknowledge the interest and support of the many local South African organisations—too many to list here—that supported the early research workshops. I hope that this new text—now a "proper" book—continues to provide them with valuable assistance in terms of improving information management and improving their prospects of success with information systems investments.

Equally, it is important to acknowledge the contribution made by my many colleagues and students here in South Africa and elsewhere. In the beginning, working with John Ward, Rob Lambert and Chris Edwards at the Cranfield School of Management was inspirational; on arriving in South Africa so many years ago, Allen Lee articulated the need for the IMBOK in his keynote address at our inaugural conference in Cape Town, in 1999 (see Fig. 1.2)—that was the tipping point at which the story really began; the support and encouragement from Busi Ngidi, Cedrick Muleya, Yvette Greef and Munira Allie preserved my sanity when it was threatened by the mild but enduring chaos of the University of the Western Cape (at that time; the university has matured since then!); when we won the funding for the original research from the Carnegie Corporation of New York Derek Keats, Karolina O'Donoghue, Fahrnaaz Johadien, Melius Weideman, Corrie Uys, Bennett Alexander, Marcel Berteler, Peter Thomas, Lauren Wildschutz and Johan Mouton all contributed to a very challenging research agenda in many different ways; Geoff Erwin made it possible to contribute to the research developments at the Cape Peninsula University of Technology following its transformation into a real, research-based, technology university, and he encouraged the early dissemination of the IMBOK; as "students" (a descriptor hardly adequate to indicate the importance of their support and involvement) I must acknowledge all the happy times with Denise Biggs, Sipokazi Bukani, Bongazana Mahlangu, Constance Mtsweni, Sydwell Nikani, Rashied Scello, Thoko Speelman, Johannes Taswell and

Sibongiseni Tunzelana. Most recently Kobus Smit and Zoran Mitrovic have been particularly encouraging in the adoption and development of the IMBOK, and Darlington Onojaefe, Edward Naa Dakora, Laban Bagui, Moira Bladergroen, Wallace Chigona and Johannes Cronje have all been extraordinarily helpful, patient and supportive as the work of a lifetime finally settled down and became amenable to incorporation in a book like this.

Finally, I have to make special mention of two people. First, Grafton Whyte, whose doctoral project was the first one that I was ever substantially involved with and who followed me to southern Africa from the UK, to do what he could to promote Information Systems study and practice here: he has done more than anyone to encourage and critically appraise the ideas that have emerged. Second, my wife Ann, for endless proofreading and constructive criticism over nearly four decades of academic endeavour; it is just wonderful to have taken this journey together, with barely a single cross word exchanged. How did we do it?

Having said all that, any residual errors or omissions must of course be laid at my door, but the door is open—please visit the IMBOK web site and join the ongoing conversation.

http://www.imbok.org

Thanks, everyone!

Cape Town, August 2014 Andy Bytheway

Contents

Part I
Taking Stock

In getting started, we need to understand *who* and *what* is involved, what the problems are, and what is needed to address them.

- We need to take a broad-based view of why information and its management is important—one way to achieve this is to start with three important stakeholder groups: *business*, *government*, and *civil society*; and let us not forget the role of the *individual*.
- Four short, simple stories exercise some of the issues, and give us something to get our information management "teeth" into.
- There is a great deal of difficulty with information technology and information systems, but also some success. Patterns have emerged over the decades, and we can learn something about success from the history of information management in organisations.
- Today, things are changing rapidly, so let us be very careful. Geo-political structures are giving way to info-political structures, and big business reaches over and beyond government and communities everywhere.
- There are, in my view, no management "theories", only management fashion and fancy.
- At the same time, technology is now commoditised and it is ubiquitous; governments have been shown to unconstrainedly and recklessly harvest intelligence data from the installed technologies around the world.
- In fact, governments have suffered some of the very worst examples of poor information management.

New information management competencies are needed, both to render government more effective from within, and to give business and civil society the tools and capabilities with which to succeed, despite the degree of contextual change and the shortcomings of government.

The IMBOK enables us to start getting all of this organised in ways that we can manage.

1 Introduction

"Information management" is an expression that needs, for the present purpose, to be carefully defined. A lay audience with no special interest in the merits of good information management would probably see the words, think nothing much about them and move their thoughts on to something of more obvious interest. A working professional seeing the words—a business manager, a travel agent and a doctor—might pause and wonder for a moment whether an understanding of information management (whatever that is) would be helpful; they certainly would agree that their work is intimately concerned with acquiring, processing and using information. An information technology (IT) specialist seeing the words "information management" would probably think of data acquisition and storage, database management challenges and (in some cases) the "users" who give him such a difficult time in defining, developing and delivering information systems that actually work well for those users.

And so we learn: *it all depends on your point-of-view*. Different people may have significantly different ideas about what information management is and how it impacts on or contributes to their lives. For everyone (from the most uneducated lay person to the most expert information systems specialist, whether they realise it or not) the flow of information through their lives has become critical to their twenty-first century existence.

What I have found interesting in collecting new material for this book is that the term "information management" is more frequently found in the writings of other professional disciplines, such as chemical engineering, port management and government[1] than in the technical software and information systems literature. As we strive to understand the junction and intersection between the worlds of information technology and society at large, this is important to acknowledge and respond to.

If we are to make the most of information in our lives then all people need to understand something about how the technology makes it available, how it affects

[1] (See, for example: Dragan (2011), Park (2012), Sheriff et al. (2012), Chaudhry (2013)).

A. Bytheway, *Investing in Information*,
DOI 10.1007/978-3-319-11909-0_1

our lives advantageously or problematically and how (if it is properly managed) it helps us to achieve our ambitions within our family, our community or our work. A recently employed and empowered graduate in Tanzania might want to buy a smart cell phone; an entrepreneur in New Mexico might want to set up a Website; a bed and breakfast business in New Zealand might want to implement a credit card payment facility; a global oil company might want to find new ways to distil the oil out of the data from their geological surveys; the government of a well-developed country might want to implement a new, country-wide, health insurance scheme. A pensioner on a cruise in the South Atlantic might not understand why the email service from the "business centre" does not work, because there is no satellite connection in place and so on. Everywhere we look, there is a dependency on *access* to information and a need to *process* it in order to achieve an outcome.

The Context

This is the context for what we will call "information management" here. The wide variety of particular scenarios, as indicated above, is daunting. The rate of change of technology is breath taking. The inability of some people to understand and accept change, and the insistence of others to force it upon us, seems to defy analysis and understanding. But that is the purpose of this book: To examine the different stages in delivering real value from information technology (for it is with *the technology* that this all starts), to present tools that anyone can use to think about it, to make appropriate plans to use it, and to act in ways that will improve their lives and their work.

The normative perspective that will be adopted here is that of the *organisation*, sometimes referred to as the *business* or the *enterprise*. The business context is the source of many of the ideas presented here, but time has shown that they are equally applicable to government, to civil society and to the individual.

In the course of this text, we will increasingly refer to people and organisations that we can call *stakeholders*. The idea that we must identify and understand all those people and organisations that can affect the way we live and work will prove to be very important. I am particularly fond of the arrangement of ideas shown in Fig. 1.1 it identifies four high-level stakeholder groups and the relationships between them.

It is interesting to see the individual separately from business, government and community, because individuals are also to be seen *within* these three "collective" stakeholder groups. Individuals are *employees* within businesses, and yet they are *customers*; individuals are *tax payers* and yet they may work as *public servants*; virtually all individuals would admit to living *within communities*, another context within which different needs and priorities emerge.

With this high-level view in mind, we can begin to understand that one technology—let us think of the smart phone, or the "tablet"?—can impact on one or all of these stakeholder groups at the same time, but differently. The impact might be

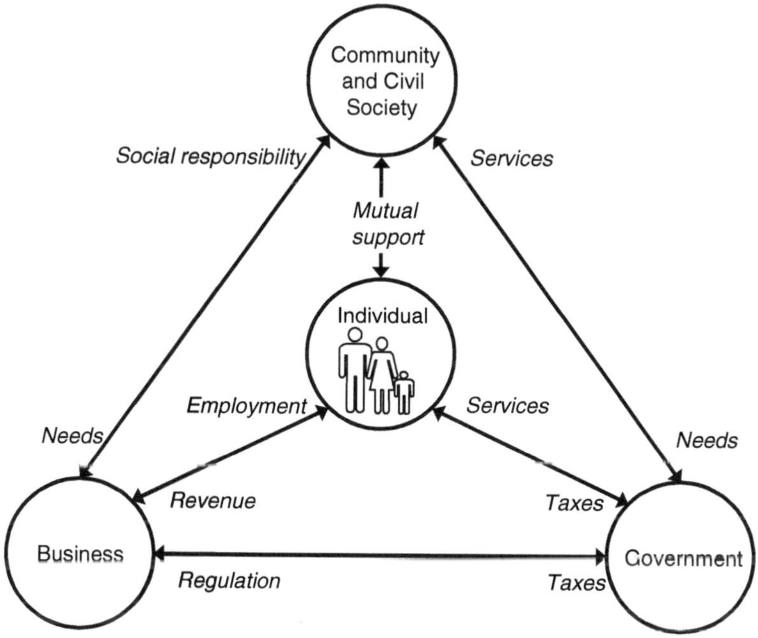

Fig. 1.1 A stakeholder context for information management

advantageous to one group but not to the others. This view of our world is a useful reminder that there are patterns of dependency within which we live, work and pay our taxes.

The pages that now follow put some flesh on the bones of this idea, in the form of short stories about life, work, people and information.

Four Short Stories

These four short stories are based on real recent experiences in:

- Courier services (the individual working with business and government)
- The legal profession (a professional business drowning in paper)
- A university (a community trying to bring in efficiency and standard practice)
- Central government (a national government unable to deliver its promises)

A Global Courier Company Cannot Find the Address

The first example, although simple, manages to combine the interests of an individual, a business, a government *and* a community, all in a single story:

Bill logged on to the Internet to check that his tender documentation had been delivered to the Ministry of Finance. He was confident that his bid for a two-year IT consulting contract would be a winner, and it would generate enough personal income to feather the retirement nest quite nicely. The consulting was required in order to further the national strategy for delivering Internet services to remote rural communities.

He was shocked to see that the package had not been delivered. "No such address" the courier company "tracking" web page said. He pulled down the file from his shelf, containing a copy of the invitation to tender and his response and satisfied himself that he had given the courier the right physical address for the "tender box" in the central government offices. Not to worry, he thought, the local courier office would sort it out, or they would call him to find out what to do.

The next day, he was doubly shocked to see that they had now failed to deliver the package three times. He broke out into a cold sweat—the deadline for submission had passed in the night and four days' solid work preparing the tender, with his wife's endless help, was all totally wasted. No chance now to feather the retirement nest-egg!

He logged onto HelloPeter.com and quickly (and angrily) complained to the whole world that FedEx had let him down. That made him feel a little better, but deep inside he was still boiling with anger and frustration, partly against himself (because he could, if he had chosen, have telephoned the courier company on first sight of the problem) but also against the couriers (after all—who, in their right mind, would try three times to deliver to a non-existent address?)

Twenty minutes later, the telephone rang. "Good day!" said a cheerful American female voice. "My name is Lizzie, and I am calling you from FedEx. Before you say anything at all, I want to say that I know that there is a problem and I want to admit that this should absolutely NOT have happened, and I am going to find out what went wrong. I am here to help you …". Bill was amazed—how could FedEx possibly have known there was a problem?

Ah—HelloPeter.com, of course!

He talked it through with Lizzie, who was continuingly apologetic and patient with him at the same time, and they agreed to speak again when the exact details of the problem were identified. It turned out that his local courier, who collected the package from his home and took it to the local FedEx depot, had not written the correct address and the necessary information was only available within the sealed inner plastic envelope.

This story combines issues concerning business, government, community and the individual. We live in an interdependent, information-connected world.

Everyone contributed to this problem:

- The local courier was incompetent and did not follow the rules.
- Bill was too lazy to make a phone call.
- The FedEx "system" failed to check that all required information was actually available, and despite their famous investment in Web-based "package tracking", at the end of the day there was a collective failure to perform.
- The government provided only a traditional "snail mail" route to submit tenders, with all the concomitant risks.

This is not a large or complex example, but it shows nicely (if there was any doubt) how organisational boundaries are dissolving, the reach of information systems is extending, and awareness of the need for good information management is becoming more obvious to everyone. HelloPeter.com and Web services like it can be effective in getting people with shared problems and interests together, in ways that were barely imaginable at the turn of the century.

The Legal Profession Battles with Huge Numbers of Documents

This second story reveals the difficulty in bringing professional people into the modern world:

> Anton watched and listened as the lawyers discussed the finer points of the case. Eight people around the table were talking about a multi-million dollar claim against a property development company that had converted a business property to residential use. It was a famous 70-year-old art deco building, and it had commanded huge market interest when the apartments were sold "off the plan" about 10 years previously. Unfortunately, the developer had failed to waterproof the exterior of the building, and rain was penetrating the walls and windows, causing quite severe damage inside. It was said that those who knew the history of the building had always warned that damp penetration was a long-standing problem.
>
> Having eight legal specialists discuss a problem like this was proving to be expensive. Anton, as the chairman of the owners association, was anxious to get full legal value for money, but he suddenly decided that the process in which everyone was involved was simply chaotic. One thousand five hundred documents had been "discovered" (from the defendant's and the plaintiff's archives) that evidenced the history of the conversion project. Some of these documents were on hand, at the meeting, in "lever arch files"; some of them were in boxes on the floor; some of them were elsewhere. On the table itself (it was a very big one) there were papers everywhere, in a state of what could only be described as documentary chaos. A junior lawyer was noting "important" sections of selected documents in his lever arch file, using a highlighter pen; the most senior lawyer was using special coloured tabs to mark pages, using a larger number of documents that he kept in a movable

bookcase (many were the same documents that the junior lawyer had, of course); an articled clerk was looking rather detached and simply made notes on a pad of scribble paper. When a particularly important and difficult document came up in the conversation, Anton reached for his small netbook computer and projected a PDF image of the document on the wall, using the data projector that he had brought with him. The meeting paused and focussed on the projected image. Anton quickly highlighted a block of text (in yellow) and added a comment in the margin that summarised what he thought had just been agreed. He then clicked something on the keyboard and brought up a list of all the names of the people who (according to the "discovered" records) had received a copy of that document.

Johannes, the senior lawyer present, stopped him. "Anton" he said, "if I had one of those" (pointing at the netbook), could I do that?" (pointing at the wall).

This story shows how even in the most professional businesses the advantages of information technology and information management are yet to be realised. It might seem extraordinary that a highly qualified and highly successful senior attorney could have failed to realise—in the twenty-first century—that technology holds great promise in the management of information about a court case. At a time when the costs of legal services are at a record high, and when there are so many people who need these services, the imperative to improve the efficiency and effectiveness of legal processes is obvious: more cases could be processed, more aggrieved parties could find redress, and if they played their cards right, lawyers could make a great deal more money.

Yes, we could note that in some jurisdictions the use of computers in the legal profession is commonplace and the benefits are understood. But in other places professionals like Johannes still choose to use traditional methods that are slow, unreliable and severely limited in dealing with large volumes of information.

Consider some of the issues that this short story raises:

- Is there a "system" that could be acquired, that would provide management, analysis and reporting of legal evidence? If not, could one be developed? It seems that Anton had rustled something up in a few days.
- Should the design and implementation of such a system be led by lawyers, or by IT specialists?
- How can the intransigence of senior lawyers be assuaged? Without their involvement the idea would never work.
- Is this an opportunity that would allow one progressive legal firm to steal an advantage over others, so that it becomes much stronger and more successful? Or, should the whole legal industry get together and develop a single shared system to maximise the benefits to everyman and everywoman?

- Would such a system use cloud services, tablets, laptops or desk-based workstations?
- What would be necessary to change in the operation of a successful legal office, and in the related staff responsibilities, in order that the benefits are maximised?

History shows us very clearly that early adopters of ideas like this can decimate an industry that is generally failing to pay attention to advances in information technology and good information management—consider the travel and financial services industries, both of which are replete with examples.

Information Management in Education

Let us move to a community perspective; communities come in many forms, and education is just one example. A university (for example) is certainly not "government", and generally universities are very unhappy to be seen as "businesses" (although that might be changing?). Education is certainly not immune from the problems that dog the successful implementation of potentially useful information systems, and education does not have the clear hierarchy of management control that might deal with these problems.

Yvette looked at the screen, which showed the student marks she had just loaded into the new "Marks Management System", and thought to herself that it would have been a great deal quicker to use the spreadsheet that she had developed 9 years previously, designed exactly as she wanted it. For her subject area, she had developed a marking scheme that was particularly clever. The marks for students' class contributions were linked to a separate spreadsheet, which showed the timetable for her lectures, the details of each lecture, and (most importantly) a class list that included all the student names and student numbers for her classes and the participation that they had achieved in class.

The new marks system had none of that, and particularly worrying was the fact that instead of working with percentages (and percentages of percentages) it would only work with absolute marks until the very end of the process, when a percentage result was given in the final tabulation of results. It had no provision for written comments. The consequence was, Yvette had had to build yet another spreadsheet, to convert her percentages back to absolutes, and at marks evaluation meetings she still had to take printouts of her spreadsheets with her.

Never mind, she thought with a smile, this new marks system will never prevail and when the university finally gives it up she would be able to revert to her spreadsheets. She had heard (in the senior common room) that in other subject areas, the new marks management system had actually delivered incorrect final marks, although whether that was as a result of careless use or errors in its logic, no one knew yet. There were strong rumblings of discontent everywhere.

She turned to her emails and, seeing an email request from the Dean's office for a copy of her teaching plans for next year, she tried to put marking out of her mind and sat down to think about next year's teaching. But she was still troubled. Next year was going to be similarly challenging, because other new "systems" were planned, including a more advanced teaching and learning content management system, further support for multimedia production and delivery, and a research publications management system. "I wonder why they cannot just use YouTube and GoogleDocs?" she asked herself, idly.

Whereas the lawyers were working in what we might think of as "the dark ages", Yvette's university is clearly working in the modern age. But it is a long way from getting everything right. It displays some of the characteristics of a community in that historically the people working there have had some discretion to do what they think best, there is a wide variety in the ways that people work, and there is often a disputed concept of academic freedom that makes it difficult to engender change.

It looks like marks administration has been implemented badly, without the participation of a representative number of teaching academics (especially those with peculiar or complex marks management needs), when in fact dealing with marks is a critical, core function of the university, that simply *must* be made to work properly. Because it does not work well, staff and students have lost confidence in the ability of the IT support function to deliver systems that work, and that work well.

This story raises further, different, questions:

- What do large, complex community-related organisations need to do, to make sure that key operational functions are properly supported by reliable systems?
- If this system was developed "in house", why did the institution not acquire an existing and reliable package from the many suppliers of educational software?
- How is it possible to build such a system ignoring the actual needs of its users?
- How can the potential interest and enthusiasm of users be harnessed, in order to get the job done properly?

Yvette's idle thought about using Web and cloud services of an appropriate kind, to deal with technically complex issues like multimedia and document version control, is entirely appropriate. At the time of writing (of this book[2]), the adoption of Web services is at a tipping point: Not just universities, but schools and businesses are realising the benefits, and the risks; we are not yet done with our assessment of the risks of going "into the cloud".

[2] "At the time of writing"—this is a phrase that will recur in this narrative, given the rapid rate of technology-driven change.

Big Problems in Big Government

Despite decades of practice, during which the required management skills should have been developed, communicated and established, it is worrying that government—surely one of the most critical sectors for automation—still cannot get it right[3]:

> A series of botched IT projects has left [UK] taxpayers with a bill of more than £26bn for computer systems that have suffered severe delays, run millions of pounds over budget or have been cancelled altogether.
>
> An investigation by The Independent has found that the total cost of labour's 10 most notorious IT failures is equivalent to more than half of the budget for Britain's schools last year. Parliament's spending watchdog has described the projects as "fundamentally flawed" and blamed ministers for "stupendous incompetence" in managing them.
>
> Further evidence has emerged over the failings of labour's most costly programme, the mammoth £12.7bn IT scheme to revolutionise the NHS. The Independent has learnt that just 160 health organisations out of about 9,000 are using electronic patient records delivered under the scheme. The vast majority of those were GP practices. New figures have also revealed that millions of pounds have been paid out in legal fees. The taxpayer has footed a £39.2m bill for "legal and commercial support" for the National Programme for IT (NPfIT).
>
> Alan Milburn, the former health secretary, said in 2001 that everyone would have access to their health records online by 2005, but it is understood that the Department for Health is still "years away" from fulfilling the pledge.

Neither a room full of lawyers nor a university comes close to this awesome story of central government ineptitude. How can a "developed" country, with more than 40 years' experience of public service information technology and information systems, get into such a managerial mess?

There are yet more new issues here. The lawyers were at the *beginning* of a systems idea, Yvette was in the *middle* of the execution of ideas, but the United Kingdom government was over-extending itself in an orgy of information technology expenditure, having had *decades* of "experience":

- We seem to be progressing from early to later days: Does this story illustrate some kind of "third stage" in the maturing of information management capability?
- Was the government misled by consulting companies that recklessly suggested impossible feats of systems development?

---

[3] This example is taken from "The Independent" in London (the Tuesday 19 January 2010 issue).

- Was politics the overriding consideration here, rather than operational efficiency, because individuals hoped to make their reputations and soar above the average? Clearly they failed.
- Being dependent on the contracts negotiated with suppliers of systems and services, were those contracts the principal source of difficulty?
- Or, was the bureaucracy simply incapable of dealing with the very high-level strategic issues involved?

This story is deeply worrying, because it is not an isolated incident and there are other variations on the theme of problematic central government computing, concerned with mass data collection, surveillance and abuse of privacy, all in a context where routine operational systems could not be made to work despite an investment of billions of British pounds and tens of thousands of man years of effort. Further, the British Government takes much of the credit for something called the "Information Technology Infrastructure Library" (ITIL) that purports to provide sound advice on how to get systems developed and installed successfully. Did they use it themselves? Can we trust them with information technology at all? We will be looking at ITIL in some detail later.

Success Is Difficult to Find

Within the ghastly mix of problem public sector projects, it is the United Kingdom National Health Service (NHS) system that stands out. British parliamentarians admitted that the NHS IT system was "one of the worst fiascos ever". Since it was initiated in 2002, the project has been dogged by technical and contractual problems, and when the British Public Accounts Committee concluded that it was one of the worst projects in the history of public sector endeavour, with a final bill to tax payers around £11bn, the project was finally closed down. It is small comfort that some of those tax payers, working in the IT industry, enjoyed enviable salaries during the project: On the other side of the contracts, much of the cost was actually easy revenue for overseas suppliers of technology and services, and for consultants. It is clear that ministers and civil servants had not learned and applied the lessons of modern history. But what are those lessons, can we now assemble useful guidance from past experience? With this background in mind, let us look at the issues from both sides.

Some IT project managers, firmly entrenched in the world of information technology, will say "*Yes, my project was a success*", based solely on the argument that their project came in "on time" and "within budget" (although the evidence is that fewer than 50 % of IT projects actually manage to do so). But talk to those who are expected to *use* the system and you may well find a different story. "*This is not what we needed*"; "*If they had only come to talk to me I could have sorted this out myself*"; "*Putting in this system has cost us eight month's production—we would have been better off without it*"; "*They put this system but provide me no support at all—I have no idea how I should be using it*"; these all might be typical comments in the difficult weeks and months following the introduction of a new system.

So, what is going wrong? It is difficult to say, and we have to admit that there is *some* success. At the time of writing, TripAdvisor, Facebook, eBay and Amazon each stands as a global, Web-based systems and information service that delivers access to massive information repositories and—more importantly—organises and catalogues the information in ways that make it universally accessible to a global audience. Further, they track usage in ways that make it seem that each of us is known to them, so that we become dependent on them, and even our inner thoughts and propensities become public knowledge if we are not careful. But few people reading this book will successfully launch an "Amazon" or an "eBay" and become multi-billionaires. There is still a huge array of other smaller successes, some incremental (consider the steady impact of information technology in education and in small businesses, as well as in community activities) and others that are "game-changing", but only within the context of a small business, a social club, or a special interest group.

For more than 50 years, experts and academic researchers have been trying to find the means to assure success (and avoid failure), and the search goes on. Later, we will examine a selection of proven ideas that have emerged over this time and position them within a tested management framework.[4]

In the meantime, these short stories are indicative of the potential difficulty that managers and others face, a difficulty that arises from investments in information technology and information systems. Virtually everyone has a collection of such stories, and we will hear more before we are done here, but with these difficulties in mind, it is worth reviewing recent history so that we can identify trends and start to organise our thoughts about managing information effectively, and investing our money, time and effort more usefully.

A Brief History

In trying to find some kind of shape to the problems and opportunities, and in trying to step back from the short-term perspective that we all have to live with, it is useful to step right back and look at the 50-year history.

The Early Days

Since the 1960s, organisations have been developing computer-based information systems. Before this era, people, paper, pens, calculators and mechanical punch card machines were the main tools available for information management. The early applications of computers were those that were the easiest to identify, such as

[4] In this text the words "model" and "framework" appear frequently, but they can be seen as different: a *model* is something that emulates reality (and can perhaps be used to predict what will happen), whereas a *framework* is merely an arbitrary separation of ideas that renders a complex issue tractable, or manageable.

accounting, invoicing and other labour-intensive office activities involving numbers and calculations. In the very early days, simply *making computers work* was deemed as "success", but problems emerged with alarming frequency.

Partly this was as a result of mismanaged expectations, but also as a result of increasing confidence and an increasing ambition to use computers in more and more adventurous ways. The cost of early mainframe computers was very high, and it was reasonable that the early management focus was on *cost saving* and *efficiency enhancements*.

The Maturing Years

It changed in the middle 1980s, when commercial organisations began to gain real *strategic advantage* from innovative applications of information technology. The window of such advantage (the period of time it takes for competitors to catch up and match the strategic advantage) became the critical issue to manage well. This window became shorter and shorter—only months not years—until the capability to *manage change itself* became the most important thing.

But organisations still struggled to deliver systems that really matched needs; they struggled to understand how to set timeframes and budgets that can reliably be met; they struggled to manage an inadequate IT workforce with scarce skills and an alarming tendency to move quickly from one job to another. Knowing that one development team somewhere had successfully achieved a competitively useful system rendered them highly recruitable, and the churn in the work force was a major challenge.

In order to deal with things in these times of change, organisations tried a number of approaches that can be seen as minor "eras", something along the following lines:

- Hire better programmers and introduce systems analysts (*early 1970s?*)
- Devise more structured methods of working (*late 1970s?*)
- Introduce project management, like in construction (*early 1980s?*)
- Impose quality management (*later 1980s?*)
- Fully incorporate IT issues in business strategy (*late 1980s, 1990s*)
- Reorganise the resourcing of IT through "outsourcing", diminishing the status of the internal IT department (*1990s*)
- Of course, IT departments fought back, admitting that IT resources were now a commodity but raising ideas of "Enterprise Architecture", and promoting organisation-wide "Enterprise Resource Planning" (ERP) systems (*2000s*)
- Organisations now recognise that technology has finally become truly ubiquitous, that corporate (and national boundaries) are dissolving and that the world begins to change in yet new ways—"agility" is the word on many people's lips (*2010s*)

These eras have caused organisational management to continually review their strategies for information technology and systems investments. We will come back to the idea of "eras" later in the narrative.

In the meantime, occasional success and improvements in new systems capabilities are evident but there still seems to be a fundamental difficulty with the chasm that exists between the world of IT specialists and the business people who simply want to improve their business performance. IT managers have difficulty communicating with executive management; research has shown that even the most senior IT management is often unable to operate credibly in the board room, where they find an alien culture, an unfamiliar vocabulary and unexpected behaviours (Chatham and Patching 2000). The division of responsibilities between the IT department and the rest of the organisation is difficult to define. As a result, there is a culture to "throw things over the wall", admitting that these two worlds will never meet. Of course, the idea of a wall is false: IT managers and business managers work for the same organisation, their interests overlap and their functions overlap, and there are strong interdependencies that have to be recognised if investments are to be successful.

The Beginnings of an Idea

Speaking at BITWorld '99, an international conference in Cape Town, Allen Lee explored the two worlds of information technology and society at large (Lee 1999). Figure 1.2 illustrates how, in his view, these two worlds intersect in a way that makes clear the joint area that is so difficult (but so important) to manage. Rather than a wall, or chasm, he suggests that there is an area of common concern that we must understand and work with so as to make sure that information technology makes a good and proper contribution to society at large and business in particular. Hence, it is the overlap between the world of IT and the world of "the business" that needs to be managed, not a chasm:

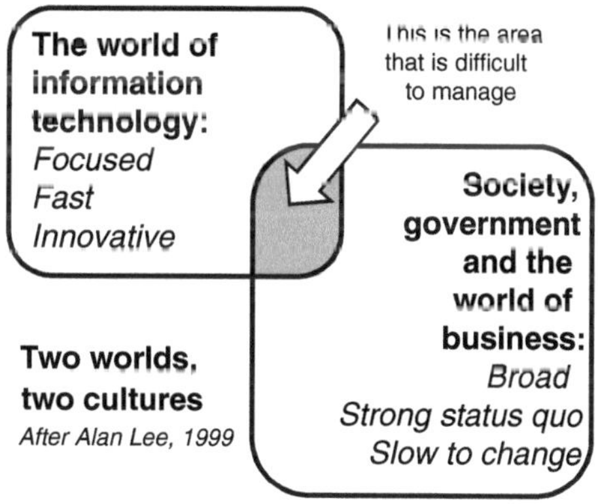

Fig. 1.2 The critical area where information needs to be managed

This figure is almost hopelessly simplistic (it has already lost the useful detail about stakeholders that we found in Fig. 1.1), but it provides the basis of the question that must be answered: *exactly what is it that is shared by, or sits between, the world of technology and the real world of business, government and community that uses technology?*

The vast majority of the issues in the early years were those associated with how to "supply" information systems to business. Information technology was a driver of cost rather than a source of new thinking and innovation. The principal problem was finding people who could do the work rather than making sure that the work was what was needed. Supply-side organisations (such as the mainframe suppliers and the emerging software industry) drove a lot of the early investment through simple marketing and peer pressure. As the supply-side issues became better understood by buyers, and with many basic business functions having been automated, attention turned to more imaginative and fruitful applications of information technology.

Attention Shifts

This shift of attention has highlighted issues relating to managing the 'demand' for information systems in organisations. No longer are organisations content to be driven by information technology capability, now they are searching for new business opportunities that might change the nature of the business and what kind of business it is. There has been a surge of interest in management tools and techniques that help to incorporate information technology into the formulation of business strategy, so that investment is based on real business needs rather than spurious technology-driven thinking. This focus on demand management has not detracted from issues of supply, but rather has broadened the range of concerns of management teams. In particular, the ability to manage recurring strategic and operational change has become all-important.

The status of the IT department in organisations has diminished. As one response to this diminution, IT people dreamed up "systematic" ways to see a business, adopting the term "Enterprise Architecture" as a moniker. At that time, an internationally known Chief Executive was heard to say (I paraphrase his exact words): "*If these IT people expect to rampage through my business and tell my people what they must do, because of some damned 'enterprise architecture', then they must be crazy. I am not letting them anywhere near my senior management team*". Another senior Director of Engineering, globally responsible for software engineering in a mobile services company (he was responsible for the software that runs cellular telephone base stations and manages the flow of voice and digital data through the networks) was asked what he thought about the "*other IT people, who develop and maintain the commercial systems. Where do they sit in the overall pecking order?*". He said "*Let me think about that for a moment ...*", he was silent for a while, and then he answered, with disdain: "*... just above the canteen staff*"!

What chance does a senior IT manager have in situations such as these? The best option is surely to get closer to the business and to help build information management skills within the business that will bring a focus on the business benefits rather than the technical problems. IT management needs to promote a better understanding of the benefits of information technology and systems investments: how they can be defined, how they can be managed, how they can be measured and finally how they can be demonstrated in a way that senior business management understands.

These are the things that we will soon attend to here, but at this point, it is important to remind ourselves that business is just one facet of society at large. This is especially so when information technology is so clearly spilling out over the boundaries of organised business and is becoming a commonplace feature of everybody's lives. As we shall see, it is not only organised business that needs to manage information technology well. Those of us who are fortunate enough to have information technology at home, or even in our pockets, need to have some regard for the way that it will enhance and not undermine the quality of our lives. Those of us in government have a responsibility to take on information technology and systems that will provide better and more appropriate services to the public.

Those of us who are *not* yet fortunate enough to have information technology within reach must hope that it is used to improve our prospects, although this is one of the more recent and most challenging questions that we face at this time: How can we ensure that the *social* appropriation of technology (whether by government policy or through the efforts of NGOs and others) is managed in an effective way? Early experience suggests that there are many more challenges here than we ever anticipated.

The world of information technology is fast-paced and very often presumes the advantages of innovation—a phenomenon the academic world refers to as "technological determinism"; it is focused on the endless reduction in size of technological devices and the increasing speed and capacity of our networks.

A Meeting of Minds

A defining moment in these shifting times was the publication of an important and frequently cited article by Carr (2003) which argued forcibly that information technology had become a commodity, it offered far more than people were competent or capable to use, and management should focus relentlessly on reducing the cost of information technology. Somehow, this article grabbed the attention of many people and really did begin to persuade business mangers (as opposed to technology managers) to think again about managing information technology and information systems investments.

At about the time that Carr's ideas were published, and in order to hear directly from the "front line", more than 70 people (from education, business and public administration in Cape Town, South Africa) met to discuss the problems in delivering the benefits of information technology-related investments. This was a structured and professionally facilitated meeting that delivered a clear consensus that probably reflects the situation internationally (South Africa is often said to display a mixture of first- and third-world characteristics, and both first- and third-world issues were very prevalent in the discussions).

There was strong concern about strategy formulation and implementation, the practicalities of developing and delivering of new systems and achieving successful exploitation of them. There was a vision of an improved future, where IT and business strategies would be aligned, the management of information systems projects would be under tight control, and business people would be empowered rather than inhibited by the systems that they were asked to use.

But, there was widely shared concern about the lack of appropriate information management capability in organisations of all kinds, and the failure of education in schools and universities to deliver appropriate competencies. Some critical competencies—all concerned with management—recurred several times in discussions: Strategy *management*, information *management*, project *management*, change *management* and service *management* all featured more than once. In this discussion, it emerged that competencies are not seen to be the same as skills, and the general preoccupation with skills training was not expected to solve problems—something bigger and better than that is needed.

Perhaps the most critical requirement that emerged from the discussions is the matter of business performance measurement: If there is no agreed framework for measuring how well we are doing (not just financial measures, qualitative measures are needed as well) then we will never be able to demonstrate the success that we seek, so as to build confidence, and win support for further investment. Success would only be evident when investments delivered measureable *benefits*.

It was from this meeting that early versions of the text you are reading now first emerged, as a response to the needs of these business people, academics and public servants.

The Situation Today

We are surely all aware that the Internet and the World Wide Web together are leading to the wholesale destruction and reformulation of economic sectors that are information intensive, such as travel retailing, publication and banking, and enabling individuals and communities to make their voices heard in ways that were never previously imagined. When we could once focus on information technology and information systems investments in *business*, we must now recognise the interdependencies with *government*, with *communities* and with *individuals*. Hence, the "wall", "chasm" or "gap" between the world of IT and the real world is much more complex than we once thought.

Allen Lee has urged us to resolve any differences at the intersection of the two worlds, because when we understand that intersection we can stop worrying about change, we can anticipate it and we can take advantage from it. But is this shared world of difficulty the same today as it was at the turn of the century?

It is not, because there has been a seismic shift in the balance of power.

IT is "Commoditised"

Nicholas Carr was very clear when (in 2003) he wrote his seminal piece on the commoditisation of information technology. He pointed out that since the invention of the microprocessor by Ted Hoff in 1968, the uniqueness and novelty of information technology inventions has dissolved into ubiquity. He argued that this completely changes the strategic and tactical options for information technology management in organisations: IT managers should *spend less* he argued (more expenditure on IT has not reliably improved organisational performance), they should *follow the crowd* and not try to lead (the longer you wait, the cheaper and more reliable is the technology), and you should make sure that your procedures and processes to fix things, when they go wrong, are bomb-proof, because they *will* go wrong and customers' perceptions of a "levelled" playing field will be determined by embarrassing failures much more than by startling successes. This all drags the IT department well down in the overall pecking order of an organisation.

Carr accused organisations of being passive in dealing with suppliers (of technology) and sloppy in the implementation of systems; he sees merit in refusing to buy functionality that is far beyond what is needed, and to stick to what is mature, reliable and economical. "*[You] need only look at Microsoft's profit margin*", he says, if you need to understand how much money is wasted with software acquisition. We might note here, about ten years later, that Microsoft has hit a few brick walls of its own since then and their profits are no longer assured. Perhaps the comments that Carr made were one factor that contributed to Microsoft's current difficulties but the point that he made still stands true. Open source software (OSS) and free and open source software (FOSS) is available that fulfils the vast majority of organisational needs.

But in this first, oft-quoted piece, Carr largely ignored one important factor: that boundaries between organisations are dissolving, the power of the individual as a customer, tax payer and community member is increasing, and so the ways that organisations *seem* to behave, and way that their investments in information technology and systems recognise rather than ignore these factors, becomes a critical success factor.

A Journey with no Map?

Despite Nicholas Carr's interesting assertion that most organisations now have all the systems that they need, investment in new systems continues. Hence, whether we are an individual looking for home automation, a 4x4 club wanting a new Website, a business needing better customer relationship management, or a government tax department thinking about introducing electronic tax returns, we still need to *think*, to *plan*, to *act* and to *check* that we have done something useful (more of that shortly).

It follows that we need to dig deeper and explore what actually happens between the acquisition of technology (or technology-based services) and the fulfilment of an individual or organisational ambition. How shall we achieve this magical alignment of technology and organisational strategies?

First, we must admit that any strategic investment will not be solely based on the acquisition of information technology and systems; there will be other strategic needs such as marketing or impact analysis, recruiting new employees with new skills, renting new or upgraded premises, acquiring capital equipment, and undertaking product development effort. Perhaps we will also need to talk to our friends in order to see what their opinions are.

These needs will colour the discussion that follows in the pages, sections and chapters that follow. However, in that discussion, in order to save time and to standardise our vocabulary, we will generally assume that it is sufficient to refer to "the business" rather than "the organisation", "the community" or "the government department". Whether it is the "business" of an individual going about their work and their life, the "business" of a community seeking new forms of entertainment, or a government department working on new tax collection schemes, the word "business" can be seen as encompassing them all. Where it is important to be more specific that will be made clear.

And so, we set out to find the map that will get us from where we are to where we want to be, but we must choose which of two different directions is most appropriate: in one direction, it all starts with an investment in information technology and works towards improving business performance, and in the other direction, it starts with the formulation and implementation of an organisational strategy that defines the expected improvement and then strives to make the best possible use of information technology through organisational change.

"It is your choice", we might say: typically (and quite naturally), people with their noses stuck deeply into information technology would choose to spend the money and then explore the possibilities; people more concerned with the business would set their targets and then look to see whether the technology might contribute to their attainment.

But let us not rush ahead. One word keeps coming up in this narrative—"management". Let us reflect on what that means for a moment.

The Management Perspective

Academics studying and teaching management often refer to management "theories". I do not believe that there are management theories, as such, but the field is replete with fashion and fancy. Management is a complex domain, and it is dealt with by choosing very limited viewpoints comparing, perhaps, just two features or qualities of management at a time. The Ansoff matrix comes to mind (Ansoff 1957), where marketing strategy is reduced to present and future customers and present and future products; would that it was that simple! Nevertheless, there is one simple and helpful model of management as a process, a process model that is to be found in virtually all introductory management lectures.

Management 101 in a Nutshell

A common view of management, often taught in early classes dealing with management theory, is that it comprises four principal activities: *Think*, *Plan*, *Act* and *Check*. This four-stage sequence reminds us that—conventionally—we have to *think* about what we hope to be able to do, *make plans* that ensure that we have all the financial, human and material resources needed, *execute* the plan by means of appropriate actions and finally *check* that all went as intended and that the desired results were obtained (Fig. 1.3).

Put into the context of information systems investments, this means that:

- we must be clear about why we are spending money on information technology and systems,
- we must have proper plans that include budgets and time scales,
- we must manage the processes and activities of implementation and
- we must be able to check that the benefits that we hoped for are delivered.

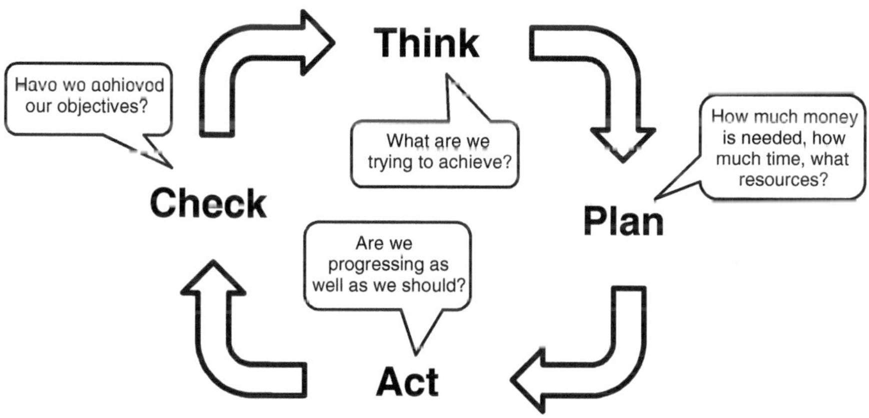

Fig. 1.3 "Think, plan, act and check": Managing information systems investments

This is a simple set of ideas, and it is equally applicable to domains other than information systems, but it makes a point: Managing is not *one thing*, it is *at least four things* within which we can see *four stages* in adding value; further, it identifies four places in a cycle of activity where we have to consciously switch from one way of thinking to another, possibly taking important decisions (such as whether to start or stop what we are doing) on the way through.

According to the above scheme of things, we first develop and deliver a plan and that in itself is *valuable* (if it is a good plan); then by means of an implementation project, we deliver an output which reveals the *real-world value* becomes to those who want it; finally, we confirm that what was produced is what was wanted—the *ultimate value* of knowing that we did well, or that we could do better next time.

But, now we begin to see some of the inner difficulties:

- Do we have the capability to think strategically and set reasonable achievable objectives for our projects?
- Do we have the discipline to raise a project plan, validate it and then perform according to it?
- Will that plan include an unambiguous specification of the information storage requirements and the required functionality of the new system?
- Have we defined the intended benefits of the investment of time, money and effort in a way that can be measured on delivery?
- Do we have the maturity to honestly assess what happened, and admit to the possibility that a project was sub-optimal in some way?

These are demanding pre-conditions that have been addressed incrementally as time has passed and experience has accumulated; there have been no magic bullets.

New Management Competencies Are Needed

It is clear that the successful deployment of information technology demands many differing competencies and capabilities, some of which are new. Experience suggests that in larger organisations, it is possible to employ specialists who sit in the middle of this spectrum of activity, and specialise in working between the extremes of technology and business, and strategy development and strategy implementation. Where once we relied upon the "systems analyst" to gather requirements and specify solutions, because the scope of our ambitions has extended well beyond the simple systems of the early days, we now need *business* analysts, not *system* analysts. The tools and techniques that these business analysts use are different. They are not just concerned with analysing business activities and designing database structures, they are concerned sometimes with wholesale business change—a different thing altogether.

But then, today everyone is an "expert": Familiarity with one's PC or tablet tends to suggest that we now know what to do, but (as has become clear) the technology might be the opportunity but it is not the main issue—people, and managing change, are the main issues.

The world of business has invested large sums of money in trying to address the "middle ground" of business change, but often in a piece-meal manner. Just "doing" project management does not solve the problem. Single role players—the project manager or the business manager, for example—cannot do the whole job by themselves. All role players must combine their efforts in this difficult territory if we are to truly improve business performance through the deployment of new and effective information systems.

The approach taken here is that we must understand the full range of competencies that deliver organisational strategy using appropriate information technology. There are at least five areas of requisite competency, as we shall see, one of which divides into two important parts; even more important, there is the challenge of moving our thinking from one level to another. That is the most difficult thing of all. We need a tested framework that organises the links between IT (as a cost driver) and business strategy (as fulfilment of our objectives) and thereby simplifies problems of communication and shows how different management tools can be applied to increase our understanding and to improve the chances of success.

The Information Management Body of Knowledge

2

Allen Lee's simple model (see Fig. 1.2) was the foundation of the IMBOK, but it masks huge complexities in the territory where information technology, business and society meet, and hence, the IMBOK is an expansion of it that begins to accommodate the different attitudes, vocabularies and expectations that are evident. The reality is that there *are* direct connections between these two worlds, there *are* shared interests that mutate from one level to the next, and it is necessary to understand them if our personal or organisational investments in information technology and information systems are to succeed.

At this first stage, we will develop an understanding of those connections here by dividing the intervening territory into six "management" segments—six areas of interest that each requires distinctly *different* management skills, competencies and techniques, but that share the vision of a valuable outcome from an investment:

- Information technology
- Information systems
- Business processes
- Business information
- Business benefits
- Business strategy

Figure 2.1 shows **information technology** at the left and **business strategy** at the right, thereby reflecting the arrangement of ideas in Allen Lee's model. We shall make the connections between the two using four specific, additional areas of management concern and action that are of concern to *both* parties: the **information system** that makes information technology useful and workable, the **business processes** that are improved by the introduction of new information systems (but which are different to information systems in that they embrace *all* aspects of what a business does, not just the processing of information), the **business information** that supports them and the **business benefits** that evidence that operational business improvements—usually articulated as performance targets embedded within the **business strategy**.

A. Bytheway, *Investing in Information*,
DOI 10.1007/978-3-319-11909-0_2

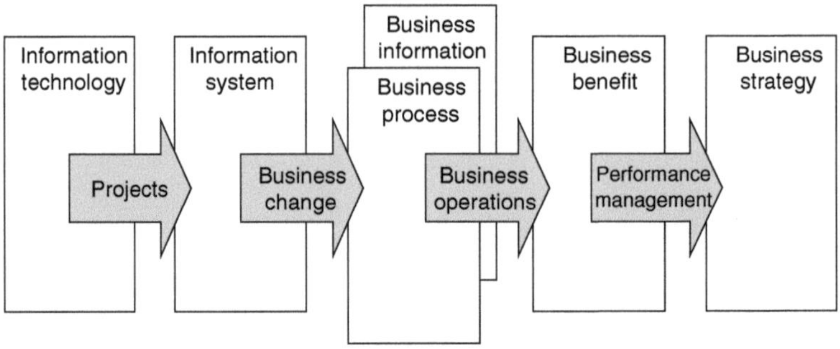

Fig. 2.1 The Information Management Body of Knowledge framework (simplified)

Hence, we see, for the first time, the outline logic that links the two ends of our intended journey. "**Information management**" is a phrase we will use here to encompass everything that has anything to do with information in business—in effect, the six areas of interest that are shown in the figure and enumerated in the paragraph above, *and* the four areas of activity that join them. Each of these six will be examined in some detail in the sections that follow. The combination of them all we will refer to as "the Information Management Body of Knowledge"—or just the "IMBOK", as it has become commonly known. Figure 2.1 presents the simplest view of the IMBOK, and we will look at some of the detail as we proceed from here.

The challenge is to find the managerial connections between IT, the information systems that serve business needs, and the strategic objectives of the business and then understand our competency to manage them. Sounds simple? It is not—it is a complex managerial challenge that cannot be met by IT people alone. Where competency is missing, there will be major challenges in putting them in place. In case you need it, another short, focused example helps to make the point.

A Simple Example

Gerry came upstairs from the computer room and met Sara, who works in marketing.

"Hi, how're you doing?" he asked.

"Fine" she answered. "We just had a great meeting discussing the new web site. We want to add some new features that will allow personalisation of the home page for our regular customers". She knew that Gerry would be interested.

He was. "That's great—when can we get started? I've been playing with XML and the new secure server platform and I'm sure we can work up some great ideas for you ...".

Sara wondered exactly what "XML" might be and whether this was the seventh or eight new server that the IT department has bought for themselves this year. She then wondered where the conversation might go next, and decided to cut and run.

"Yeah, sure! Let's meet soon and talk about that" she called as she turned to go down the corridor to her office in the marketing department.

What do you notice about this example? Although it is short, it is quite believable and it makes one or two things clear.

- Gerry gets a clear message that there is a need in marketing, but the implication is that there was no one from IT at the meeting. *Is that what you would expect?*
- Sara gives a short, sharp description of the need, but Gerry fails to engage with her concerning the details. He seems to assume that it is a good thing. *Is that what you would expect?*
- Gerry talks of XML and secure servers. Do you think that Sara would or should understand what he was talking about?
- Sara did not challenge him to explain about either XML or security in server platforms. *Do you think she should have done?*

Neither person made any attempt to examine the interesting middle ground between the information technology (that is clearly "home ground" for Gerry) and the needs of the business ("home ground" for Sara). The casual exchange between Gerry and Sara might be typical of your experience or it might not. The example might be from a large business or a small one, it does not matter, but we are reminded that there is often a place called the "information technology department", and there is "the business", and they might have difficulty communicating.

Let's explore the middle ground of Gerry and Sarah's situation briefly, so that we can see how the IMBOK begins to bring shape and size into an understanding of the situation. We can do this by asking the sorts of questions that we might ask ourselves, whether in the context of our work, our community, or our government:

- What exactly is the *information system* that will serve our needs in a more personalised way? Does Sarah actually need an order entry system? An order status checking system? A cataloguing system? Or, is the personalisation about providing customers with only the web functionality that they need? Is it an existing system, or will it be a new one?
- What is the *business process* that will benefit from such new systems? Is it "customer order fulfilment"? Or, "new customer acquisition"? Or, "customer relationship management"? Or, will it embrace all activities that relate in any way to customers?
- What *business information* will be derived from Gerry's XML data structures? Data is not the same as information, and because a majority of people are

process oriented rather than *information oriented,* there are perpetual difficulties in identifying and organising the right data that will deliver the right information. How might we relate XML data to business information?
- What will be the *business benefits* of the new system? Are we concerned to increase the number of customers? If so, how can we be assured that this will happen? Are we aiming to get more business from existing customers? If so, the same question arises: How can we be assured that this will happen? Are we simply trying to retain existing customers?

When managers make decisions about information technology and the information systems that are built with it, there is a very strong tendency to decide on an arbitrary basis. "*Our main competitor has done it, so we must do it too*". "*Gerry thinks it's a good idea, and he is good with IT, so let's give it a try*". These are not reliable arguments with which to justify spending large sums of money.

It is now time to move on. Before moving into the detail in the heart of the book (in Part Two), this first part concludes by unpacking, introducing and explaining the elements of the IMBOK.

The IMBOK Framework Step by Step

It is critically important to understand the logical connections between technology capability (and cost) and strategic need (and benefits), and this is what the IMBOK does.

The basic outline of the IMBOK framework has been seen already. A more complete version of the framework shows the *knowledge areas* (the white boxes) and *processes* (the grey arrows). Further, because of the central importance of business *process* management and business *information* management, the central domain *business systems* is divided into those two parts. This is an important difference between earlier versions of the IMBOK in the published literature and the version that we will work with here.

- Information technology
- Information systems
- Business process
- Business information
- Business benefits
- Business strategy

In Part Two of the book, each of these domains has its own section, making six sections in all. In this second part, the tools and techniques that help to make things manageable are presented and discussed—they map quite tightly to the processes that link these six areas of management activity.

First, some explanatory notes about the main components of the IMBOK—the *knowledge areas* and the *processes* (that is, the processes of *managing information*, not the main processes of the business).

The Knowledge Areas

Information technology: The world of technology is constantly changing and presents special challenges to those who would wish to understand it. An IT support group in a large organisation should know all about the different technologies that are used—the communications kit, the database software, the operating systems and even the physical infrastructure that houses the technology—but what can a smaller business do to protect its interests? And, what do we all need to know as individuals if we are to make the best possible use of technology? If new technologies appear every three months on average, do we need to update our investment every three months? If we do not, what will the consequence to be? This becomes an exercise in managing time horizons.

Information system: We make sense of technology by engineering it into information systems that include not just the hardware, but all the components of a working system *including* the human capability to work with the system to deliver outputs. Information systems have traditionally been developed and maintained by the "systems development department". There we find systems analysts, database designers and specialists who can test systems and make sure that they work according to the specification. But today, things are changing. Progressive organisations realised some years ago that they share information systems needs with other sibling organisations, so why should everyone suffer the cost of designing and building a unique solution to a shared problem? The *software package* has emerged as the preferred approach to the fulfilment of routine needs. From small personal productivity software that costs a few hundred dollars to huge enterprise-wide systems that cost millions, the expectation is that we will buy a ready-made solution rather than struggle to build our own. But exceptions are still to be found where a business has a truly unique requirement or where a business sees an opportunity that has not yet been exploited by others.

Business processes and **Business information**: Information systems are applied to business processes in order to improve them, and they bring data to the business that becomes useful as business information—it has already been argued that business systems are not the same as information systems. We may wish to make more widgets or to make them more cheaply or both; it is new business systems that will achieve this, not information systems alone. We may wish to increase the information content in our processes that deal with customers, so that we can relate to customers more closely—large businesses have become very interested in how they can use information technology to appear smaller through more intimate relationships with their customers; it is an improved business system that will achieve this, not a just a new database. Hereby, the differences between information systems and business systems become clearer. However, business *process* management is a relatively new idea, it is not universally adopted, and it has been difficult in many cases; business *information* management is even more of a challenge, and it is a resolutely difficult idea (that we will address here in new ways). A simple view is that a business process is something that extends from one boundary of a business to an opposite boundary, for example "customer order fulfilment", or that it delivers an outcome that is of direct concern to a specific stakeholder, for example "supplier management" or "shareholder relations". Those organisations that have adopted business process thinking would say that processes are the responsibility of functional managers: sales managers look after the activities that make up sales; production people look after production; senior management look after finance and corporate administration. However, there is always confusion about the difference between process management responsibilities and the organisation chart (the "organogram" as some people would call it). We must examine these differences and clarify them. In the same way, business information is something that enables an informed business decision to be made and that needs to be harvested from available data and structured as data in databases. Functional management must determine information needs, in order that effective database designs might be provided. It has been said that any organisation has only one information model, but that there is an infinity of process models that would serve it: we might be selling widgets (that will not change), but we can sell them by mail order, over the phone, on the Internet, or over the counter. More about this in due course.

Business benefit: Here is an interesting one. What *are* the benefits that we are seeking? Can we even anticipate them properly at an early stage in the investment analysis cycle? Will the benefits be evidenced through business performance improvement? How are the actions of managers and functional departments currently judged? By financial measures? Sales statistics? Transaction volumes? This complex area needs to be understood and effectively managed if we are to all work to a common end, but is there a single point of responsibility for the *delivery* of business benefits? As may be judged from all these questions, the management of business benefits from information technology investments is not well understood. In recent years, since the emergence and popularisation of the Balanced Score Card (Kaplan and Norton 1996), there has been huge interest in business performance management. However, not much serious effort has been made to relate business performance management to the benefits of information technology investments and the introduction of new information systems; where there has been research, the results are not clear and some analysis shows that the highest "IT spending" organisations (3 % of turnover or more?) do *not* perform as well as those that spend much less (say, 1 % of turnover). There is much more to this than just reaching into the corporate capital account (or into our personal savings or our donor funds).

Business strategy: Most organisations try to work with a strategy that guides and gives direction to their efforts, although the quality of typical organisation strategies varies widely. A business strategy is usually the product of senior management deliberations, but do senior managers really understand what is going on in the business? Sometimes (often, even?) they do not. And, how can we persuade people to act upon a strategy when it is decided and agreed? Developing strategies can be great fun: interesting meetings, challenging arguments, time with consultants and fully expensed weekends away from the office and away from home. At the end of the day, a handsome document with a refined analysis and clear targets for everyone to work to, but implementing strategies can be a nightmare. People worry about how strategy will affect them and they do not want to understand how it is dependent on *their* efforts to deliver some of the components of a strategy. Strategy formulation is easy; strategy implementation is extremely difficult.

The Information Management Processes

Suppose that we know all about the six knowledge areas. We have experts who know all about the technologies that we use. We have competent systems development staff that can work reliably to deliver good systems that meet the specification of the requirements. Functional management in the main business areas is strong and amenable to change, and the senior management team is well informed and sets reasonable targets.

Things can still go wrong. The problem lies in the *migration* of ideas and information management value from one area of competency to another, as indicated in Fig. 2.2.

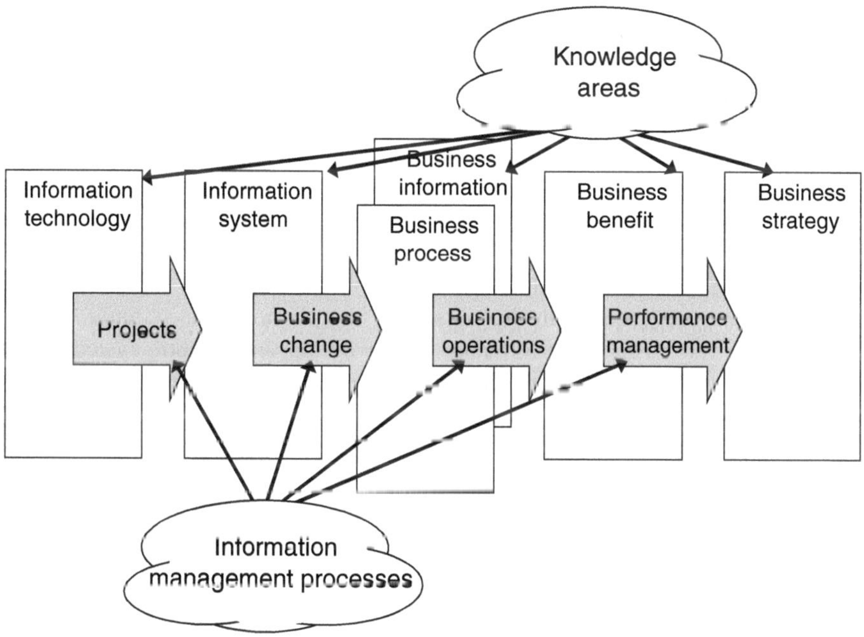

Fig. 2.2 Six management domains, four intersections of necessary alignment

Projects: Information technology is useless until it is engineered into information systems that meet the needs of the business systems (business processes and business information). Getting business people to articulate their needs can be extremely difficult. Consider the case where a new customer relationship management system is to be developed, based on Web technologies. Customer relationship management is not happening right now, at least not in any formalised sense. So, how can anyone tabulate and describe the facilities and functionality that might be needed? *Project management* is the information management process that delivers systems, and project management is still difficult. Project managers tend to focus on tasks, milestones, deliverables and budgets. Success is seen in "coming in on time and on budget" irrespective of the actual outcome at the level of the business. It is a rare project manager that can see how all the detailed work in a project will produce the business benefits that represent the fulfilment of strategy, but that understanding is necessary to achieve.

Business change: The best information systems succeed in delivering benefits through the achievement of change within the *business* systems. But people do not enjoy change, especially when it makes new demands upon their skills in the ways that new information systems often do. Consider the case where a new sales system allows sales staff to deal with sales orders over the Internet or over the telephone, where previously they were solely concerned with mail and fax orders. The previous expectation was to deal with an order within a week (say), but now customers expect the order to be dealt with in minutes. Telephone and computer skills that were previously needed only to deal with queries and complaints now need to be extended to deal with sales details and with the negotiation of terms and discounts. At the start that is not seen as a problem, but in the event, it causes staff stress and they will resent this kind of change unless it is properly managed.

Business operations: With new systems in place, with business processes and business information improved, and with staff finally ready and able to work with new processes, *then* the business can get to work. "Business operations" is the business at work: producing its goods and services, delivering value to customers and others, performing to the expected level, and earning revenue as well as delivering happiness to customers. We are now beyond the scope of the direct involvement of information technology and information systems staff, but we are still very much concerned with the benefits of new information systems, as seen through improved business performance. The way that information systems have impacted on business systems has changed markedly over the years: from the early days, when all that was needed was a demonstrable improvement in throughput or a marginal reduction in cost, we have progressed to the point where systems will sometimes dramatically change the ways that we work. In some retailing businesses, supply-side companies (such as the food producers or hardware suppliers) are now expected to manage the stock in the large retail stores directly, providing fresh stock when it is needed rather than waiting for the store management to place replenishment orders. This requires extensive information sharing and information management at a very operational level. The retailer may be asked to make a commitment to pay for supplied goods without an invoice on the grounds that the price and the terms of payment are already agreed. Retailers operating as "acquirers-and-breakers-of-bulk" become "renters-of-shelf-space". And now, just in case we thought we had solved and optimised the problem, Internet shopping is decimating the high streets of many cities. Who wants to trek into town and battle to find a car parking space, when they can buy everything that they need from the comfort of their home?

Performance management: There has been a dramatic rise of interest in the way that we manage business performance. From the early days, when financial results were everything, we have moved to a much more sophisticated regime where we strive to balance financial success with internal efficiency, with customer satisfaction and with organisational learning and development. It is no longer sufficient just to make money, we have to make the customer happy, we must work to improve internal operations so as to be "best of breed", and we have to ensure that all the time the organisation is moving forward in terms of capability and competencies. Performance management is where business strategy meets business systems and where the benefits of our investment in better business practice are finally seen and delivered.

Summary

There are always many ways to see a business, and the Information Management Body of Knowledge is only one way. It is important to see how other areas of business activity will also contribute to strategy—it is not only information technology that moves a business forwards. Human resource management, product development and marketing will all have an important role to play in strategic ways, and we must not see one domain of activity alone as the sole source of strategic success. On the other hand, human resource management, product development and marketing are all dependent on effective information management, and so in the final analysis, our competency to manage information well can be said to be predominant.

We have found six knowledge areas that stand as separate domains of management competence, each of which must be mastered if we are to succeed with information technology and information system-related investments:

- Information technology
- Information systems
- Business processes
- Business information
- Business benefits
- Business strategy

These are not six areas for sequential managerial action—they must rather be seen as parallel activities requiring continuous attention. Starting at the left-hand end or the right-hand end, they are six domains of expertise that could not all be easily dealt with by a single person—they must be the responsibility of different people with different management skills and backgrounds. It is the movement of ideas from one domain to another and from one person to another that has proved to be so difficult.

For years, now we have had a strong managerial interest in information technology and business strategy. What has emerged (and is not yet widely understood) is the importance of the intervening domains: information systems, business processes, business information and business benefits. We are therefore concerned here to identify and describe "best practice" in the six knowledge areas and the transfer of information value between them, as seen by experts around the world.

Part II
Exploring Information Management

The interest in aligning information systems and business strategies has prevailed for more than 30 years. Here, the alignment issues are divided into six areas or domains of management competency, with attention to the interfaces at which value is transferred from one domain to the next.

- **Information technology** is not the same as information systems, it is just the building blocks with which we work. As time progresses, it becomes increasingly possible to outsource information technology management, most recently into the "cloud", where applications continue to emerge that will handle most routine requirements.
- **Information systems**, sometimes called applications, are the vehicle for enabling improved business performance. The development of information systems in-house is a way of achieving differentiation and competitive advantage, but increasingly outsourcing eases this burden where information systems are not critical to success. There are significantly different approaches to systems development that are determined largely by a portfolio approach to their management. Seeing models that elucidate the design of processes and information structures is critical to success.
- **Business processes** and **business information** are both fundamental to how a business is seen and how it operates. Improving existing processes and identifying new ones, and designing information structures, is not the business of the information technology department, it is to be done by means of stakeholder analysis and deep reflection on the fundamental things that define the business and about which information is needed for effective operations and management control.
- **Business benefits** are often the poor relation of information management, given that a majority of businesses make no real effort to ensure that the promised or expected benefits of information technology and systems investments are delivered. In recent years a discipline for correcting this and pro-actively managing benefits has emerged and has raised great interest.

- **Business strategy** is often considered to be all about alignment but here we describe the process in detail and identify tools that can be used to formulate and implement viable strategies that deal with both the technology and the business. The applications portfolio is a key component of successful strategic management.

3 Exploring Information Technology

What Is Information Technology?

Information technology is a phrase used to refer to specific technical components, normally organised as hardware, software and communications, which are used to make up an information system. But that is an almost hopelessly simplistic view of what information technology is.

We often say "IT", without thinking about what it really means. For many years, "information technology" was a phrase that was used to refer to almost everything in the realm of computers and systems in business. As the IMBOK makes very clear, it is a long management journey from investing in raw information technology components to delivering the benefits of that investment, and by themselves information technology components may have no useful function at all. They need to be engineered into usable and useful *systems* that serve a real organisational need.

Nature of Technology

"Hardware", "software" and "communications" are the traditional categories of information technology. Teaching texts of the 1980s and 1990s often tabulate endless examples of each, such as the (limited) lists in Table 3.1.

But, what is the significance of these "information technology types" today? When you can acquire a sophisticated smart cell phone for just a few hundred dollars (even less "up front", in conjunction with a service contract), do we care what components there are within it? The fact is there are many thousands of components in the average cell phone, in each of the above categories—by some definitions, there are millions of components. A GPS (geostationary positioning system) facility that was once a separate device is now integrated into your smart cell phone. By the time this book

A. Bytheway, *Investing in Information*,
DOI 10.1007/978-3-319-11909-0_3

Table 3.1 Some examples of "traditional" technology types

Hardware	Software	Communications
Central processing unit	Operating system	Modem
Disk drive	Job scheduler	Multiplexer
Printer	I/O controller	Networking switch
Keyboard	Program code compiler	Terminal
Magnetic tape drive	Device driver	Communications line
	Database system	Optical fibre

gets to print, things will have moved on—at the time of reading, bar code reading, face recognition, and incorporation of smart phone capabilities into spectacles are all current developments. It is fruitless to wonder what specific miracles of technology might be still in development as you read this … what is more useful is to step back and think about the trends, and the patterns of technology innovation and obsolescence that will endure for a long time to come.

Experts are arguing that information technology is now so commoditised that it is no longer important to know its details. It is pre-engineered and pre-packaged so that we can buy information technology from a catalogue and, almost literally, plug it together and have it work for us without any real effort. Certainly, putting up a complex Website to support (for example) a cataloguing and retailing system is the work of a few hours. The acquisition of much new software is now a matter of logging on to the Web and downloading it—even if it is hundreds of megabytes. However, loading the *content* (the catalogue itself and other essential details required to make a working system that will sell your products and services securely) will take a good deal longer than the original installation and configuration of the system, because new human endeavour is required.

Context for Use

An important distinction is between the technology that is for our *personal* use (the PC together with end-user productivity software such as comes in an "office suite"), that which is aimed at small businesses (small client-server networks with applications suites such as Pastel and AutoCAD, and Web components such as Apache and MySQL), and that which is aimed at larger organisations (larger hardware configurations with enterprise suites such as SAP and PeopleSoft). There is also a vast range of special purpose technology—principally software—ranging from engineering to financial and medical (and back again).

There is an endless list of devices that now routinely include information technology that we might not be aware of: it is said that more than half the cost of developing the Boeing 777 airplane was for software development, more than for the airframe and drive systems; most modern motor vehicles contain engine control systems based on software and associated automatic controls. Bank cards and ID cards now contain processors, input–output facilities, and so on. The context within which information technology is now applied is huge, complex and expanding, and the impact on us all—as individuals, businesses, communities or public administrations—inculcates fundamental changes in society. Managing change is a matter of *strategy*.

Strategic Issues

Where we once talked of the strategic value of information systems, the commoditisation of technology makes that more difficult. Just having technology that another organisation does not have is no big deal—it is generally (but not always) easily available. As Nicholas Carr points out: "*What makes a resource truly strategic —what gives it the capacity to be the basis of a sustained competitive advantage—is not ubiquity but scarcity*" (Carr 2003). This will always be true. What becomes more interesting, from a strategic point of view, is how good an organisation is at recognising the potential of technology, acquiring it safely and deploying it through innovative information systems and organisational change management. Carr might be right about raw technology becoming a commodity, but he cannot argue that information systems and business processes are wholly commoditised, therein lies one of the principal opportunities for competitive advantage today, new business models and an organisational agility and culture that welcomes them.

Recognising Technology Potential

One of your author's favourite pastimes is recounting tales of missed management opportunity. The automatic teller machine (ATM or "cash" machine) is an old but good example that I was personally involved with. We all take ATMs for granted today, but when the idea was first conceived, specified and documented in the late 1960s, by a group of three salesmen working for the National Cash Register Company (NCR) in the NCR London banking division, the idea was met with derision at Corporate Headquarters in Dayton Ohio, USA. A formal and properly motivated product specification had been prepared wherein the very last paragraph suggested that the proposed terminal device could be weather-proofed, and fitted to the external wall of the bank. A droll reply came by telex the very next day: "*NCR is* not *in the business of knocking holes in the walls of banks*". Two years later, NCR headquarters was striving by all means possible to get an ATM onto the market and the resulting product generated an extremely useful cash flow. Some said that it saved the business from bankruptcy.

Another, even more astonishing story, concerns the invention of optical fibre technology, also in the United Kingdom. A young physicist called Charlie Kao, working for Standard Telephones and Cables' research laboratory in the UK, had devised ways to pump coherent light from a laser (then a very new and somewhat unreliable invention) down extremely narrow glass fibres—so narrow that they had to be contained within other glass fibres with a different optical refractive index. He published this work in 1966 but he was also derided—this time by his peers—because he ventured the unexpected opinion that, *if the glass could be made sufficiently pure*, information signals could be sent down fibres many kilometres long. It transpired according to one report that the local management had never approved his research, and they declared it a "bootleg" project and closed it down. Dr Kao went back to Hong Kong where he eventually became a successful senior academic and Vice Chancellor of the Chinese University of Hong Kong, but still maintaining his links with business in the USA. In 2010, he shared the Nobel Prize for Physics for this work, which was thereby finally and publically acknowledged. Neither STC nor any of its successors earned any licence revenue from this ground-breaking research work.

Such stories as these are amusing to relate, especially when one has been personally involved, but what is the significance for the average business, government or community? At one level, they simply make clear that, however, clever, motivated and organised you are, technology-based opportunities might pass you by; at another level, you might be the one that stumbles upon an idea that truly has the potential to change the world, but you are warned that people might not understand the merits of your idea. Most recently, your author (working with a colleague) developed a scheme for the application of advanced barcodes, containing structured information about people, places, products, services and other things, but we could find no financial support for some simple academic research into the need and the potential. Within just a little time, the two-dimensional "QR" codes began to populate advertisements, business documents and the Web, and a smart phone now has the capability to scan the codes and take actions according to their content. If you have the energy and time (and money) to investigate the commercial and societal benefits of these new codes, please feel free to take the idea and play with it. (Here is a hint: it is something to do with the "Internet of *things*" … but more about that later.)

So, what should be done to manage information technology opportunity properly? In any progressive organisation, two things need to happen:

- There must be time for innovation: selectively, people need to be motivated and capacitated to think about new technologies and to explore their potential.
- There must be a process for the evaluation of new ideas: organisationally, there needs to be a defined procedure whereby new ideas can be presented, discussed, tested and approved (or rejected).

These fundamental needs apply to information technology, information systems *and* business processes, and as we progress through our examination of the IM-BOK, the means to achieve them will become clearer.

Acquisition of Technology

The evidence points to a worrying mix of challenges relating to information technology supply. Apart from the obvious potential lack of appropriate skills and competencies within an organisation to negotiate effectively and to assure a proper contract of supply, infrastructure is sometimes inadequate and not well managed; that itself mitigates against successful acquisition. The rapid change in the nature and capability of information technology products and services also undermines our ability to manage information technology successfully. Many organisations have chosen to rely on outsourced supply, thereby accessing the skills and competencies of external specialist companies that have chosen to specialise in technology competencies. Some are good, but other suppliers tend to "drop the boxes and run" or charge high fees for the supporting services that make the technology usable and useful. Recently, a cloud services business that provided software development and program code library management services was hacked, and clients developing complex software systems lost all their data—live data, backup data and everything. The cloud service provider was left in an impossible situation and simply closed its business the next day. Organisations must learn to manage the relationship with technology suppliers to their advantage and to recognise and mitigate the risks.

Can we trust the "IT department" to do this for us? Do they have the right skills to negotiate well, and are they the best custodians of our interests as they fine-tune supply contracts for us? Not necessarily. There are different models for procurement —adversarial, negotiated, shared risk, and shared reward—one needs to be sure that one is adopting the best for one's circumstances, and IT skills alone are of no use when negotiating with adversarial or self-seeking business partners. Ian Angell—a radical academic based in London—has warned that the modern organisation is wholly dependent on its information technology and information systems and considers that information security is of paramount importance (Angell 1997, 2000). Anyone who believes that managing the consequences of information technology is just a matter of "getting organised" needs to read Ian Angell's arguments that there are severe problems ahead—it is necessary to get management thinking out of the minutiae of the technology and into the higher (metaphysical?) levels of information management strategy and change management.

Summary

Managerial Issues Concerning Information Technology

These worrying information technology supply issues are matched by problems with developing a forward vision. Effective project management, fulsome communication between role players, application of appropriate standards, proper planning and effective management of technology and technology suppliers all feature in any debate about a vision of good information technology management. We need strategies to deal with technology supply as just one component in a broader overall strategy for the organisation. Although in a book such as this, we must step lightly over specific issues of information technology because things are changing so fast, people working in the real world with real management responsibilities have to understand more about the specific issues of the moment. Take staffing: technology skills may be available but staff must be motivated to work well and not to seek employment elsewhere. Having said that, is "crowd sourcing" a viable approach to getting access to the best technology skills? What opportunities are offered by "open source" software? How can "bring your own device" be incorporated into the work of a busy organisation with real concerns about security of data? What is the reliability and the true cost of "software as a service"? The answer that will emerge here is that *it all depends* on the kind of information system that we have in mind, the specific information that is involved and the strategic significance of the business process or processes that they will support.

Perhaps, the most important single aspect of information technology management today is simple: to ensure that IT is used well. It is frightening to reflect on the power and capability of the modern personal computer and then the extent to which it is actually used in the typical organisation. Does that matter? Yes, it does. Although the cost of a typical PC has reduced markedly, the total cost of ownership including all support, consumables and maintenance and has been estimated as high as $50,000 over the life of a PC—and this is dramatically greater than the $1,000–2,000 that represents the original capital cost. Carr reported in 2003 that an estimated $2 trillion is spent worldwide on information technology each year. How much of that investment is *well spent* and how much of the technology is *well used* are interesting questions to ponder. It behoves every organisation to find a way to monitor the usage of technology and to weigh the demand for investment against the benefits. We shall come to that again in due course.

By way of summary, here are some of the managerial issues that we must deal with in the domain of information technology:

The scope of technology management: Increasingly, technology is becoming something that other people manage for us, that we do not acquire and that we have no need to understand in detail. It follows that senior management must be appraised of the risks and benefits of outsourcing (and all its variations) in order that the benefits of bringing technology in, and managing it internally, are known and used to determine the scope of in-house technology investment and the appropriate level of investment, not only in the hardware, software and communications equipment but also in the people who must be employed and trained to incorporate it into the infrastructure, operate it and maintain it. As noted, the cloud stands as an exceptional facility that dramatically changes the scope of internal technology management needs, but it carries risks of availability and security. We have yet to understand all of the consequences of this approach to systems implementation, but the extensive literature on outsourcing evidences a lot of expert analysis and opinion; for example, John Cross describes the early experiences at BP Chemicals (Cross 1995), Mary Lacity and colleagues provide a detailed review of research in the area and discuss the research that is still needed (Lacity et al. 2011), and a trades union in the UK even commissioned a more general review of outsourcing in the UK National Health Service (possibly with a degree of self-interest?) (Lethbridge 2012).

Managing suppliers: We need to understand the kind of relationship that we could most usefully have with our technology suppliers and then build it. Generally, it might be most appropriate to have a simple transactional relationship, but sometimes, there is merit in working more closely with suppliers. Different kinds of supplier relationships need to be recognised and managed appropriately, and the cost of dealing with suppliers must be understood and managed. For example, the City of Cape Town decided some years ago to acquire SAP enterprise resource planning software, despite the fact that originally, this was developed for manufacturing businesses. They negotiated directly with SAP, developed modules applicable to local government needs and now own the intellectual property in those modules. Was that a successful move? We await further reports, but the key message here is that it is sometimes important to be a good *customer*, and pushing suppliers to the point of abuse is not always a good idea.

Acquiring technology: More specifically, we must manage the acquisition of technology well. It is so very easy to spend excessively on technology "just in case", because of the difficulty in anticipating its effective use and the benefits that might arise. Justification and tendering procedures are needed and must be well managed. Clear criteria are needed for deciding what kind of supply arrangement to choose, in difference circumstances.

Managing the technology portfolio: It is useful to see the current investment in technology from a portfolio viewpoint: some technology will be working for us right now, and some will be the basis of future technological success. A portfolio view will ensure that technology requirements are well aligned with business strategies. It should also ensure that an organisation knows what technology it owns and where it is located —that can be a very real problem as the size of technological components reduces and its potential value increases and then declines.

Technology competencies: Even if relying heavily on suppliers to be skilled in dealing with technology, it behoves every organisation to maintain appropriate competencies in order to track technological developments and to understand what information technology is and where it comes from, and then to encourage a degree of experimentation, innovation and evaluation.

Budget management: It is unlikely that a single budget will be the best way to manage the acquisition of new technology. In some cases, it will be most appropriately funded through centralised capital budgets and in others through local (even departmental) budgets. Policies need to be in place and need to be understood. This is something else that we will come back to.

Finally, because of possible linguistic confusion, we need to be careful to use the term "information technology" to refer to the technology alone: information technology is the hardware, the software, the database systems and the communications networks that comprise the automated components of an information system. Any one of these—hardware, software, databases and communications—breaks down into its own complex hierarchy of components. For example, software includes operating systems, middleware, application software, browsers, language systems and so on. A full "family tree" of information technology components would be very complex and need not concern us here. Here, we are interested in how we manage these things, not how we engineer them.

Having said that the skills required to engineer these technologies and to make useful systems out of them are difficult to learn and do not sit well with the requirements of business people who just want a system delivered to their desks and who are not interested in the complexities of technology. Hence, if we are to manage information technology successfully, we need to encourage the proper use of the phrases "information technology" and "information system" to indicate that there are two layers of different activity and management concern that are related but separate from each other.

Information Technology Management Competencies

In order to assess the level of competency to deal with information technology management, here following are some of the competencies and preconditions that have been found to be required.

- An understanding that information technology investments are—in the end—driven by customer's and other stakeholder's needs.
- Well-defined policies and standards for sourcing technology, and clear criteria for deciding what kind of supply contract to choose, making sure that experimental or innovative initiatives are encouraged but ring-fenced.
- Well-defined relationships with technology suppliers, defined according to circumstances.
- A good understanding of the cost of dealing with suppliers.
- An established portfolio of existing and future technology requirements.
- Monitoring the effective usage of technology and managing its effectiveness.
- Defensible justification for the acquisition and cost of technology.
- Access to people who maintain a good understanding of technology.
- Provision of training in technology when and where it is needed.
- Good information technology support for business users.
- Avoidance of lock-in to specific technologies and vendors.
- Effective use of outsourcing in the provision of technology, systems and related services.

Research Side Note: Chasing the Hottest IT

Wang, P. (2010) Chasing the hottest IT: Effects of Information Technology fashion on organisations. MIS Quarterly, 34 (1), pp. 63–85.

Wang Ping has looked at what happens to organisations that follow or even lead information technology "fashion", and therefore favour the very latest information technology. Wang looked at 109 large companies' performance over ten years. What was found was that such behaviour creates an impression that the organisation has a good reputation, and that the levels of executive pay in such organisations are high (that is interesting!), but the actual organisational performance **is not better** than industry averages in the short term, only in the longer term. Hence managers responsible for information technology need to find a balance between simple business pressure to perform, and their innate need for the admiration of their peers.

Research Side Note: Yes, Technology Is Cool, but Don't Forget the People

Schwarz, A., Chin, W.W., Hirschheim, R. & Schwarz, C. (2014) Toward a process-based view of information technology acceptance. Journal of Information Technology, 29 (1), pp. 73–96.

For a long time, academic research has looked at the way that people react to new information technology in their work, because resistance to new technology and new systems is a source of common difficulty. The "Technology Acceptance Model", familiarly known within academic work simply as "TAM", has prevailed since it was first published in the late 1980s. But Andrew Schwarz and colleagues have dug deeper and propose a new model, based on the stages that people go through. They show how people behave when they first hear about a new technology, learn more about it and how it works, form an opinion about it, and then either accept or fight it. This is an example of a very academic paper. As it stands, this research merely cautions us that there are stages that people go through, and understanding those stages at least gives a focus to the actions that managers can choose to take in different circumstances. Further, this paper provides copious evidence of the negative thinking that is likely to emerge amongst users. It helps us to understand, at this early stage in our discourse, that the acquisition of new information technology might be the beginning of a whole new raft of problems, not necessarily just happiness.

Exploring Information Systems

4

What Is an Information System?

An information system is not the same as the technology upon which it is based: it is the totality of technological and human components that work together to produce the information services that are needed, for organisational purposes.

We usually use the words "information" and "system" without thinking what they might mean. Just take the word "system" alone—it has many uses and many nuances, from talking about national politics ("political system") to possibly obscure aspects of science ("eco-technology systems").

And then, "information" is one of those words that make less and less sense the more you think about it. The combination of the two words—"information" and "system"—is often seen as synonymous with "information technology" or just "IT", but here we must make a very clear distinction, as indicated above.

Nature of Information Systems

An information system, although it is a combination of information technology, information systems engineering and human capability, has to be a reflection of the organisation that uses it, the organisation's style of operation and the work that it actually does, just as a house is a reflection of what we want to do at home and the way we want to live. The analogy with housing is a useful one: to design a house, we need an architect and possibly an engineer; to build a house, we need bricklayers and carpenters. To design an information system, we need business analysts; and to build it, we need software programmers, database designers, and systems integrators.

A. Bytheway, *Investing in Information*,
DOI 10.1007/978-3-319-11909-0_4

This analogy with houses is not intended to "put down" the skills of programmers and database designers, because as soon as you investigate what makes up an information system and compare it with what makes up a house, you realise that information systems are infinitely more complex than houses. (And, on the other hand, there is much to admire in the skills of a good bricklayer and a good carpenter that is often missing in the finished work of programmers and database designers). Just as the supply of building materials is a completely a different kind of business from one that constructs houses, the manufacture and supply of information technology are completely different to the design and construction of information systems.

Whilst the housing analogy is useful, it has its limitations and there are other aspects to information systems management that are important to understand. For example, there are different ways in which we can classify systems. We can organise them according to:

The degree of formality: Some information systems are almost entirely informal, or ad hoc. For example, in an organisation, much information is communicated through social processes, whether by face-to-face conversation or by using email messages. Are we to regard this as a kind of information system? Yes, surely we must.

Such conversations become more formalised when they are brought into "discussion forums" and "electronic conferences", where there may be someone who moderates and organises the contributions to the discussion, because now everyone can see what others have said. And, there is a formal record of what has been discussed and—in some cases—decisions that have been reached.

As we progress our thinking to the core high-volume information systems such as those that process sales orders, invoices and payments, there is clearly a much higher degree of formality because of the rules of doing business with others. On the other hand, some strategic information systems, for example those that support customer relationship management, may need more flexibility and less formality in some functions, for example where sales people are expected to make open comments about the relationship with a customer or to record the outline of a telephone conversation. As we reflect on the different levels of formality that may be involved, we begin to realise that the users of information systems need to understand something about the level of formality and may need to be trained in order that they can use them appropriately. Clerical staff who have been trained in specific data entry techniques might really struggle for a whilst when they are moved on to work with systems that have fewer rules and no constraints on data entry—front-line staff who have worked unsupervised, and relied on their innate knowledge and capabilities, will react badly when given systems that take control of what they can do.

The degree or extent of automation: Historically, the more routine and formalised a system is, then the more likely it is that it can be automated—possibly to a very high degree. However, this is no longer always true. Consider the case of call centres, where there is an interesting combination of structure (most call centre operators are working to carefully designed scripts that guide them through their tasks) and informality (call centre operators are working with people, and there must always be some latitude in dealing with people who might be angry, anxious, or frustrated). Consider the differences between an ATM cash dispensing system that is almost completely automated, providing four or five basic banking services, and a telephone banking system where skilled operators are able to undertake almost all conceivable banking transactions. The degree of automation is very different because of the different scope of what is offered. There is a limit to what can be automated in most businesses. Health care, for example, is becoming much more automated, but the human contact is absolutely critical to providing satisfactory health care services.

Their relation to decision-making: For many years, there has been very specific interest in the way that information systems support decision-making. It has become a common remark that "data, when read, becomes information; information, when understood, becomes knowledge". The next step is to ask: what is knowledge, when it is deployed? But for most of us, knowledge deployed is simply a decision that is taken—a *well-informed* decision, one hopes.

It is interesting to look at models of how businesses work, plotting the movement of information from one point to another, and to realise that decision points are not always fully informed so that good decisions can be taken. In one model of an international supply chain, decisions taken by large-scale fishing operators were based on a single informal, in accurate memorandum from a different continent, that purported to communicate the level of retail demand in Europe but in fact was based on a single manager's whimsy.

Management decisions need to be properly informed and are often seen at different levels: *strategic decisions* that will affect the future performance of the business must be based on information that probably comes largely from outside the organisation; *control decisions* that affect current operations at the level of production control and forecasting must be based on information that comes from within the organisation on a daily and weekly basis; finally, *operational decisions* that affect working on the ground on a moment-to-moment or hour-by-hour basis, based on information about current operations and according to well-defined rules.

The value to the organisation: Perhaps the most interesting classification of information systems is the way in which a system provides value to the organisation. Some information systems are deployed only for regulatory purposes. For example, every business must manage its books of account and the only sensible way to do that in a business of some size is to automate them. But, what is the value? Statutory requirements are satisfied, and directors of the business can relax in the knowledge that they will not fall foul of the law; on the other hand, an information system that is truly strategic and that wins significant new business delivers *real* value—to the business, to its shareholders and to its employees.

How odd it is that so many businesses try to manage *all* information systems projects *in the same way*, without recognising the significant differences that can arise from the nature of the *value* that the system will deliver. Management thinking has migrated over the years from investing in systems that provide purely internal (and relatively limited) benefits, to investing in much more ambitious systems that stretch beyond the boundaries of one organisation and may in the end involve whole industries. Today, there may be debates about the commoditisation of information technology, at the same time that there are debates about the criticality of information systems and the need to secure them (see the discussion of Nicholas Carr's and Ian Angell's writings, earlier), but in the final analysis some information systems will always be strategically important to progressive organisations. This is a theme that will underpin much of the narrative in this book.

Information Systems Maturity

The above ideas that characterise information systems are helpful, but they reveal little about the longer-term trends that are important to an understanding of the proper management of information systems. A better way to see longer term trends is through two important characteristics of information systems that have been changing over decades and that continue to change today: first, the *scope* of information systems, and second, the nature of the *s* that are sought, or expected, from an information systems investment. Both of these characteristics of information systems progress over time: the scope of some information systems, once confined to a single organisation, now reaches right across the world, joining businesses to businesses, businesses to government, and individuals to everyone and everything else. This expanding scope arises from a rising confidence in our collective ability to conceive, develop and implement systems with vast scope, to embark upon ever more adventurous information system designs, and a rising willingness amongst key players in different sectors to share their collective interest in good systems and invest in them on an industrial scale.

The 3x4 figure (Fig. 4.1) shows one view of the way that the nature of information systems has evolved over the years, based upon the change in the benefits that have been sought (the three columns) and the scope or reach of systems (the four rows).

System **benefits** were seen in the beginning as a matter of simple *efficiency*, within a single organisation. With maturity and experience, organisations begin to seek *effectiveness*, not just by simple efficiency (if you have never done so, think about the differences between "efficiency" and "effectiveness" for a moment), and effectiveness often derives from working beyond the limits of the single organisation by sharing systems and benefits with partners. Ultimately, a progressive organisation may seek to evolve its very form and nature (and that of its industry) through more advanced use of information systems that radically change what the business is, and how the industry works. Having said that, we must note that truly radical innovation as evident in the operations of Amazon and Google does not come from within extant organisations, it more often comes from frustration and hours imagining and developing new ideas in back rooms and garages. Evolution is as much about step change and paradigm shifts as it is about incremental evolution.

The **scope** of information systems was initially confined within single organisations but with experience progressive businesses sought to link their systems with

	Efficiency	Effectiveness	Evolution
Company	Departments within organisations see the opportunity to save a little time and money by "computerisation".	With experience gained, people see the possibility to achieve a better output, or outcome from organisational activity, and business process re-engineering begins	Success breeds ambitions to change or extend what the organisation is, based on information-based products and services. Industries are re-engineered.
Community	Communities of commons interest get together to share the benefits of common systems in (for example) EDI and supply chain management.	Industry processes are rationalised and the role of the different players in a business starts to change. Operational information is shared rather than hidden.	Widescale rationalisation and disintermediation of role players begins, and new entrants disrupt normal practice in a radical way, especially on the Web.
Country	Radical national investment in IT infrastructure and the rise of regulatory systems. Endemic use of the Web.	Globalisation of business systems. Governments struggle to maintain control and excess (as in banking) leads to crisis.	Rise in the sovereignty of information, and the gradual decline of geo-political structures.
Cloud	Personalisation and detachment of systems begins as mobile technology and the Internet of things spreads.	The influence of global providers of software as a service rises, and challenges the idea of national identity and regulation.	A shift from single, actual personal identity to multiple "constructed" web identities – the rise of the virtual world.

Learning 60s Rationalising 80s Restructuring 00s

Fig. 4.1 Scope and benefit of information systems

those of key partners, such as suppliers, customers, banks and logistics operators. Thus, we begin to see a community or industry effect that delivers the shared benefits referred to above. Ultimately, systems are seen that extend beyond a single business, or even industry, and take on importance at the regional, national or global levels. At the time of writing, the cloud has rapidly become critically important to organisations of all kinds, at all levels and for the moment we can nominate the cloud as the one idea that extends beyond company, community and country.

The combination of these two things, benefits and scope, allows us to define the eras through which information systems have gone (and continue to go): first, *learning* about the potential of information systems to improve business performance, then *rationalising* how a business works, in order to improve performance and deliver better services and outcomes to stakeholders, and then to much more radially *restructure* the way that things work. Figure 4.1 illustrates (selectively) how this has happened, and how it might continue to happen.

In this way, these two things—benefits and scope—characterise the change in the nature of information systems over the decades more than any other characteristics of information systems. The combination of the two, as each progresses from early to later stages, reveals much about how management thinking has developed over the years. The notes below discuss some aspects of each of these many stages, in chronological sequence, as they might apply to an imagined business (but by no means *all* aspects—that would be a huge task); whilst much of this is now history, there are important messages in the trends that can be observed.

Internal efficiency: Initially, say 50 years ago for the "early adopters", information technology and systems investment were justified with the expectation of improved internal efficiency. Tasks that were already undertaken by clerks were computerised with the intention of reducing staffing levels. Tasks such as invoicing, accounting and order processing were developed to mimic the manual activities replaced. The "DP (Data Processing) Department" had been born. Information technology tools were developed to meet the needs of such systems. Large numbers of technicians were recruited. System flexibility was not especially important, as the systems developed did not change very much through time.

Internal effectiveness: As time passed, attention turned towards using the information stored in the early systems to improve the effectiveness of the work of the organisation, especially in management. "Management Information Systems" were born. The information related to the internal workings of the organisation was summarised for the purposes of better management.

But major problems developed, because the tools available to develop systems were those first used for data processing. New levels of flexibility were required but were not really available. The underlying systems and the tools for systems development were inflexible and difficult to use.

On the other hand, things got better for customers. For example, airlines could provide ever more personal services, thereby justifying premium prices for those travellers wanting them, yet they could still contain operational costs by means of key operational systems for flight management, crew allocation and maintenance. Add to this a high level of customer service based on maintaining information about premium travellers and their use of airline services, and suddenly, it is not just about appealing to discerning customers, it is about extending revenue earning and increasing customer commitment across the board.

Internal evolution: Moves to integrate information systems, and the confidence that was ultimately gained in developing systems, led management to understand that systems could change the very nature of the business. Not only could information services be added to conventional products and services, but new revenue streams could be generated and—in exceptional cases—the "Data Processing Department" was floated as a separate business unit or entity offering data processing services in the open market.

External efficiency: The horizons seen by businesses began to widen, and the boundaries of the systems that serve business widened even more. Organisations realised that it is inefficient to print out an order on paper and to post it to a supplier, just so that suppliers can key the details into their systems. Systems owned by different organisations were connected to form "electronic data interchange" (EDI) networks that overcome these inefficiencies. Orders, invoices, product specifications and other information are now routinely transferred electronically. Efficiency is the main benefit, but now it has an external focus and is shared by whole communities of businesses.

External effectiveness: With experience of EDI efficiencies, and having achieved internal effectiveness through second-stage systems, progressive organisations then realised that there was potential for improved effectiveness at the industry level. For example, rather than two organisations carrying stock of a particular item, it would be advantageous for stock information to be shared and for all stock to be kept in a single place. The first signs emerged of supply chain and industry restructuring, for the mutual advantage of all role players (except perhaps for employees, who were further threatened by the economies of scale and the rationalisation of business processes). Large manufacturing companies took millions of dollars of cost out of their supply chains.

Industry evolution: Sharing information and optimising stockholdings led to a change in the structure of industries. In fast moving consumer goods, there was rationalisation of warehousing and transportation arrangements. The very question of who owns goods as they move through the supply chain was challenged so that the original manufacturer could retain ownership (and responsibility for stock management) right through to the point where a consumer buys it over the counter. A business-making tooth paste, that earns no revenue until the toothpaste is finally sold to the consumer, has to seriously change its view of business operations. Suddenly, it is not about chasing payment of invoices to retailers, it is about a fine level of stock management at many levels in the supply chain. Huge rewards and cost savings can be gained if such improvements can be made to work. With this new kind of thinking, customers can raise invoices on themselves, and suppliers can raise purchase orders on behalf of their customers. It started to happen in the 1990s, and it still happens today. The same is even truer in the service sector: for example, in the travel industry, there has been widespread rationalisation and disruption with the emergence of information services such as online booking (that excludes the travel agent), and traveller rating systems that allow one to choose a hotel or restaurant based on guest reviews and price, and make a booking forthwith.

National and international efficiency: There are examples where whole countries have adopted information systems at the national level, to improve efficiency and to create an attractive environment for inward investment and to attract international businesses to come and work there, rather than in other countries. Singapore comes to mind immediately, as an early and classic case of national investment in information technology, right back in the 1980s. It has paid off handsomely. Singapore has highly efficient banking and trade management systems, and more than half of its GDP is generated through *other countries' trade*. At the same time, the World Wide Web emerged as a primary force for computerisation on a national and trans-national basis and suddenly rendered the Internet an accessible and universal medium of working for everyone.

National and international effectiveness and evolution: We are now close to the modern day. Considering the effects of globalisation and the supremacy (in informational terms) of global organisations, we begin to ask whether we really understand what a "country" is. The idea of the *community (of practice, of interest ...)* comes to the fore, and it begins to be more important to know what information privileges someone has rather than what country they come from. From Internettrading, where one is almost entirely unconcerned with where your purchased goods might be coming from, to the present level of terrorism, which has become a trans-national affair and which is very concerned with information technology and information management, many of us are becoming less sensitive to national issues and more concerned with global issues and information privileges.

In this new world, one needs high speed broadband Internet access, because a traditional modem is not sufficient to browse and buy at the pace we wish to. Community usage of information technology and systems becomes a primary driver for the IT industry, and the formalised markets for "traditional" IT services begin to fade as commoditisation takes over. Interestingly, information technology skills become more ubiquitous, just like the technology itself, and the long-held shortage of skilled personnel is suddenly not such a critical reality. Ordinary people begin to do extraordinary things with Web technologies, and a whole new approach to information systems emerges.

At the same time, there are millions of people in the world who live in poverty and who in their lifetimes will never enjoy the benefits of free and unfettered access to information. Although there are many initiatives that strive to bring information technology to the poor, only some are successful and many conclude with no benefit other than some kind of reputation (and possibly cash flow) to the non-profit organisations that promote them (and their agents). It must be noted that the "digital divide" is a reality and a challenging one.

The cloud: At this point, we start to look to the future. Everyone in business seems to have heard of "the cloud," but few people seem to know exactly what to do with it. Is it secure? What are my rights? Is our data safe there?

And just around the corner we have the "Internet of things", wherein every *thing* will be connected, every *thing* will generate data and every *thing* will take on its own persona. At the same time, as sentient human beings, each one of us can already adopt multiple identities and personae so that we can present different images to the world in different situations. Web service providers become expert at profiling our activity and connecting us to our friends, in ways that governments never dared imagine. One wonders, where will this all end? It will end with winners and losers, as always, and that is why we need tools and techniques to analyse and understand the directions in which we are headed so as to manage better.

What do we learn about information systems, from this complex evolution-arypicture? It is important because many organisations are still stuck in the very early stages, and this framework allows an organisation to position its thinking in a strategic way. In some, information systems are managed strictly within the organisation, and there is no expectation to evolve or re-engineer the business, and the benefits of information technology and systems investments are strictly limited. For some organisations, the stimulus to think more progressively comes from external influences, such as suppliers (who have, for example, started to publish their catalogues online), customers (who now demand a web site that supports the business and avoids the need to telephone or email with routine enquiries) and even from the tax authorities (who begin to insist that tax returns are submitted online, rather than by post). Many individuals are now familiar with Internet banking and most enjoy the benefits; the banks benefit because customers now do the basic data entry themselves, dramatically reducing some key internal operating costs within the bank and moving the responsibility for accuracy to the customer.

The extent to which an organisation or an industry (or even a whole country) has developed its thinking within this framework is a good indicator of its information technology and information systems maturity. By examining the application of information systems in this way, it is possible to see the kinds of benefit that are being achieved and the benefits that could be achieved in the next major phase of strategic investment and information systems development.

We learn that the *maturity* of thinking about information systems can be graded and these things will prove to be key indicators of other aspects of the IMBOK: the nature of business *processes* and the organisational *culture for change*, the *kind of benefits* that are sought from information technology investments, and the *kinds of strategy* that might prevail. But before we press on to look at these "higher" level domains of the IMBOK, we must examine some specific aspects of information systems: how they are specified, how they are deployed and some of the current management issues that they raise.

The Applications Portfolio

Because attitudes to information systems shift with the maturity of organisational thinking and with attitudes in business and society, we have to find a way to manage information systems differently from one case to the next. An information system that is a source of competitive advantage presents certain challenges, and one that just shaves a few percentage points off operating costs presents other challenges. For years, this was acknowledged, but there was no widely understood scheme whereby the *differences* between systems could be explained at a strategic level, and the consequences for management could be understood.

One approach that has found almost universal favour amongst those managers that have studied it is to work with a *portfolio* of information systems. Warren McFarlan takes the credit as the first to point out that just as we expect a business to have a portfolio of products and services, every organisation can improve its management of information by recognising the need for a "portfolio" of information systems. As early as 1984, he argued that through an understanding of their current and future strategic significance, the risk of information systems projects, separately and together, can be supported by better informed decisions that will deliver more successful outcomes (McFarlan 1984).

The essential idea that McFarlan worked with originates from the realm of marketing, where for many years, there have been ideas that highlight the differences between products (in the general sense) at the early, middle and late stages of their effective life cycles. The idea in question is the "Boston Box"—a portfolio model that organises the life cycle of a product into four stages, each of which is named in a way to reflect the status of the product at that stage: *wild cat*, *rising star*, *cashcow* and *dog* are the names normally given to the four stages, broadly relating to innovation, adoption, deployment and decline of a product. First, let's look at the general features of the Boston Box, and then we can examine its application to information systems as the internal product of a specialist provider: the information systems department.

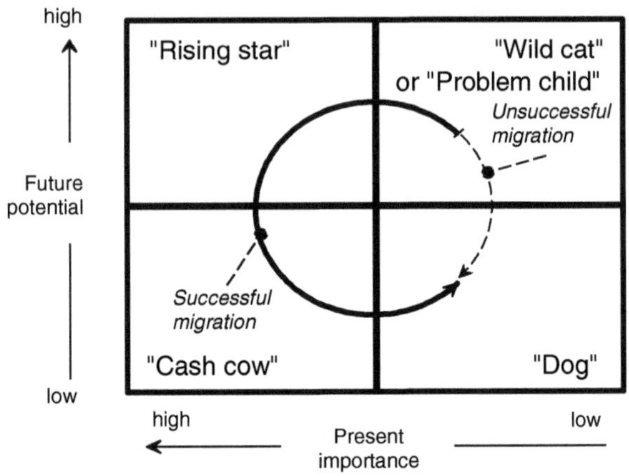

Fig. 4.2 Introducing the Boston Box

(The Boston Box will be examined again, in a later section dealing with strategic analysis tools.)

As indicated in the figure, a product has a life cycle that starts with innovative thinking (Wild cat), if it is a good idea, this, in turn, becomes strategically important (Rising star), and if all goes well, it turns into a product that generates revenue and repays the cost of innovation and development (Cash cow). A product that is past its time becomes a Dog. Note that new ideas that are adopted but then fail can migrate *directly* to the Dog quadrant—the "unsuccessful" migration in Fig. 4.2. The message is that every business dependent on product sales needs to manage a portfolio that ensures it has a constant flow of new ideas and ensures that products past their time are recognised and managed appropriately.

This idea is not as complex as it seems at first sight, because it exercises only two questions:

- How important is this product in terms of its *future potential*?
- How important is this product to our *present success*?

An example will help. In quite recent history, say in the 1990s, the *overhead projector* was a cash cow. Every school, college and university needed one in every classroom, every business needed one in every meeting room and even churches used them to project the words of hymns on a screen for the congregation to follow. The overhead projector was a "cash cow", because demand was constant and those businesses making them had a steady way to make money. But their technological features were fully developed and there was little that would further advance their performance or desirability, and so when the digital *data projector* emerged, it took the idea of classroom projection into a completely new place. In the beginning, the data projector was a complex, expensive and unreliable device that was far beyond the budgets of typical businesses and colleges. But, some businesses and colleges began to buy them, and as they became cheaper, smaller and more reliable they became the norm in the meeting rooms and classrooms of the world.

So what comes next? Soon, no doubt, people at meetings and in classrooms will see the material of a presentation as a "head-up display" in their digital spectacles, yet another idea that seems (at the time of writing) to be a "wild cat", but one with a bright future.

The simple move that we must make in our minds is to recognise that *information systems can be seen as products*, and they also have a similar life cycle. When applied to information systems, the portfolio model is generally known as the "Applications Portfolio". By regarding an information system as a "product", that migrates and matures through four identifiable and quite different stages in its lifetime, we might find that many managerial issues start to fall into place.[1]

This is indeed the case, because information systems were seen for at least twenty years in a very *singular* way, when in fact they are not a "singular" problem. In the early days, differences between different kinds of information system seemed to be of no great concern (and were in any case less marked than they are today). More recently, the differences are very significant, and there are endless examples where information systems that were innovative or experimental in nature were forced through a conventional systems development lifecycle, so that they succeeded only with great difficulty or sometimes failed completely.

In the face of difficulty, the tendency in the past has been to introduce more particular *standards* for information systems design, more *rules* and more *procedures*, in order to "tighten up" the way that systems were being produced. This is appropriate in some cases but not in all. The applications portfolio makes clear that there are at least four different kinds of situation that we might find, each requiring a significantly different managerial approach.

Of all the ideas that have been introduced into management education about information systems and information management, the applications portfolio is the most useful, the most enduring and the most enjoyed by students, and so here we will adopt it—not only to explore the differences between different kinds of information system, but also to resolve issues of how they should be managed.

In line with the current literature about information system management, we name the four quadrants as follows (as shown in Fig. 4.3):

- **Turnaround**[2] (Wild cat)
- **Strategic** (Rising Star)

---

[1] It is unfortunate that terminology now presents a small challenge, because we seem to have the interchangeable terms "application" and "information system", which may or may not mean the same thing to different people. In conversation today, we also have the diminutive term "app" something that works with your tablet or smart phone. For the present purpose, we will use these terms interchangeably.

[2] In other literature, "Turnaround" systems are sometimes referred to as "High Potential" systems, but that seems overly optimistic—not all experimental systems certainly have high potential, they have to be turned around in order to test their potential.

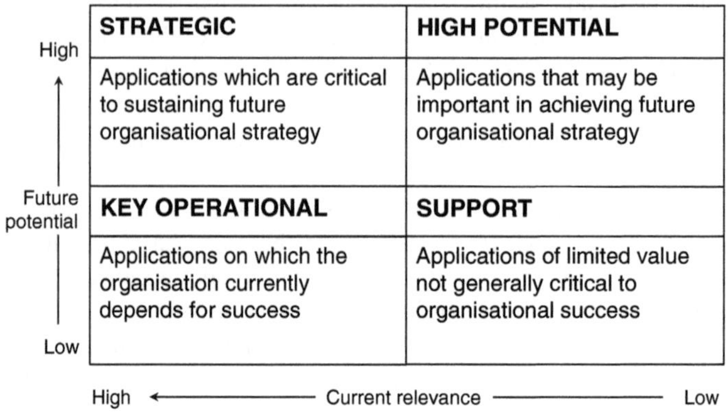

Fig. 4.3 The applications portfolio

- **Key Operational**[3] (Cash cow) and
- **Support** (Dog)

These chosen names are not so evocative as those of the Boston Box, but they are clearly indicative of what is intended. The paragraphs that follow discuss each in turn.

Turnaround Information Systems

> Applications that may be important in achieving future organisational strategy

A small proportion of turnaround applications might ultimately provide strategic opportunities and help to secure the future of the company, a larger proportion might turnout to be a waste of time and resources. A progressive organisation recognises this and finds a way to encourage innovation by investing in the future. Laggardly organisations do not recognise this, and generally wait until competitors have established a new information system idea before making the move (by which time the system idea is no longer "turnaround", nor even "strategic, perhaps?). An organisation that refuses to enable turnaround activity will always lag, whereas one that nurtures and sustains experimentation will never be short of potentially useful systems ideas.

[3] In his original writing, Warren McFarlan referred to these as "Factory systems" but time and usage have determined that they are better referred to more simply, as "Key operational systems".

How does one go about systems development in this quadrant? Not with meticulous attention to standards, nor even with large teams of specialists drafted into assist. Development in this part of the applications portfolio has to be done by (or in very close conjunction with) the person whose idea it is, and that person may be a "user" rather than a technical specialist. The objective is not to change the world, nor even to actually implement a working system, but to work up an information system idea and *test its true potential*. Once this potential is tested, when there is a consensus that the idea is useful and important, and when the rest of the organisation has agreed to take it on board, then the style of development will have to change. But until it is approved as a legitimate strategically relevant idea, development needs to be fluid, exploratory and as rapid as possible. There is no benefit in protracted development and a search for perfection; every effort should be directed towards the qualification of the idea, as quickly as possible. If the idea proves to be a good one, then it can be progressed, but if it is not, then it can be discarded. Turnaround systems development activity is as much about recognising and enjoying failure as it is about success.

Strategic Information Systems

Applications that are critical to sustaining future organisational strategy

A strategic information system needs to have the support and commitment of more than just a few users. Such a system will not be strategic unless and until all involved staff agree that it is so, especially senior management or organisation leaders, because changes to business practice will be involved and the management of change requires a high level of commitment. The specification of requirements must be done with the business in mind and with more attention to what *might* be done in the future than what *is* done now. Thus, we might say that *business* analysts are required, not *systems* analysts. Good business analysts are difficult to find because they must straddle the divide between the worlds of technology and business; some of the best examples of success can be attributed to talented people who acted in this role and did well, in other cases, people have failed in this role and disaster has ensued. Even the best technical specialist will probably fail, if given responsibility (by design or default) for the conception and specification of a strategic information system. Business analysis is difficult in the strategic context because of the need to explore new territory, where users will not be able to articulate their needs straightforwardly and yet an understanding of needs (and potential benefits) is critical. A degree of experimentation and a good deal of business change management may be required.

The tools that are used in these cases may be different. The challenge is to formulate and test new ideas about the business in order that they can be realised by means of new systems. The ideas may originate from the turnaround quadrant of the portfolio, or they may be seeded in corporate strategy: organisational objectives, critical success factors and the other stuff of strategic analysis. It is therefore important that the communication of business ideas (using appropriate models and possibly prototype systems) is not just encouraged but *driven* by means of energetic management activity and commitment. In this way, all those involved will be able to assure themselves that the proposals are appropriate and sound. Strategic systems are demanding of management time, principally because of the effort that is required to grow an idea, test it and then settle it down and stabilise it to the point that it can be incorporated into a new system design.

The construction of a strategic system also needs a particular approach. The trick is to work quickly, because one is seeking competitive advantage and this is only possible within a window of opportunity that might be usurped by competitors. Clearly, a new strategic system must work at a functional level, and to some extent, it will have to integrate with existing systems, but one cannot afford to let the IT team dwell upon fine points of technical detail. It is important that strategic systems are built quickly and competently, but in most cases, their parts will be re-engineered later, perhaps over extended periods of time, so as to achieve efficiency of operation. At the start, efficiency in operation is not as important as innovative functionality, but nevertheless the development team must try to forecast the workload levels and ensure that there is enough capacity in the infrastructure to sustain the system in use, even if it is planned to re-engineer it later to make it more efficient.

Websites are a good example. Most large banks are now well past the early stages where the critical objective was to get a web site up and running, knowing that the demand would actually be quite low but that the important thing (strategically) was simply to be able to say that a web site was up and running, to be credible and to appear progressive. Then, famously, a number of banks were embarrassed by the exceptional level of interest, leading to overloading of limited infrastructure, system failure and seriously unhappy customers. It is all a balancing act, and we are reminded that strategic information systems *demand* a culture and a context that is willing and able to deliver change. Without that an organisation might be better advised not to even start, but to wait until the merit of a new idea has been adequately demonstrated by competitors (there is nothing wrong in being a laggard rather than a leader, provided that a business has other strengths).

Key Operational Information Systems

Applications on which the organisation currently depends for success.

Key operational systems are different again. There are fewer mysteries here because the area of application is likely to be well known, it is probably already common to all the main players in a certain industry (and therefore *not* strategic), and there may well be off-the-shelf packages available, which provide a suitable vehicle for implementation (although they are not always cheap—when consultancy assistance, support and training are taken into account, six- and seven-figure US$ prices are common for the larger enterprise-wide software packages).

Clearly, there is a pattern emerging here. Larger, more forward thinking companies often find themselves blazing a trail with new ideas that are, in the beginning, strategic. They put the new strategic systems together despite all the challenges because they can afford the very high development and management costs involved—others cannot. They can justify the expense because it consolidates their dominance of a market. When the ideas begin to be adopted by the majority of players in that market, then systems tend to become available from independent software suppliers (sometimes in the form of a modification of a system first developed by one of the main market players). At the same time, these systems can be replicated in competitor businesses more cheaply because the nature of the application has become well known, and there will be people around who can be hired for their experience and knowledge of the information systems that deliver it.

Thus, the information systems that comprise the basis of key operational applications may be found as packages and may not require bespoke (in-house) development. The requirement still needs to be specified, however, because a good package will offer many options and there will be work to do in setting it up and configuring it properly. Even if a package is the primary vehicle for implementation, it still has to be evolved or manipulated into the form and function that the business actually requires. It is a mistake to confuse the two. If a business decides that using someone else's system can easily solve their problems, then they will almost certainly find that this is not the case. Even the best packages require substantial implementation effort because they will have to coexist with other key operational systems and interfaces will be needed. As many organisations have found, adapting an existing system can be *much* more difficult than building a new one from scratch.

On the other hand, acquiring a world-class package and then fitting the business around it can be an effective route to real benefits at many levels, provided that all necessary changes to working practices are made. For example, many large retailing companies around the world have chosen to use the same package for their core stock management and purchase order processing (a US-originated package called "World Wide Chain Stores"). This does not mean that the businesses had to be the same: the package just deals with the core information processing requirements at the operational level. Here, competitive edge comes from the ability to implement such packages well and to manage the adaptation of the business to make the best use of it. There is still plenty of scope for competitive differentiation within other application areas.

It follows that the key skills for the successful implementation of key operational systems tend to be technical (concerning the set up and configuration of the package) and managerial (for the implementation of operational changes); but senior management does not need to be heavily involved because we are not changing the world, and we are merely optimising it. Efficiency and reliability in key operational systems are extremely important and require technical competencies. Depending upon the hardware and software environment, skilled database and teleprocessing specialists will be needed to set up the right infrastructure and systems programmers are needed who can tune the environment to give the last percentage point in efficiency with the very expensive infrastructure that is involved.

Key operational systems are not merely advantageous (as a strategic system will be)—they are essential. Generally speaking, without the requisite key operational systems businesses will simply not survive because they will not have the basic capabilities that are necessary to be a viable player in their chosen industry.

Support Information Systems

Applications of limited value not generally critical to organisational success.

Support systems are the fourth and final category in our applications portfolio. In many ways, they are the most difficult to characterise because this fourth quadrant tends to be something of a mixed bag.

Here, we put systems that have little or no *strategic* relevance. As indicated by the definition (above, and in the figure), they are of limited value for some smaller reason, but not critical to general organisational success. Examples are: local systems used by only one department, for example HR systems that deal with remuneration and sick pay; low-level systems that might be widely used but are not critical to business operations, for example budget and expense management; systems that serve statutory needs such as import and export statistics reporting; even pervasive service systems such as email would be most appropriately categorised here when they are not being used for strategic or key operational purposes, which seems to be true in most cases. But let's be careful—access to a fully functional email service might be critical, depending on how the business chooses to operate.

A good approach here is to invest a minimum of money and effort, and wherever possible to go for absolutely standard packages even if they do not fit well—the presumption being that we can change the way we do things to fit the package. Using a package obviates the need for any detailed design or analysis. A support system needs only a minimum of analysis, first to be certain that it is truly a support system and then to establish the basic fit to the business requirement. Interfaces with other systems must be investigated because any strong links to key operational or strategic systems might affect our view of things. Perhaps, if it generates operational data, the support system is not a support system at all?

We will soon look in more detail at the different styles of management that are most appropriate for these different quadrants of the portfolio, but it should be obvious that for support systems the management effort must come from the local or departmental management concerned. There is a strong argument that the funding for the acquisition of support systems must come from departmental budgets: if the benefits are confined to one small part of the business, or one small area of the overall business activity, then why should central budgets be deployed? Hence, local commitment must be assessed to ensure that the system is really required and that those concerned are willing to manage the implementation project and all that goes with it. Support systems do not justify the use of scarce, skilled systems development resources that are more usefully deployed in the other more valuable quadrants.

Having said this, we might note that there are classic examples where support systems were recognised to have strategic potential. The (apocryphal?) American Hospital Supplies case study has been very widely quoted as a strategic example, but (according to the story) it started with a single buyer in a hospital who decided to go online only because his sales representative noticed they used the same kind of IBM terminal. A support project, surely, as it was originally conceived? Who is going to get excited about a buyer who sets up a link with one of his salesmen? But this was so clearly strategic when later seen in the competitive context.

Classifying Applications

Using the portfolio to position present and future information systems investments is not primarily a deterministic process. According to the rules that are implied by the explanatory notes above, it is a matter of discussion and consensus. In either case, in order to decide in which portfolio quadrant to place an application its present and future value must be assessed in some detail. For example, an application might:

- have high future potential, which is currently under exploited;
- have the potential to be extended or enhanced to be of more value;
- be more valuable if integrated more effectively or used more extensively;
- be critical to the business but suffer from poor-quality data;
- need to be redeveloped to meet changed business requirements;
- be transferred to more economical and up-to-date technology;
- provide more functionality than is needed, thereby allowing simplification and reduction;
- have no current or future value at all and therefore should be discontinued.

Based on such an assessment of its value, a plan can be developed for each application: the portfolio model helps us to see the investment in terms of resources, funds, risks and even management style. We can see where effort is currently being deployed and where it should be deployed in order to ensure that plans better suit corporate objectives. For example, most companies would wish to focus on strategic and key operational applications, but it is surprising how often effort is dissipated in the support category. Remedial actions might include reducing the resources used for support systems, buying off-the-shelf packages to service support applications, bringing in outside manpower, or simply a real reduction in overall investment if neither funds nor staff are available.

The Need for Discussion

The decision as to where an application fits in the portfolio is not dependent on a simple set of rules that we can apply to determine the outcome. A decision will only emerge from a management discussion about an application, and its current and future potential. In many cases, this will be debatable and may, in the end, depend on quite arbitrary management arguments.

For example, in most organisations email is something that is seen as useful but not critical. "*Every business seems to have it, and our people expect it, so we must have it.*" However, a different viewpoint may emerge from management discussions. Email might be seen as the primary vehicle for the movement of operational information and a conduit for a new workflow management system; the intended benefits might be very strategic, being based on new levels of internal business performance that will outperform the competition and set new standards for pricing and delivery of customised products. This is no longer a support idea. It requires that the business be significantly changed and the challenge is not merely to install an email system, but to change the way that people work. The same might be true in the case of a maintenance support system, but for different reasons. A major electronics company regarded its maintenance management as a support activity (with support systems), and then decided to outsource it to an electronic components supplier. What was a support system to the major international business became a critical strategic system to the outsource service provider, and we see that a shared system might be in one place in the portfolio of the first partner, but in a quite different place in the portfolio of the other, threatening some confusion in discussions between the two.

In summary, some of the key management issues in each quadrant are gathered below, together with a brief explanation of the outcome of successful management.

Turnaround applications: The basic philosophy of turnaround applications is more in the nature of "research and development"—controlled experimentation to identify the potential benefits, opportunities and costs involved in a new idea. Only when these things are understood it is possible to decide whether further investment is worthwhile, and how the next stage of application development should be managed.

The outcome of a turnaround application is new understanding, not necessarily profit or competitive advantage.

Strategic applications: Strategic applications are "business driven", and management thinking about information systems in this category must be driven by the business imperative. The principle risk is that of missing a time-dependent business opportunity. It may be about developing new capabilities before the competition do, and the most critical aspect of such systems is managing business change.

To be considered as strategic, any application must address critical success factors and the outcome is new capability and competitive advantage.

Key operational applications: Key operational information systems have, quite properly, been the traditional domain of the IT department, for which tools and methodologies have been developed over the last forty years and more. However, with new technologies and with new expectations the nature of key operational systems within whole industries is changing. Development needs should not be compromised for business expediency—it is critically important that these systems work efficiently and work reliably. Often today, packaged solutions will be chosen as the enterprise solutions available are all capable and can be seen as defining best business practice.

The outcome of successful key operational systems is increased efficiency, lower costs and more contribution to profit —shared with upstream and downstream partners in many cases.

Support applications: Support applications are determined by simple economics. Probably local in nature, or contributing at a low level across an organisation, cost control will be the main reason for deciding whether to go ahead. This is also the area in which the most packaged software is available because support applications are often generic, or common to all industries.

The outcome of successful support systems is that a local- or low-level need is served well, and needless expenditure is avoided.

Issues in Managing the Applications Portfolio

Migration Around the Portfolio

By reference to the Boston Box and the early ideas of Warren McFarlan, we have established that information systems (applications) have a life cycle and maturity, just like products such as data projectors, refrigerators and motor vehicles. We are not talking about the systems development life cycle, the cycle of program coding and testing that delivers a new system, we are thinking of the *complete life cycle of the idea.*

In the beginning, there may be an idea that is understood and championed by only one person: a *turnaround* application. The potential for the idea has to be explored and appreciated by the organisation at large before any substantial investment is made. The idea may be rejected and if already implemented, it falls directly to the *support* category and becomes an avoidable cost.

However, when the organisation at large has agreed to adopt an idea for good reasons, it becomes *strategic* application. It will need senior management support, and it will be expensive in terms of resources required as well as funding.

Applications that have become widely used in an industry are known as *key operational*, because they are critical to the core operations of a business. Key operational applications are like cash cows; they are critical to the generation of revenue and profit.

Applications that are important to just one department (such as a specialised budgeting system), or which are pervasive in nature but not seen as strategically significant (like email) are known as *support*: it is necessary for some reason to have them, but they are not critical to current or future success.

In this way, we must remember that the categorisation of information systems can change over time, either because of a change in the business context, a change in strategic positioning, or because we simply choose to manage a system differently when it makes business sense to do so. Even the humble support system can find its moment of glory and might lead to the initiation of a complete new cycle of strategic thinking.

Portfolio Management in Complex Businesses

With all management tools, it is important to realise that they may have to be applied in the context of a *single business unit*—the imperatives and needs may be greatly different from one business unit to another in any organisation that is not trivial.

Organisations can be seen at different levels: at one level, we have the whole organisation, and at the other end of a scale, we have the individuals who work for it. In the middle, we have departments, divisions and other units that may have different names in different specific situations. Here, by "business unit" we mean *a single part of the overall business that has a single family of products, with like characteristics, identifiable competition, and is at a known point in its business maturity life cycle* (Fig. 4.4).

What works well within one area of a business might not be applicable in other areas of a complex organisation. Consider a telecommunications service provider. This kind of business comprises many different subsidiary businesses: network engineering, domestic services, business services, data transmission, and so on. Each unit within such a complex business should assess its own needs and develop its own strategic analysis. Data services might be a new business unit with an innovative and rapidly developing product and service portfolio; domestic services might be running down; data transmission might be in the middle of replacing its core infrastructure but otherwise stable. Hence, you should be able to see that the portfolio model is a good example of the sort of tool that only works well within a single business unit.

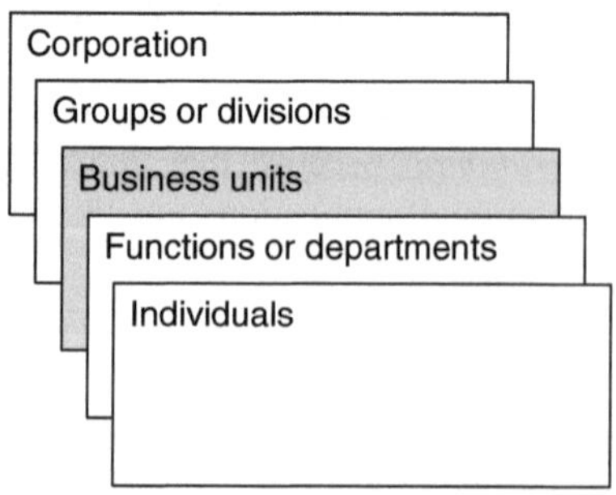

Fig. 4.4 Business units in context

The significance of a certain information system—even if shared between all units—might be quite different from one business unit to another. Email could be strategically important to a sales office that has decided to use email as the primary vehicle for communication with its customers, whereas for a production unit, email is a minor issue that does not affect the outcome of their efforts at all. An executive management dashboard draws on and relies on operational data, but it is of little interest to a facility manager who is solely responsible for managing procured inputs.

The different business units in an organisation are not only concerned with operations, of course. There is the matter of the corporate centre, where policy is made and where periodic targets are set according to overall organisational performance. Information systems strategy for the corporate centre is likely to concern a minimal set of centralised systems, but with an overall concern for the infrastructure that no single operational part of the business would want to pay for all by itself. The wider needs of the operational units within the organisation will all be different and will need different approaches to the management of information systems. For example, one unit might be in a heavily strategic phase, deploying new products based upon a four-year product development plan; another might be at the end of a cycle and striving to drive all possible cost out of their operational budgets. Another might be working on strategic issues with industry partners, but on much longer timescales than the other parts of the business.

Having said all that, if the business is predominantly in one industry where synergy is a potential source of advantage, a separation of strategic thinking would deny the advantages of that synergy. Individual business unit strategies must be supplemented by some central planning of shared information systems (probably key operational systems) and a firm hand on acquisition and delivery of new systems, in order to avoid proliferation and incompatibility of data.

Thus, strategic analysis might be undertaken in each business unit individually and also (separately) in the corporate headquarters. These analyses will identify unique needs but also similarities of need, and thereby the most economic route to overall fulfilment. For each corporate situation, a suitably structured mixture can be arrived at. An applications portfolio, for example, would be developed for each business unit separately but has the additional advantage that the analysis of need across business units can be consolidated where needed.

Support applications are likely to address similar administrative requirements across the whole organisation and software packages are a common choice: there could be extensive consolidation of systems requirements here. Other areas are less likely to share similar application requirements although the approach to implementation might be common. Take key operational systems: these need to be competently implemented, and some of the critical skills are independent of the application itself. For example, project management will be critical to implementation success and might well be provided from the centre; training of operational staff demands training skills as well as application knowledge and might be handled in a central training facility by corporate training specialists. Strategic systems are going to be tightly focused on the parts of the business that are affected, but it might be that the parts in question are subject to new levels of operational integration—that is a common benefit of strategic systems—and central management will have to ensure that operational changes are implemented even in the face of local protest. Turnaround systems have the least synergistic potential, but different uses of the same idea may work in different business units.

Even if the business units are different, the use of similar technology in the different units will enable better quality key operational solutions for all, and therefore, a central point of expertise in technology management will be needed. Sharing the advantages and experience gained by one unit with another will accelerate the development of strategic applications and help promote an understanding of how to achieve strategic benefits and how to manage business change, even though specific requirements vary.

Shifting Attitudes

At the same time that the applications portfolio matches demand for information systems in different business units with the most appropriate means of funding, supply and implementation, we must remember that the four segments are driven by different factors and need different approaches to their development and management. The role of systems will also evolve over time, and they will need to be migrated from one portfolio segment to another, requiring a change in the style of management over time—sometimes more rapidly than one would expect. Consider again this notion that there is an *outerlife cycle* to a systems idea: if at some point in time, a new idea emerges, and it may be misunderstood by most but championed by a few (turnaround); as the viability of an idea is established and competitive advantage becomes evident, it is adopted and approved for wider implementation (strategic); as competitive advantage is negated through industry-wide adoption, it becomes something that all industry players have to do (key operational); finally, as new ideas emerge and take over, what was once a radical new concept fades into history (support).

The automatic teller machine (ATM), already mentioned earlier is a good example. We take them for granted today, but when the idea was first mooted and rejected within NCR it was only when IBM was nearly ready to launch such a terminal device onto the market that senior management in NCR realised what had to be done. An example of "Turnaround"? Yes! The terminal device that resulted—the NCR770 Automated Cash Teller—was not only better than the IBM equivalent, it sold in thousands and saved NCR from possible bankruptcy.

Benefits Vary Around the Applications Portfolio

There are many stories in the same vein. Although most of us still use ATMs after more than 30 years, with Internet banking and smart cards we can now anticipate the time when there will only be a few people who still want to use ATMs; they will be seen as laggards, in a world where the majority have chosen to move on and use alternative forms of electronic banking—probably "e-wallets" in smart cell phones. The important point to realise, yet again, is that *there is a life cycle to most systems ideas* and that management recognition of the life cycle is critical to exploiting the benefits of an idea. These benefits are very different at different stages of the life cycle.

Turnaround: At the beginning of an idea, the benefit is *understanding*: something that was a mystery to most (but a startlingly good idea to a few) becomes tested and approved for wider implementation.

Strategic: In the strategic phase, a system delivers *competitive advantage*: for a period of time (not necessarily a long one), such systems deliver a distinct capability that is not available to (or from) others in the industry, and new business of one kind or another is won.

Key operational: As a new idea becomes widely adopted, then there is a period of *improved efficiency*: those organisations that are best able to squeeze efficiency out of the system will improve profitability, retain customers and contain costs.

Support: Finally, as an idea becomes less significant, the benefits tend to be either very localised or vanishingly small, and it may be worth discontinuing operation of the system or letting others take it over on an outsourced basis.

This evolution of systems over time, and the changing nature of the benefits, shows clearly that information systems need to be managed differently over time.

Information Systems Project Management

What we learn from this examination of the portfolio and the way it illuminates the life cycle of a systems idea is that different factors affect each stage in that life cycle. Information systems have to be developed and implemented, and the usual means to achieve that is the *project*: project management must also adjust to the circumstances of the systems idea.

Management style: Generally, management can be supportive of systems work and commit a good deal of time to it, or they can decide to minimise their involvement: at some points, *business* management needs to be the most involved and at others *technical* management is more important.

Project style: The specific question of *project* management is even more interesting. Because the implementation of a new system must be in some accord with its impact and potential benefits, the approach to project management will be quite different at different stages.

Risk management: Project management is often explained in terms of balancing *time*, *quality* and *cost*. It is interesting that the nature of risk from one quadrant to another runs around this triangle of concerns (with the exception of turnaround projects, where the risk is really more to do with the quality of the experiment that is testing out a new idea).

Funding: There is always competition for budget allocation, and new information system investments are no exception. The portfolio model provides approaches to financial justification that suit the context and the expected benefits of each quadrant. The difference between corporate and local funding becomes very clear.

	Management style	Project management	Risk management	Funding
Turnaround	*Loose.* Work with the energy and commitment of the "champion" and insist on closeness to the actual business.	*Light touch.* Set clear time and budget limits and then back off, but insist on a final review to explore promotion.	*Open.* Contain over-spending through time and budget limitations. Close down projects that fail at review time.	*Minimise*: rely on the ingenuity of the champion but provide some seed funding where appropriate.
Strategic	*Focus on the business:* and its ability to tolerate and adopt change. Prevent the IT Dept from taking over.	*Intense:* focus on achieving business change. Needs attention to business change issues.	*Time is the greatest risk*: If time is lost then advantage is lost.	*From corporate funds*: these will be expensive, both financially and in terms of management time and commitment.
Key operational	*Focus on process*: needs technical excellence. Allow the systems department to lead where appropriate.	*Tight and traditional*: this is the traditional area of information systems department activity.	*Quality is the greatest risk:* Key operational systems must work reliably and efficiently.	*From revenue*: in principal, these systems should be funded from existing revenue sources.
Support	*Lean and mean*: limited benefits means that local management should look after these systems.	*Limit to essential needs*: contract out if useful to do so and acquire packages-do not use scarce resources here.	*Cost is the greatest risk:* Work with strict budgets and timescales. Some argue to use "scarce resourcing" here.	*From local budgets*: if the canteen wants a new canteen system, then the canteen must pay for it.

Fig. 4.5 Summarising management around the applications portfolio

Figure 4.5 summarises some of the management issues that must be faced according to each of the four stages of the systems life cycle, as represented by the four quadrants of the portfolio (see the Fig. 4.5 for the details).

Communicating Information Systems Ideas

It is clear that communications is a key problem in dealing with the diverse issues inherent in good information management. Partly, this is because of the very abstract nature of information systems. How do you visualise a system? How can we judge the size of a system? A system has to be engineered, whether by the "using" organisation itself or by a software package supplier, and therefore we have to have some means to communicate our ideas and to specify the requirement in order that a solution can be designed and built.

Consider again a more familiar domain of specification and realisation—house building. We all know what an architect does (do we not?), and we all know how the craftspeople work from the architect's drawings (do they not?). Well, no, they do not always do that. And no, we do not always understand the implications of an architect's drawing because it gives us such a limited view of what the end result might be. So, although we do not always get it right, a house *is* something that we can easily visualise and quickly sketch on paper. The question arises: *what exactly is a quick sketch of an information system going to look like*? The hardware can be visualised easily, whether it is a tablet, a desk workstation, a network server or a multimillion dollar mainframe, but hardware such as this is just a part of the total system. The part that has to be developed afresh every time is the software—the intangible and invisible collation of instructions to the computer that tells it how to work. These instructions are the smallest building blocks of a computer system, but how do they relate to the familiar parts of a house: bricks, slates, timber and internal fittings? A quantity survey of a house is relatively easy to achieve. However, a simple count of the number of "components" in a computer system is notoriously difficult to estimate—indeed, it is even difficult to agree on what the basic components of an information system actually are.

Our problem is something along these lines:

- Just as with a house, we need a means to design the form and function of an information system, but *unlike* a house the building blocks are not at all clear.
- A house is comprised of bricks, mortar, windows and doors that can be easily quantified and costed, but an information system comprising program instructions, database definition language and job control statements cannot be easily quantified and costed.
- When building a house, the state of completion is very clear, simply by looking at it. There is little to see in an information system that tells you reliably how complete it is, nor when it will be ready.
- If there are faults in the construction of a house, they are visually evident, mostly even to an untrained eye, but the faults in an information system may only become apparent when the associated program code or data structures are exercised and that might not be for a year or two after it was thought to have been completed.

It follows that understanding the business requirement, and then specifying the function and form of an information system unequivocally and reliably, is a critically important thing to get right; or, when the requirement is not clear (as in the case of turnaround and strategic systems), a staged approach including some prototyping will be helpful (if not essential). Getting it right requires a medium of discourse that may be very alien to the business audience, especially in terms of vocabulary and conceptualisation of ideas. Someone who has been working successfully as a credit control clerk for 17 years will not thank some bright young thing from the data processing department for wasting their time trying to understand and document how credit control works, when (to the credit control clerk) it is just second nature. To the analyst, in the first instance, it is a mystery. Add to that the suspicion that a new information system for credit control might put you out of a job, and we have the makings of real problems.

Describing how information systems can be documented is far beyond the scope of this book, which sets out to try and deal with the *management* issues not the details of business and systems analysis. So, what do *managers* need to know about systems specifications? Should they understand them? Should they be able to critique them? Can they be expected to sign them off as "correct"?

No, they will not know about systems specifications, they will not understand them and it is dangerous to expect them to sign them off as correct, which all leaves us with a big problem. First, however, let us try and summarise the principal tools with which we can try and specify a system and what it will do.

The notes that follow take a brief look at the traditional approach to requirements specification and then examine why this traditional approach does not always work, and how the process has changed in the era of modern Web technologies and other important factors.

Managing Systems Development

It would be irresponsible to try and describe the issues of systems development in detail here. Indeed, there are many books that do so to which the interested reader should refer. However, *managing* systems development is something that must be addressed.

There are many different models that set out to describe how information systems might best be organised and managed. The earliest and most widely promulgated model is probably the "waterfall" model. Larman and Basili's (2003) compact but authoritative review is a good source that traces the history of how systems have been conceived, designed, tested and implemented over the years. It describes early work at IBM, the adoption of the "waterfall" model, the use of "pilot" projects and "spiral" methods, and then the emergence of iterative methods that they judge to be the most appropriate for complex projects; in their review, the waterfall model is deemed suitable only for very simple projects and its unfortunate predominance in practice for many years is blamed on the United States Department of Defense's military standard DoD-Std-2167 (DoD 1979), which included the waterfall model as a standard contractual requirement of DoD projects.

A significant step forwards can be found in the "V" model, which makes clear how systems development starts with an idea in the business and finishes with benefits arising from acceptance and implementation in the business. This model takes the key stages in the waterfall model and turns the later part—those stages following the system build stage (when program code is generated and tested at the model level) and turns them back up to reach into the giddy heights of the project initiation, when happy and enthusiastic managers and staff met, perhaps even excitedly, to discuss the possible features and benefits of a new system. In fact, too many conventional projects end in misery and dissention, and this revision to the waterfall model reminds us that through all of the testing period (which must be organised to test *at different levels* according to the technical and function requirements of the system) we are endeavouring to climb back into the world of

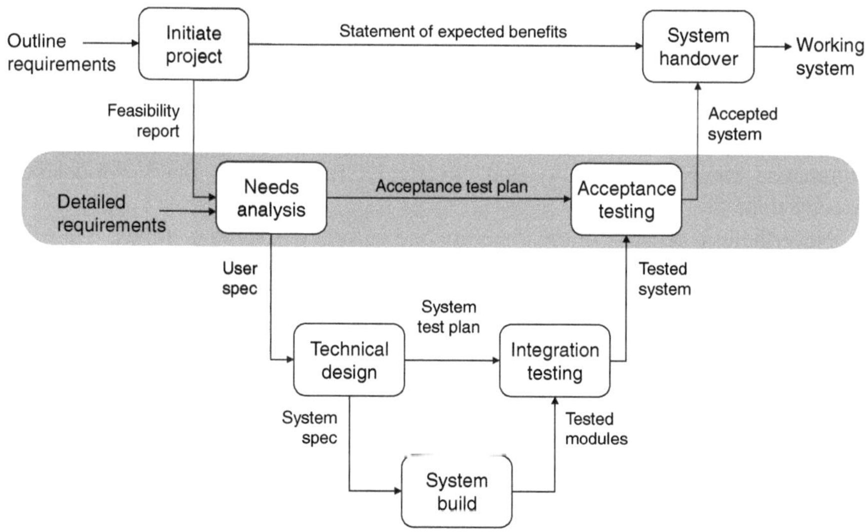

Fig. 4.6 The "V" model for systems development

the business and to ensure that we are actually delivering (or taking on) something that will be useful and beneficial. The grey area in the middle of the model is the area that challenges us to achieve effective communication between the two world views and that is what we shall look at next. If anything needs to be managed carefully, it is this: without care and attention at this important interface, communications will deteriorate into a slanging match where work is thrown over the "wall", and never properly understood on either side (Fig. 4.6).

Critics argue that the V Model is too simple to deal with the realities of systems development and that it reflects a management view rather than that needed by programmers and users who are directly involved in implementation. Well that suits our present purpose, but it reminds us that management must acknowledge the need for more detailed, different perspectives on the task for the benefit of those working on the details. Although it is seen by some as inflexible, this is not so—it can stand as the start of a discussion about how systems might be developed, and then adapted to include much more *detail* about each stage, and *iteration* where requirements are not certain and have to be tested through joint design and prototyping, and *short timescales* where agility is needed in the development process. As noted by the proponents of "agile development", there is often difficulty in establishing exactly what is required, especially for strategic systems, and so an iterative approach on very short timescales is appropriate, delivering minimum but fully working modules of system functionality so that all concerned can learn and judge which way to go. Even so, rapid iterative development will still progress through all seven stages of the V-Model, but at a much finer level of granularity; at the end of the day, rapidly developed fully functional components of large complex systems still need integration, and later developments might impact severely on the early installed and operational components that then have to be changed. It is impossible to eliminate complexity, and it will always be true that equivalent complexity must be evident in the solution as well as in the problem: Stafford Beer's law of requisite variety comes strongly to mind (Beer 1984), but management will always be a matter of abstraction, and managers need simple models that summarise complexity reliably and effectively. In my view, the V Model does exactly that.

Nevertheless, because of the visibility and currency of agile methods, it is worth summarising its characteristics. The "Agile Manifesto" reads:

> We are uncovering better ways of developing software by doing it and helping others do it. Through this work we have come to value:
>
> **Individuals and interactions** over Processes and tools
> **Working software** over Comprehensive documentation
> **Customer collaboration** over Contract negotiation
> **Responding to change** over Following a plan
>
> That is, while there is value in the items on the right, we value the items on the left more.
>
> Kent Beck, Mike Beedle, Arie van Bennekum, Alistair Cockburn, Ward Cunningham, Martin Fowler, Jim Highsmith, Andrew Hunt, Ron Jeffries, James Grenning, Jon Kern, Brian Marick, Robert C. Martin, Steve Mellor, Ken Schwaber, Jeff Sutherland, Dave Thomas
>
> © 2001, the above authors. This declaration may be freely copied in any form, but only in its entirety through this notice.
> (From Wikipedia, July 2014)

Each of these four "values" has great merit, of course; I would argue that none of them are incompatible with the V Model, which still stands as an axiomatic statement of the stages that a collective systems development effort has to go through. As is so often the case, much of the dissention that is seen in the current discourse derives from the posturing of "experts", and their failure to see all sides of an argument.[4] Management must find a way around this by ensuring a consensus view amongst all role players, by means of good management. The applications portfolio is the tool that begins that process by making clear the varying need for detail, speed, agility and particularity.

---

[4] For a short but informative discussion of the differences between traditional and agile working, Paetsch et al. (2003) provide a useful overview and critical appraisal, highlighting the role of documentation and other factors.

Needs Analysis and Acceptance Testing—The Key to Success?

It's time to have a closer look at the interface between the world business and the world of technology: the stage identified in the V Model as "Needs analysis" and its companion, "Acceptance testing".

In the early days of systems development, requirements analysis was a "black art". It was so poorly understood that it was barely visible in the average project plan—programmers were simply set to work on programming "solutions", without any attempt to understand first the real needs. However, nowadays, requirement analysis receives as much attention as any other stage in systems development, and the methods and techniques employed are very refined. Graphical techniques are used to represent models of how a system will work and how its data will be organised. We might not be able to draw a picture of a new information system in the same way that we can draw a picture of a car or a house, but we can draw diagrams of how the information will move from one task to another, and how the information will be structured.

The early graphical techniques for modelling systems were based on flow charting symbols signifying disk files, magnetic tape files and obsolete elements such as paper tape and punched card files. This is equivalent to presenting the house buyer with a detailed view of a house, one room at a time, with so much technical annotation about building materials and instructions that it is impossible for the inexpert eye to make a judgement about what is proposed. Happily, today, we have a richer array of diagrammatic techniques to help. The general approach is to present a business-level view of proposed systems that can be readily understood and debated, built to rules which are rigorous, repeatable, and which improve the quality of the work. The models that are used provide sufficient discipline to optimise the problem and avoid obvious traps at the same time that they make the specification process more visible to the users.

Consider one of the traps. A strong temptation is to use an organisational model to shape our thoughts about systems. The "warehouse system", the "personnel system", the "head office system" or the "Newcastle system" are all typical nomenclatures given to information systems and their projects. However, it is no longer sensible to set the boundary of a system using organisational or geographical limits. The systems that will provide an enterprise with real commercial advantage today are those that are shared *across* the organisation (thereby permitting it to operate in a more integrated and timely way) or across a whole industry (leading to the same benefits but on an even larger scale). The organisational model of an enterprise is not adequate as a foundation for the conception and definition of such information systems, and it actually leads to severe difficulties where function and data are to be shared.

A more considered approach to business modelling deals separately with:

- The organisational elements (departments, units, individuals).
- The jobs that the people do (business functions).

- The information that people work with (files and reports).
- The things of concern about which information is kept (customers, products, employees, branches).

Diagrammatic models can give an accurate representation of these different perspectives on the business. Just as we need to be able to see a new house from different perspectives, if we are going to learn all about the internal, external and constructional arrangements, we need to see systems from several different points of view.

The key to good information systems requirement analysis is the ability to break free from traditional business models and to focus on information as the driving paradigm for business design. Diagramming techniques have been developed that deal with this need, and they have been incorporated into defined methods for information systems development, redressing some of the historical imbalance towards the technical issues. Of course, there are also software tools with which to build these models and manage the different versions that emerge over time—changes to requirements is the most common problem to be managed, because changes wreak havoc in large complex projects.

Methods, Techniques and Tools

A good "method" for information systems requirements analysis will use a defined set of analysis activities and techniques that will, by and large, deliver information system solutions in an orderly, manageable and repeatable manner.

Historically, methods have been offered on a proprietary basis and have been packaged with consultancy, technical support and training, but the detail of different proprietary methods has converged and is now increasingly within the public domain. The UK government brought one particular method into the public domain and required its use on all non-trivial central government projects—it is known as "Structured Systems Analysis and Design Method" (SSADM). However, it has not always succeeded nor has it always been used well. Recent reports indicate that the public sector in the UK still has horrible problems delivering functional systems to time, and within budget. Perhaps this is because of a persistent reliance on external resources (consultants) who have no long-term commitment to the business of government, or perhaps it is because of a reluctance to educate people in the necessary tools and techniques. What does seem to become clear in the confusion is that an agency within government that takes responsibility for its own affairs, sets its own standards and works to sustain its competencies and capabilities internally, generally delivers itself systems that work well.

As confidence in information systems analysis methods increases and as more people gain the required skills, it can be expected that their use will become familiar to a wider variety of people in an organisation. The general move to the use of software packages that can be adapted or parameterised to the needs of the organisation has allowed them to avoid this need, but the parallel problems of assessing packages and understanding the true impact on the working of the business suggest that we still need a means to visualise information systems and their capabilities, even if we are "buying one in". Would you buy a new house "off the plans" without seeing the plans? Of course not. It is therefore surprising that businesses will buy very expensive software "off the plans" without even understanding how to read the plans and match them to actual needs, if those needs are even known. This is an area that has been troublesome for decades and clearly still warrants more research and more management attention.

Business and Systems Analysis

There are two principal ways to visualise an information system, namely *process analysis* and *information analysis*, sometimes referred to as *activity analysis* and *data analysis*. This variation in terminology is, of course, extremely unhelpful, but we have to learn to live with it in dealing with the world at large and then to adopt consistent terminology within the organisation.

Both techniques can be learned by business people as well as by technical specialists, but information analysis proves to be much more difficult for most people to comprehend—it is too conceptual, and people tend to be activity-oriented not concept-oriented. Proprietary methods for analysis are based upon these two approaches and may show a bias towards one or the other. For example, in history proprietary methods from the USA are predominantly process driven; in Europe, there has been a much stronger interest in information or data analysis, especially in the UK, France and The Netherlands.

Terminology is not universally agreed, and there are conflicting uses of terms such as "process", "function", "information" and "data". In particular, the advent of such strong interest in business process management (and business process redesign, and business process re-engineering) has put a new focus on the word "process". There is no universal definition even within the BPR literature.

Here, we shall use certain key words as follows:

"Entity" refers to any element of a business *about which we wish to keep information* (for example: customers, suppliers, products, employees, sales, problems)—in the vernacular, we could call this the "stuff" of the business.

"Information" refers to the aggregation of data that—when it is interpreted and understood—*provides systems users with knowledge of some kind* (for example: invoice, pay slip, stock exception report).

"Activity" refers to a task that accomplishes the processing of information at a low level and *delivers an output* (for example: check customer credit, process sales order, deal with stock enquiry).

"Process" refers to that collection of activities that *delivers an outcome* (not just an output), that is typically something that is valued by an external organisational stakeholder (for example: sales order fulfilment, new product design, employee management, and so on).

Hence, we can undertake "entity analysis", and out of it, we should expect to have an agreed set of entities that define the very "stuff" of a business, or we can undertake "information analysis" and get the outline design for a database—not quite the same thing at all. In the same way, we can undertake "process analysis" for a very high-level view of what a business does, or we can undertake "activity analysis" for a much more detailed view.

Hence, we see that analysis can be undertaken at higher and lower levels. When determining information systems strategies, it will be useful to lay down high-level entity models that help to delineate the boundaries of the business: a retailer might wish to explore what the consequences will be of extending the business systems to include customer information (by no means normal in retailing), as with the introduction of "loyalty cards". When analysing the detail of one critical business process, it will be broken down into lower level processes until we have the level of precision that will properly deal with discounting rules, shipping arrangements and quality control procedures. If the retailer is only concerned to introduce new point-of-sale services, then lower level activity analysis alone might suffice, but there may be severe implications in terms of the customer information that must be captured and stored and that makes for a much more complex job.

Note the potential confusion that can arise when these terms are used by different people to indicate different meanings—communications will only become more difficult, and it is *always* worth negotiating the meaning of key terms such as these when working in multidisciplinary teams or when working with strangers from a different organisational context.

The notes that follow provide simple examples of process/activity and entity/information analysis and examine some of the practical issues involved.

Process (Activity) Analysis

A detailed discussion of the specific tools of process and activity analysis is beyond the scope of this text, but it is worth noting that there are at least three kinds of diagram frequently associated with function analysis, namely the *process decomposition diagram*, the *data flow diagram*; a more modern variation is the *use-case* diagram. The first shows how high-level processes are made of lower level activities (in accordance with our chosen definitions), and the second and third show how information flows between them. The overall function of a business application can be very complex, but the process viewpoint is a very natural one for people working in the business and the analysis of business processes often provides the most fruitful starting point. Business people tend to be action-oriented and warm more quickly to a discussion about *what they do* than to a discussion of the structure of *the information they are dealing with.*

Read the example that follows and thinks about what you see within it. It illustrates the sort of conversation that might eventuate when a systems analyst sits down with a departmental manager to discuss how things work.

Why don't you tell me what goes on here, then?

OK, if you really want to know! I have a number of people reporting to me dealing with selling, cold calling, re-ordering and sales reporting. They change so quickly, though. As soon as we have someone up to speed they rush off and get work with someone else. It follows that we spend a great deal of time recruiting new staff—it's a terrible problem round here and we have to go the full round of advertising, interviewing and so on. I've got salesmen on the road (and women—Janet is in day-to-day charge of the sales force), I've got sales assistants in the showroom and one trusty clerk who keeps me on the straight and narrow. She's called Susan and she's excellent! I couldn't manage without her—she takes charge of the adverts for new hires, and writes all the rejection letters for me. She also arranges the interviewing schedules and deals with the personnel department when I want to offer a job.

Sometimes when there is a crisis I get involved with the travelling and I let one of the sales folk come in and interview the salesroom candidates; nevertheless it's still my responsibility to oversee the interviews and to have the final say in offering jobs. Really I leave most of all that to Susan.

But that's just the staff management side. The selling is what it's really all about. We've got people on the road as I said, who are chasing up new business and dealing direct with the big clients. The staff in the salesroom do the over-the-counter business which makes up the majority of our revenue. I insist on approving all the sales trips and I sometimes insist on going along, for example when the salesman is new or when the client situation is critically important. Then when a big deal is struck I generally go along to join in the merriment! I have to sign off all deals over a certain level, and all those closed by the junior sales people. That's the part I enjoy most. The paperwork is a real drag though. Can't stand it myself. Leave all of that to Susan—she chases up the monthly sales reports from the sales folk and does the area and regional analyses which lead to a summary report for me and my boss. I'm supposed to check it before it goes off but I don't bother. Susan does it all beautifully. What I do have to do is chase up the damned sales people. They never do what they're told, even by Susan and for Susan.

I was talking about the sales effort, wasn't I? Yes well, when a salesman is organising a trip they have to make up their own minds how to go about it and I just check it over (mostly so that I can keep a check on the expense accounts). Susan helps with the travel arrangements when bookings have to be made and she is very involved with the deals. When we are getting near to closing she prepares the draft contracts for us. Sometimes we even have to prepare tenders. Anyway, it falls to Susan to do the paperwork and luckily she's a real whiz with the word processor. She whips out the last one we did and changes the odd word here and there. Terrific stuff, this technology, eh? …

I guess so. I'll get this written up and get back to you—thanks for your time!

Discussion of the Process/Activity Example

What we find in the example is a rather confused explanation of an undisciplined sales operation. There is no view of *process* here, because the outcome (sales that delight customers?) is not even mentioned. The focus of the respondent is entirely upon the chaotic details of the sales operation, and mostly concerning the mobile sales force, even though (as indicated) more than half of the revenue comes from over-the-counter sales in the showroom.

A second interview with someone in the showroom might produce the sort of model given below. It shows (in a roughly clockwise sense) how the needs of a customer are related to available products and stock availability, and then how stock is picked and paid for. The different symbols used are marked in Fig. 4.7:

activities: the transformation and movement of information (and goods)
flows: information on the move (or material, indicated by the thicker lines)
stores: information (or material) at rest
outsiders: people and organisations outside the system boundary.

Data flow diagrams are developed using rules, which govern how they are drawn, how they relate to one another and how they relate to the more detailed specification material which supports them. Whilst management will not be involved routinely in

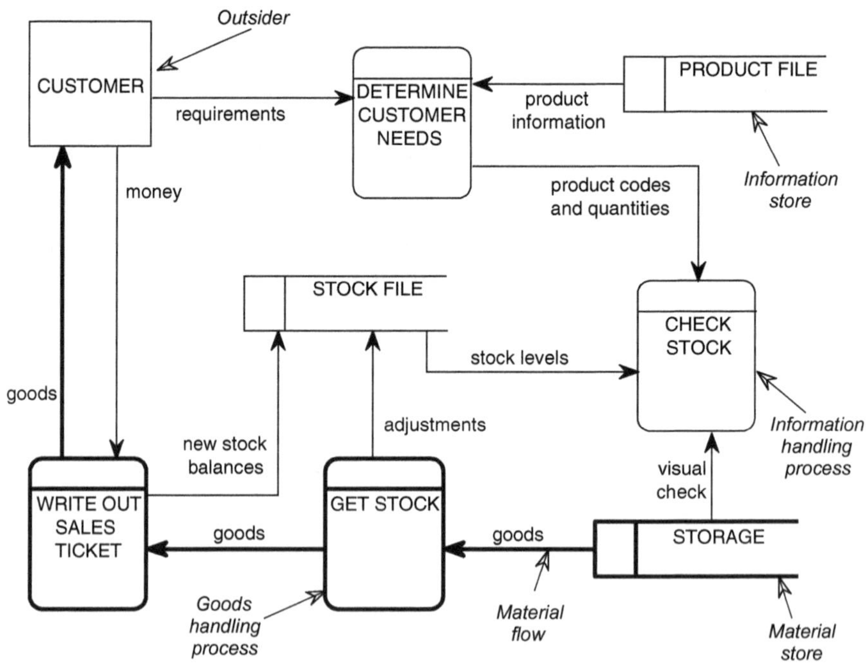

Fig. 4.7 A data flow (process or activity) model

creating them, it behoves everyone in a business to learn how to read them and how to make judgements about their quality, cohesion and completeness.

The example given here merely illustrates the way a data flow diagram is used. In a real case, a full analysis would reveal fifty activities (in a small system) or several hundred (in a large system). There might be twenty data flow diagrams in a medium-sized system, showing details of about one hundred and fifty processing elements and the information, which flows within and amongst them. The total number of detailed system components (processes, flows, stores and outsiders) in these twenty data flow diagrams could be as many as one thousand—process and activity analysis quickly produces a large volume of analysis material. The discipline of managing all this material is critical.

Entity (Information) Analysis

The other kind of analysis is concerned with entities, and the information that is needed about them and draws upon all of the content of documents and reports that are evident in a business. It produces what is generally termed a *data model*. This process of information analysis, at a fairly low level, is often called "data modelling". Data modelling is a demanding discipline that requires a particularly abstract view of a business.

Look at the example interview below, where our analyst learns about some of the information that is used in the business.

Hi Susan—it's good to meet you, I heard a lot about you already.

I hope it was good!

Yes, don't worry about that. I wanted to hear something about the that you work with here. Why don't you start by explaining what information you have about sales orders?

Sure, no problem. What we have to do is record what our customers buy from us, and in the show room we do that with an entirely conventional invoice. Do you want to hear about the big customers, and the tender documentation, or shall we do the showroom first?

Let's do the showroom and move on when I understand that.

Right. It is a perfectly normal invoice that we use. At the top of the invoice we record the essential customer information—name, address and contact information. Also at the top, we record the invoice number and the date of the transaction. The body of the invoice is made up of all the individual items that a customer has bought on the occasion in question.

OK—I recognise a invoice here. What information do you have about the products that I see listed in these examples?

We have a product file in the back office. The showroom staff can access it whenever they need to, to find out a suppliertelephone number, for example, or to get more details about the product. Usually, it's just to find the bin or shelf number where the goods will be found. But I have supplier files separately, that tell me exactly who we are purchasing from, and how much or how many at a time. When I have time I try to analyse how much business we are doing with each. That way, when we review our supply contracts, we have a negotiating position to work from.

Sounds good, and it sounds like a little automation would help!

Quite so. I look forward to that, but I won't hold my breath …

Discussion of the Entity/Information Example

Whilst this example is not complex, it is not immediately obvious how the information that is referred to might be organised. The simplest model of someone buying something would look like this (Fig. 4.8).

However, because customers buy many products, and products are bought by many customers, we have to "resolve" the many-to-many relationship otherwise we will have nowhere obvious to place the data that Susan refers to, specifically the invoice data.

Now look at the information model below, which separates the Customer and Product entities and includes additional entities to accommodate data about the purchase (as seen in the invoice and the invoice details), and the store, the supplier and the kind of customer (she refers to the "big" customers, implying that there will be categories of customer that need to be noted, for analysis purposes). The clarity of Susan's thinking shows through. No confusion there, and again, this is typical of what one will find in real cases. She quickly describes what is termed a "normal invoice", and when analysed, the result will be something like the model given below. Note the symbols used for entity models—they are different from those used in the data flow model but you will find (or you will already know) that different methods of working, many of them proprietary, use all kinds of variations in the symbols used. The rectangles now represent the entities about which information is kept: customers, products, invoices and the rest. In each case, there will be a variety of more detailed information that is required, for example names and addresses dates, product codes and the like—at this level, we begin to talk about data, because here we have the building blocks of a database (Fig. 4.9).

The connections between the entities are *not* flows, but they are *relationships*—here begins the difficulty that many people have in understanding the entity-relationshipmodelling method. A relationship shows that one entity is *related* to another through the words adjacent to the relationship line. Note the use of a

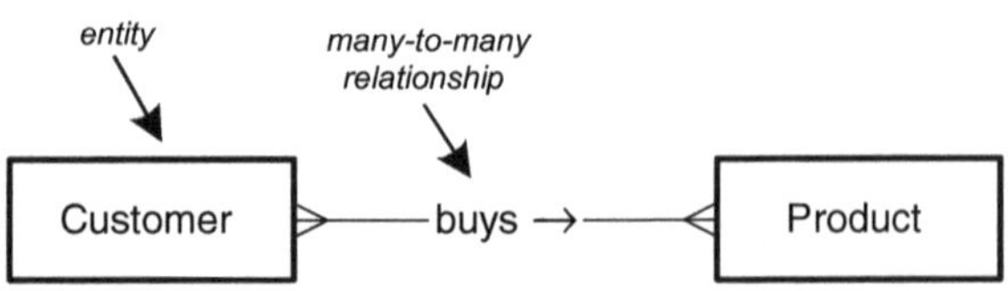

Fig. 4.8 A simple information model

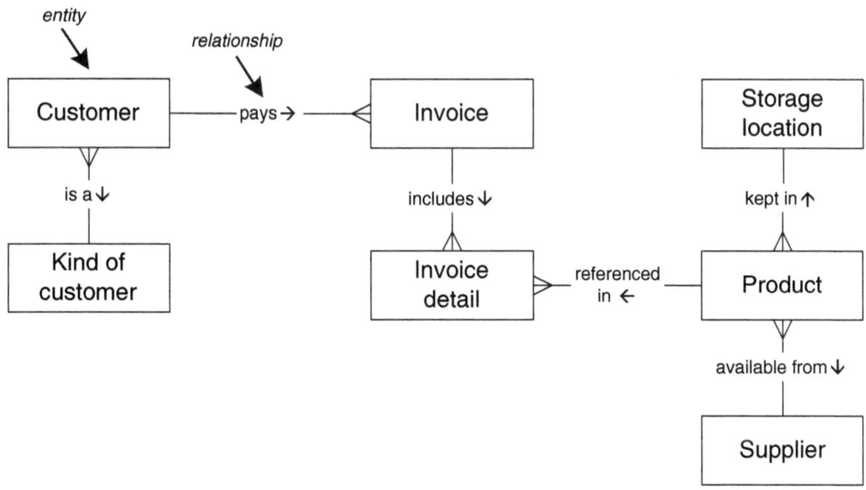

Fig. 4.9 The simple information model expanded

"crow's foot" to indicate multiplicity: a *customer* pays many *invoices*; an *invoice* has many *invoice details*; a *supplier* supplies many *products*. Here, we begin to see the structure of the information that will be invested in a database, and the relationships show how it will be possible to navigate through the information contained therein, if we design appropriate queries with which to work the system. You will note that there are no many-to-many relationships and it is necessary to explain about "cardinality", as it is called.

The Issue of Cardinality

Resolving many-to-many relationships must be done, although it might seem to be of more concern to the systems analyst than the business, because it is fundamental to database design. In fact, it also has a direct impact on the ability of an organisation to provide the management information that is needed. Consider the example above again (Fig. 4.10).

These many-to many relationships must be resolved for two reasons: first, if they are not the database design will be a compromise, because implementation will require a dummy table to cross reference customers to products. Typically, databases simply cannot handle many-to-many relationships. Second, and more importantly, the many-to-many actually indicates that we are missing a critical idea *in the business* that joins a customer record to the products purchased, where we record the details of the purchase. The "thing" that does that is the invoice, or more specifically, the *single line* on the invoice that shows one thing that we bought and

Fig. 4.10 Many-to-many relationship

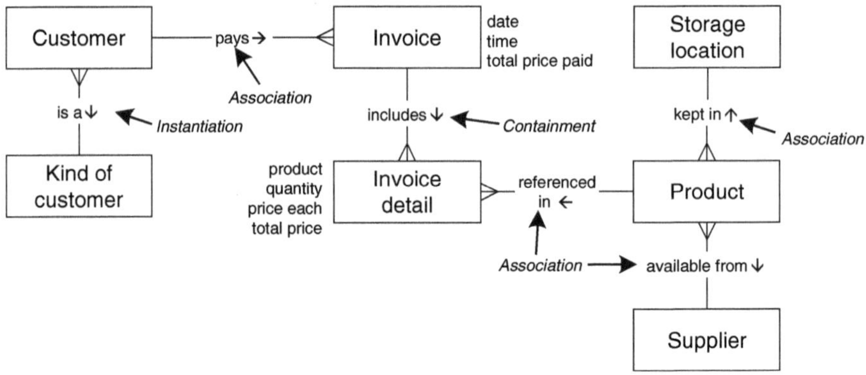

Fig. 4.11 More about what is in an entity model

what it cost. Clearly, there will be some data about the invoice itself (the date, the time, the total amount), and some data about the individual purchases (the product description, the quantity, the unit price and the total) (Fig. 4.11).

The information that is used to identify the *kind* of customer will vary from business to business, but customer information has been central to the retailing industry in adopting loyalty cards for customer profiling. With customers suitably "categorised", one retailer reported that they were able to see that "one-bag shoppers" actually bought just as much as "Volvo shoppers" when everything was all added up (these are their expressions, not mine); another retailer decided that as many as 30 % of customers *were not even profitable* because of the overheads associated with them—an astonishing revelation that made the marketing management think again about how to develop personalised marketing promotions.

This example helps to make clear that it is the low-level, high-volume data (such as transactional data in retailing, messages on the social Web and telephone records in the communications industry) where the analytical potential lies. "Analytics" is a word that is on many lips today and it hints at a near future where more organisations of all kinds (especially security agencies) will harvest data about the minutiae of our life and work. "Big data" is the data that is derived from these low-level transactional records, and it is the source of what we could call "big information"

It is worth taking this short discussion of a fundamental issue in data and information management one stage further: the relationships that join entities are of only three different kinds:

- There is **containment**, whereby one thing (entity) is a part of or contained within another.
- There is **association**, where there is a functional dependency between two things (entities).

- There is **instantiation**, where one thing (entity) is a specific instance of a kind of thing (entity).

Look again at Fig. 4.11, that illustrates how these ideas occur in a real model. Note also that the relationships can be named in either direction, and the small arrows indicate the direction of the chosen descriptor.

Working with Entity Models

An entity model tells us little about the detailed way that a business works, but it tells us everything about the foundations upon which it is built. The essential definition of an entity is: "any*thing* about which we may wish to keep information". This sounds simple but people still have difficulty understanding what these ideas convey. One problem is that in an entity model, all things are seen in the same way, *but they may represent quite different kinds of "thing"*: people (customer, employee), organisations (operating company, regulatory body), product (stock item, non-stock item), locations (shelf, head office), moments in time (approval, sale) or even completely abstract notions (project, idea). This ability to render such disparate things equal, in information terms, is the main strength of the entity model, because it helps us to break the mould of conventional thinking that prefers to think about just one kind of thing at a time. Instead of arguing the case for a new system for the financial controller, or for the Scandinavian warehouse, we can see the system for what it really is: a means of manipulating information in support of business processes which may transcend departmental and geographical boundaries —customer order fulfilment, stock replenishment or sales analysis. It is for this same reason—that it is able to render completely different things "equivalent"—that it is a difficult technique for some people to accept and understand.

An important property of an entity model is that it reduces our vision of the business to just one page of paper (but perhaps a large one). Even for the most complex businesses, it is usually possible to accommodate a complete view of the things about which information is needed on a single page. Process and activity models require many hundreds of pages, leading to all the consequent problems of understanding and checking of details; to have a view of the business on a single page is a huge benefit.

The Importance of the Associative Entity—Visiting the Zoo

A personal anecdote might help to ground the ideas that we have at hand here, and make them just a little more real. Some years ago, I was lecturing about entity modelling to a visiting group of students from Malaysia, predominantly Chinese. Whatever they were actually thinking they were polite and attentive, but on this occasion, I realised that the lecture was going nowhere—under the surface, they were hopelessly confused. I addressed them about this (which discomforted them) and decided that we would deal with it differently. I asked which of them had

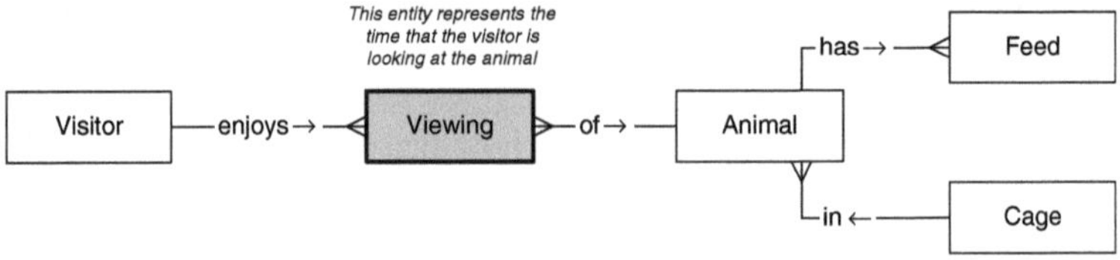

Fig. 4.12 The beginnings of the Zoo entity model

the most unusual job. Everyone looked at a young man on the front row, who explained that he was the director of the Zoo in Kuala Lumpur—let's call him Charles. I broke out into a cold sweat—I know banks, I know retailing, I know manufacturing, but I have *never* analysed or worked with a Zoo.

Twelve minutes later, we were having a great time, and Charles was on the edge of his seat. We had identified all the key things in a Zoo that are important and the *most* important thing that the Zoo needed information about was "*viewings*"—the moments in time when visitors were actually looking at animals in their cages. Information that is not necessarily easy to obtain, in real time, but this gave Charles all that he needed to go home and start investing, strategically, in new information systems. This is the heart of what we had developed (Fig. 4.12).

"Prof …" Charles said hesitantly "… have you ever *run* a Zoo?" There was laughter all round the room. We had connected at last. There can be no greater compliment than this, that after just a few moments the "client" recognises someone who can understand and improve the client's own business. It's all about having the right tools to use, and using them well. We will return to the Zoo example later in the book, when we examine business process modelling.

In the meantime, let us note that the low-level *transactional* entities such as this one—"Viewing"—are very important to identify properly because it is there that the transactional data is stored that leads to useful management information. These entities usually resolvemany-to-many relationships (as did "viewing", and the "Invoice" and "Invoice detail" in the earlier example), and they are called "associative" entities. These are things that your systems development staff need to understand, because without proper data design, good information will never be possible.

Relating Business Analysis to the Portfolio

So, we find that there are different ways to describe an information system idea, using both process and information models, and we might wonder: what is the most appropriate approach in a particular case? The applications portfolio comes to our assistance yet again.

Full analysis of a business requirement is easiest with key operational systems. Here, we are working with ideas that are already well understood, they are working for us, and they may be common across our industry. Without a suitable suite of key operational applications, we would not be a viable industry player—a bank cannot operate without systems to receive, manage and lend money; a car manufacturer cannot operate without stock control, production control and distribution systems; a university cannot teach without systems to register, assess and examine students. No real need for agility here, just a full understanding and basic systems development competencies.

It follows that here, with key operational systems, we may well want to just acquire a software package: why should we start from scratch when others have gone before us, and when concepts of good practice are already in place? Business models such as those above would, in this situation, be a way for a software supplier to explain what a package is able to do and what information it accommodates, so that we can match it to our detailed requirements. There will be a strong bias to process models, because we will want to know how the new system will impact on current procedures, but it is important to understand what information falls within the scope of a package so that important aspects of the business, such as customer information management, are assured by the acquisition of a new software package.

Analysis is more difficult for strategic systems. Here, we have a situation where there is "an idea", but it is not a familiar one. The business community that wants the system is interested, but they cannot explain what their requirements are. Experience suggests that the deeper insight that comes from entity modelling is more appropriate here than the process view, simply because people have no idea yet about the process. The fact that (at the level of entity analysis) the whole of the business can be represented on one page is very powerful. It is easier to identify and organise entities and collect process ideas around them, than to specify the process and then decide what information might be needed. The introduction of Customer Relationship Management is a good example: by introducing the *customer* as the central design feature of the business, we immediately adopt an entity perspective. What we need to *do* for customers may not be immediately clear, but the information that we can choose to keep about them (and their orders, their enquiries and their buying habits) is very clear indeed and comes quickly to mind. Once the information design is in place, then rapid and agile development is entirely appropriate here.

Horses for Courses

What we learn from the applications portfolio is that there cannot be and must not be a *singular* view of the way we manage information systems. It is essential that there is managerial flexibility, so that the profile of each system implementation project and its management can be specified individually, with appropriate tools and technical skills, and with the right degree of user involvement.

The typical business does not always see it this way, but those organisations that have invested in learning about information systems management using the applications portfolio have all welcomed it for the way that it makes the differences between different information systems and different information systems projects clear. By way of summary, consider some of the options.

Buying a Package

It is quite common to argue that it would be better to acquire a package than to build a bespoke system "in house", especially as "enterprise systems" of one kind or another become more common and infinitely capable, but the argument will flounder without some appreciation of the way the portfolio works. For example, there are no packages that deliver turnaround systems—this quadrant is the seedbed of new thinking that originates entirely new ideas. However, support systems should almost always be acquired as packages, because there is no purpose in developing yet another unique solution to a widely recognised and already-solved problem.

The case of a key operational or strategic information system is not so clear. In recent years, there has been a very strong move towards packages, ever more complex and ever more capable, providing functionality right across the whole of an enterprise, and ever more likely to provide for all key operational needs. Today, we see a trend in using the cloud for everyday applications, and we must expect this trend to extend to the most sophisticated needs of organisations of quite different kinds—there is no reason why a vast number of key operational needs should not be accommodated in the cloud but we cannot yet see what the consequences might be, and many organisations will feel strongly that some aspect or another of their work is unique and not amenable to standard solutions. Thus, the dangerous game of adapting and re-engineering standard packages and processes begins—this is not a good idea for the faint-hearted. On the other hand, there is *some* strategic potential in the deployment of a large and complex package, especially if competitors have floundered in the effort to get it up and running; the opportunity thereby exists to be the *only* business that has successfully gained the benefits of such a large package.

Take the "Enterprise Resource Planning" package known as SAP. Of all the SAP implementations that have been analysed, the majority have been found to have some degree of significant implementation difficulty. Hence, the successful implementation of SAP (and the successful adaptation of the business to work with it) will deliver considerable competitive advantage through cost reduction, improved management information and increased efficiency of working. There are many reports that SAP has *increased* costs, *impeded* the flow of management information and *reduced* the efficiency of working, but these are likely to be cases where there was no willingness to manage the changes with the necessary clarity and vigour. There is an unhappy tendency to rely on the use of consultants in these situations and that is not always a good way for management to declare their commitment to the idea of change.

One interesting consequence of a decision to acquire a package is that new dependencies on third parties are introduced—the package supplier and their partners. Worse, the relationship with the package supplier is likely to be managed through a contract that must be drafted and approved, and which will include quality controls, service-level agreements, deliverables, progress reporting procedures, and even penalties. Who is best placed to negotiate and manage a contract like that? Not the IT department, in all probability.

Outsourcing

As we learn to work with third parties at the relatively simple level of software packages, the rather more ambitious idea emerges that we can contract out whole areas of our activity, wholesale rather than piecemeal. As organisations decide to focus more and more on strategic aspects of their work, it seems more and more appropriate to let the mundane work go out to external specialists who could deliver the advantages of economy of scale and particular knowledge about the activity in question. We refer to this approach as "outsourcing"—a client organisation outsources a part of its operations to an "outsourcing services provider".

In one case, a petroleum company outsourced the whole of its accounting operation. Staff had to pass all accounting activity to a third party that then dealt with all things financial on their behalf. Seems like a risky idea? At the time of writing, the jury is still out on this one. In another case, one of the smaller banks in the UK outsourced nearly everything: cheque handling, ATM operations (including cash handling), credit card services and even information technology. All IT operations were outsourced to a single outsourcing services provider. So, you might ask, what was left? They would answer "customer relationship management". This is an extreme case, but for a small bank we have to admire, the courage involved in deciding to put virtually all key operational activities out on contract, leaving only the most strategic area of activity—customer relationship management—within their direct control. No organisation would wish to outsource critical strategic operations of any kind, but it makes a good deal of sense to outsource non-critical maintenance and support work. As it happens, at the time of writing (again), the small bank is in quite severe difficulty arising from challenging management problems. It is not clear to what extent the difficult might have arisen from the wholesale outsourcing of key operational activities. With appropriate trust and reliability in the partnership, it is clearly possible to go a great deal further, but the most recent analysis of the small bank suggests that its future is not secure.

Let us not dwell upon the details here, rather let us note that there are many outsourcing service providers who can, if managed intelligently, undoubtedly help a business to improve the quality of operations. The detailed reasons for outsourcing will vary from one case to another, but would typically include:

- Reduction in operational costs
- Access to scarce specialist skills
- Improvement in reliability of service
- Deployment of the latest technologies with real economies of scale

Of course, outsourcing presents its own risks. Suppose you have negotiated a seven-year outsourcing deal, and then, suddenly the seven years are done. You may have no internal staff who still fully understand critical details of your information systems operations, you want to make a move to a different outsourcing services provider, and you suddenly realise that the one provider—the new one—will have to rely on whatever the other will do to help. But, this other is the old one, they have just lost your business, and you are expecting them to cooperate with another party that is a competitor—what do you think is going to happen then? The best that you can hope for might be to make a completely fresh start, but does that fit well with other aspects of your business strategy?

There are more obvious risks to outsourcing that might already have come to your mind. For example, your chosen service provider might fail. They, after all, are taking up many of the risks that you would otherwise have to carry yourself. Their key staff might relocate elsewhere, where they could inform your competitors about critical aspects of your plans and strategic activities.

Clearly, it is once again a question of balance and risk management. These things cannot be left to the IT management alone.

IS/IT Partnerships

One more possibility that has found some currency amongst progressive organisations is to *partner* with an external organisation, where the synergies are good and where the combination of the capabilities of both promises to deliver large-scale strategic benefits.

This goes beyond software packages and beyond outsourcing. One consulting company has organised its thoughts about partnerships and relationships at three convenient levels, which help us to get started:

First, there can be a *transactional* relationship, where one party provides services to the other and charges for them: this is more or less at the level of outsourcing as discussed above, where fees will normally be a combination of fixed periodic payments and additional fees for extra services where needed.

Then, there are *partnership* relationships, where two (or more?) parties decide to work together in a single project (probably a large one, of course) in a way that allocates responsibility for the different tasks within the project according to the skills and competencies of each: this will never be easy in the first instance, but where there is a track record and where there is enough clarity about what must be done to enable sensible work plans to be put in place, then this is an option that should be seriously considered.

Finally, there can be a *risk and profit sharing* relationship, where the unknowns are acknowledged and where managements agree to invest despite the risk, in a way that spreads the risk between those involved; should there be a profit (and usually there will be some optimism about this, of course!) then that will also be shared.

There are examples of such partnerships all around us, not only in the systems industry, and there is evidence that they are not always easy. Even if managements on several sides agree that the idea is a good one, shareholders can upset things by refusing to support some of the more adventurous ideas. As soon as shareholders realise that there are real risks, possibly because the risks are evident elsewhere (and which shareholder does not watch market conditions carefully?), they will not wish to be exposed within their own portfolio of investments.

Agile Systems Development

As we already noted, there has been considerable recent interest in the idea of systems development agility. As an answer to endless demands from businesses that were constantly looking for the next advantage, information technology and systems managers have sought to develop systems rapidly, flexibly, and reliably. These three ambitions are not entirely compatible, and the applications portfolio helps us to look critically at the areas of a business where it is likely to be helpful to develop systems in an agile way. Turnaround systems? Well, yes, but then our whole conception of turnaround working is that one works quickly and flexibly, but *only to establish the viability and merits of a new idea*—that is not what a business is generally talking about when they are looking for agility. Rather they are looking for strategic systems that, if implemented quickly, would deliver the competitive advantage that all businesses desire.

But rapidly developed strategic systems that leave some things undone, loose ends, and weak points in the logic of the way a business is supported, are not necessarily a good investment. As soon as we think of developing strategic systems with agility, then we need to recognise the need for a "long tail" of work that follows, to re-engineer and secure the work that is done in a way that renders it suitable for the long-term.

Support systems? Absolutely not. This is the level of system development where end-users work with their spreadsheets, or their single-user databases, producing what must be seen by management as support systems; seen as "agile working", there might be the seeds of a good new idea, but the correct way to promote it would be through the portfolio as a new turnaround idea. Then, established processes for evaluating and adopting new systems can be brought into play.

Crowd Sourcing

Crowd sourcing is an interesting phenomenon that has been taken *very* seriously by key players such as Google and Amazon, organisations where any innovative approach to sourcing program coding and systems design skills is relentlessly investigated.

Crowd sourcing starts with the persuasive observation that "the cleverest people always seem to be working for someone else"[5] and continues with the exciting prospect that armies of clever and highly motivated experts will bid to work with

[5] This is "Joy's Law", attributed to Sun Microsystems' co-founder, Bill Joy.

you on the implementation of new ideas, as freelancers and working at a distance. This is perhaps the highest-risk and highest-reward situation that we can presently imagine, because once the work is done, it must be paid for, and the contractor might be someone in a distant country who you will never see and who might never be possible to contact ever again. But the idea is not to be ignored, and we might agree that it is an extremely interesting option for turnaround and strategic systems implementation—provided, again, which we have a long-tail process to clean up, document, and secure the program code and systems implementation options so that they can be sustained.

Summary

Managerial Issues in Information Systems

We have moved a long way from simple thoughts about information systems. We are touching on much wider issues that need to be revisited elsewhere, particularly in the area of business strategy. Although business strategy is not solely concerned with information technology and information systems, it has to embrace the problems and opportunities arising therefrom, and we must return to this interesting discussion later when we have laid out more of the groundwork.

It should be clear from the above lengthy discussion that there are many issues that managers face in dealing with information systems. Even if information *technology* has become commoditised as some experts are now arguing, this does not help us to deal with the many problems and opportunities that present themselves at the level of information *systems*. Too many typical businesses are stuck with 1960s and 1970s thinking about information systems, having no understanding of the strategic potential of good information systems and having no managerial processes that encourage staff (at all levels) to come forward with new ideas that can be tested.

This is the critical issue: if an organisation wants to be progressive with its use of technology and systems, then how is it to become so? We already have some of the clues before us, time will tell us what else we must learn if we are to make the best use of the multifarious opportunities that sit just around the corner.

In summary, here are some of the managerial issues that we must deal with:

System development capability: Although much can be achieved with software packages, any organisation wishing to be progressive will need the capability to develop its own systems with its own resources. The nature of technology continues to change and many larger organisations are now handicapped by the fixed and out-of-date thinking of their IT departments; it is time for them to hire some new staff who will be able to take up the challenge of working with the new technologies—especially with Web and cloud technologies that are radically different from what we have been using over the last thirty or forty years. Despite these changes, the ability to specify and agree requirements by some means or another remains a critical issue.

Information systems will continue to be fragmented and diverse until we learn to scope them and specify them well, in relation to the needs of business units at different levels.

Relationship management: The relationship between information systems specialists and the organisation at large needs to be carefully nurtured. It is too easy to devolve responsibility to a low level and to allow chasms of misunderstanding to develop. An organisation that has managed to bring the two parties together through sharing of ideas and ambitions is an organisation to be envied.

Investment justification: Often the problems start right at the beginning, when a decision is made to invest in a new system without proper consideration of *all* of the consequences, especially in terms of the benefits that are to be expected and allocation of responsibility for delivering them. A decision to invest must be supported by a proper justification, based on benefits.

Benefits management: The different kinds of benefit arising from different kinds of system must be understood, and then, systems must be managed appropriately, especially in their early days when they are conceptualised and then realised. There needs to be an effective way to categorise information systems according to their contribution to organisational strategy, and by other means.

Performance management: At the end of the day, the benefits of information systems are seen through the improved performance of the business. Without performance management that renders these improvements visible, the delivery of benefits will always be uncertain. And, it is interesting to note that business performance management is itself a matter of information systems delivery: without management information systems that evidence performance the situation will be unmanageable.

Encouraging new thinking: Any organisation that wishes to be progressive (a leader, not a lagger) needs to ensure that there are procedures that facilitate the development of new ideas and then prioritise them so as to manage the allocation of resources and funds. Further, such an organisation needs to have a culture for learning that will accept (and even encourage) failure, for the reason that there is so much to be learnt from the ideas that do *not* work. Whilst there will always be something to be learnt from watching others, the best strategic opportunities will come from within and from the accumulation of internal experience and learning.

We have looked at the nature of information systems, and we have exercised the idea that the maturity of an information systems idea is a critical one to understand. Through the 3x1 "evolutionary" matrix, and the 2x2 "applications portfolio", we can see trends in information systems thinking extending over decades (in the first case), and then, the trends within a single organisation over shorter periods of time —months or years (in the second). The applications portfolio is a particularly effective tool to use, and we shall be visiting its details again before we are through with the IMBOK.

Deciding how to reconcile the managerial approach to information systems with the applications portfolio is no trivial task, but the general nature of what can be done should now be clearer. When everything comes together properly, the results of good information systems management can be spectacular. The important message is that it is not appropriate to treat all information systems in the same way. The incorporation of different analysis and development tools and the judicious use of software packages are indicative of the decisions that will have to be made. Where bespoke systems are critical to organisational success, sound information systems engineering methods and tools are needed; where reliance is placed with external parties, as in the case of software packages, partnerships and crowd sourcing, then contract management skills will be needed; where systems are not critical, a more casual approach may be in order.

Information Systems Management Competencies

In order to assess the level of competency needed to deal with information systems management along the lines discussed here, there are some competencies and preconditions that are required:

- Discussion and negotiation of the present and future significance of different systems, and the different kinds of benefit arising.
- Clear relationships between the applications portfolio and the divisions and departments that comprise the organisation—beneficial systems are designed for *processes*, not for *departments*.
- New uses of information systems to be seen elsewhere should be monitored.
- Proper methods for justifying decisions to invest in new systems, recognising their positions in the applications portfolio.
- Systems with future strategic potential, and those with relatively little strategic significance, are recognised, funded and managed appropriately.
- Corporate information, and the data structures that accommodate it, is defined once and shared across the organisation.
- Success criteria for new information systems investments exist and are pursued; measures are used effectively to confirm that new information systems deliver what was promised.
- Lessons learned are valued and incorporated into future practice.

Research Side Note: Understanding Organisational Agility

Overby, E., Bharadwaj, A. and Sambamurthy, V. (2006) Enterprise agility and the enabling role of information technology. European Journal of Information Systems, 15, pp. 120–131.

As an early step in researching enterprise agility more exhaustively, Eric Overby and his colleagues have studied the way that organisations sense impending change, and then respond to it. By assessing how good organisations are at sensing, and then responding, they identify four types of organisation: those that lack both (don't invest there!), those that sense but fail to respond, those that do not sense but respond well when the need arises, and (the ideal?) that can do both. They observe that this leads to good R&D, the best application of IT, good governmental relations, excellent marketintelligence, and so on. This allows an organisation to detect the environmental change that comes from new technologies, regulatory changes and so on; these problems can be turned into opportunities.

They consider that a firm's IT capability is directly related to sensing and responding components of enterprise agility. They refer to the emergence of the Web and the way that only some businesses were able to sense and respond, essentially because of their level of IT capability that rendered them able to anticipate and sense changes arising from advances in IT. They refer to a wide range of other work in this area, for example Haeckel and Nolan who more than 20 years ago referred to "managing in conditions so turbulent that sense making and action are impossible" without what they called "IT enabling, managing by wire".

"Effective use of IT is one method for firms to kick off and sustain [a] virtuous cycle [of agility], as IT enhances both sensing and responding capabilities. When investments in IT serve to increase the process and knowledge capabilities of a firm, they create a powerful platform of digital options that can enable the firm to sense and respond to rapidly changing environmental conditions."

Research Side Note: The Consequences of "Enterprise Systems" on Organisational Agility

Molla, A. and Peszynski, K. (2012) Enterprise systems and organizational agility: A review of the literature and conceptual framework. Communications of the Association for Information Systems, 31 (1), p. 8.

This is a rather academic (and therefore quite difficult) analysis of existing literature about agility. It concludes that agility comes from a range of factors:

- The use of enterprise systems (such as ERP, CRM, SCM) in building and renewing their sensing and responding capabilities.
- Better alignment and higher levels of enterprise systems-enabled sensing capability and enterprise system-enabled responding capability.
- A high level of enterprise system technical competence.

They also conclude that organisations working in fast-changing environments are more likely to develop high enterprise system competence, and a high enterprise system-enabled sensing and responding capability, than those that operate in a relatively stable environment; probably a case of the blindingly obvious, but it is good to see that serious research supports it!

Research Side Note: The Consequences of "Enterprise Systems" on Organisational Agility

Grover, V. (2012) The information systems field: Making a case for maturity and contribution. Journal of the Association for Information Systems, 13 (4), pp. 254–272.

Varun Grover provides a personal overview of the emergence of academic thinking about information systems capability that can be compared with what is written here. He identifies four eras: an early era before the need for academic treatment of information systems management (other disciplines such as electrical engineering and mathematics dealt with the basics of how computers work), initial agonising about what should be done following the first ICIS conference in 1980, rapid theoretical and methodological development of the field in the 1990s, and fragmentation with the emergence of specific topics such as mobile technologies, e-business, and value-based management of information systems investments since then. I rather enjoyed his analysis of information systems research as …

- an aggregator of terms
- a complex adaptive system
- a knowledge market, and
- a biological organism.

This is an authoritative overview of information systems research over the ages, adopting a particularly interesting perspective.

Exploring Business Processes 5

What Is a Business Process?

A business process is a logical envelope that coordinates and gives purpose to organisational activities; generally, whereas an activity delivers an output, a process delivers an outcome—a result that is evident to stakeholders outside the organisation as well as those within.

Of all the concepts that we are exercising here, the business process is, for some people, the most difficult to embrace. We are all familiar with where we fit into the organisation from the point of view of the organisation chart (sometimes called the "organogram"), but when it comes to seeing our work in the context of the total work of the organisation, we have some difficulty. We all know who we work for, but we are not always clear how our contribution combines with the work of others to deliver an outcome to the outside world.

There is a useful distinction that is evident in the definition above: "*activity*" is a word we will reserve here for the lower levels of what we do; "*process*" is a word that we will use for the higher-level view. Thus, "customer order fulfilment" and "acquire new customers" are very high-level views of what goes on that would typically qualify to be seen as processes. "Check customer credit" is clearly a detail within customer order fulfilment that combines with an unknown number of other activities to deliver what the customer wants. The customer (as an external stakeholder) is not interested in credit management, only in getting their orders delivered. Until, of course, credit management causes us to refuse to do business with a particular customer; then, we will find ourselves in a different process, something to do with "manage customer relations" perhaps?

A. Bytheway, *Investing in Information*,
DOI 10.1007/978-3-319-11909-0_5

Two definitions that we will use follow from this:

- A *business process* is a high-level component of a business that is comprised of a number of lower-level business activities; it delivers value to organisational stakeholders.
- A *business activity* is a low-level component of a business that makes up a part of a business process; it consumes resources and drives costs.

This establishes the idea of a hierarchy of activities and processes and cautions us about the volume of detail that we might have to deal with. A business may see itself as having only five or six business *processes*, but it is likely to have thousands of *activities*. Set an analyst to work to find and document all the activities in a business, and they will be lost forever; set a management team to deliberate and decide on high-level processes, and we can get a grip on things.

Nature of Business Processes

It is some thirty years since the world of business management first became excited about "business process re-engineering" and yet the idea is still a distant novelty to many working in businesses and other kinds of formal organisation. For some time, experts argued about the differences between "re-engineering" and "redesign", and huge sums of money were earned by consulting companies that deployed "methodologies" for achieving "BPR", whatever that might have meant from one moment to the next. Some of this thinking has since been discredited. Once it was the target of excessive "hype", but interest in business process management rose rapidly before the early excitement gave way to the difficulties in making ideas about business process management really work. Many organisations that toyed with business process ideas gave up, and reverted to the organisation chart as the highest level view of "what the business is".

However, the idea of the business process is still important and out of the experiences of those fewer organisations that succeeded with it, we now understand more about how to deploy process thinking to our advantage. A lot of the ideas about processes come from thinking about systems, and for some people, business process management is an extension of systems thinking and systems practice. Let us start with the transition in thinking from the organisation chart to the process.

Processes and the Organisation Chart

The organisation chart is, for many of us, still the most familiar overview of "what a business is" (Fig. 5.1).

Commonly, the organisation chart connects one part of the organisation to another through a hierarchy of *control and reporting* and may indicate who is managing each part of the hierarchy. Figure 5.1 shows a simple representation of an organisation chart and the way in which business processes cut across it. The connecting lines in an

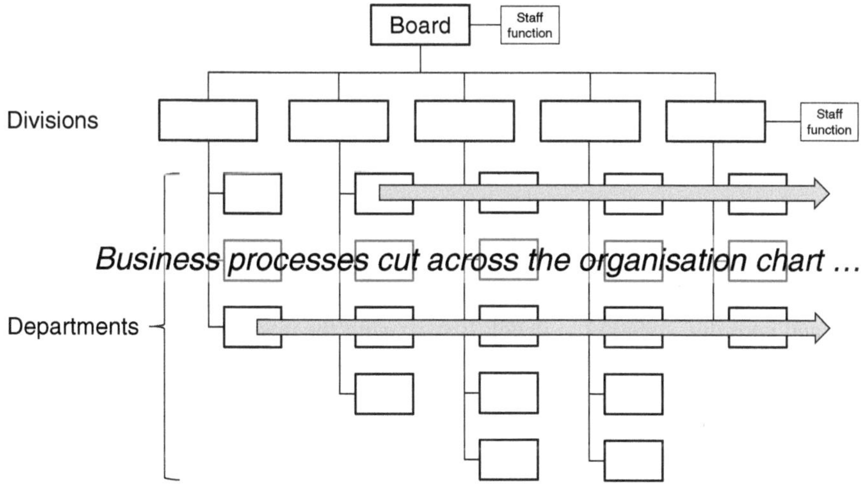

Fig. 5.1 Business processes and the organisation chart

organisation chart therefore tell us "who reports to whom" but not *what people do*. If you are ever offered an organisation chart on the basis that it will tell you who does what, be careful. It does not necessarily do anything of the sort. You have to go and talk to people to find out what they actually do, and then, you have to join together what different people tell you and track the flow of work from start to finish.

A business process delivers something useful to the outside world, as we have noted. But it does this by calling on a range of organisational components such as the sales office, technical support, production, engineering, quality management and so on. A business process is therefore the sum of all the effort that goes into delivery of the outcome, wherever the effort might have come from. As individuals, the people working in organisations that have adopted a process viewpoint therefore have two concerns: firstly, they need to know who they work for (and which functional area of the business they are in), and secondly, they need to know what their contributions are to the processes that they are involved with.

This is how people become confused. As soon as there are two lines of reporting—one to the departmental manager and one to a process manager—there is the potential for conflict and disagreement—another case of difficulty for the faint hearted. Firm and clear management policies are required to avoid the stress of many lines of involvement and reporting.

Identifying Business Processes

So far so good—we have a simple understanding of what a business process might be, and where some of the problems lie. The question arises: where do business processes come from, and who defines them? It is amusing to look back at some of the early writings about business processes, where there was a presumption that an organisation could "*set to and work out what your core processes are*" with little detailed guidance. What if an organisation was uncomfortable with what it was doing now, and wanted to find a different way, or make a completely fresh start? What if it was looking for a new core idea that would "break the mould" and "get out of the box"? Some of the early thinking was very lightweight and laid far too much emphasis on radical change without taking account of the timidity of the typical management team and the reactionary attitudes of the workers. Radical change is extremely difficult to deliver, and we have long since reconciled ourselves to the understanding that business process-related change must be done with a degree of care and with due attention to detail. It starts with the question "*what is our vision and mission, and what have we set out to do?*", and it follows through with very careful consideration of *stakeholders* and their expectations, as we shall see.

In the context of change and uncertainty that faces businesses today, it is important to be able to develop and agree a clear understanding of what a business sets out to achieve at a high level: mission, vision and "all that good stuff". From the high level of the corporate vision, which provides a rationale and a general direction, down to the definition of operational activities, an organisation needs to be able to understand what is to be done and how it is to be done. Only with an understanding of what stakeholders expect from an organisation can we derive idealised processes, and then get to work on the difference between what we *are* doing and what we *should* be doing.

The Value Chain as an Early Indicator of Process Thinking

Let us remember that we are striving to establish where and how we should invest in information technology and systems in order to improve organisational performance, whether by improvement or replacement of existing information systems.

History tells us that it is just too easy to take a blinkered view of needs, to confine our arguments to one particular part of the business, and to fail to recognise the benefits of a broader view of things. One of the early tools that has been used to explore information systems opportunities that still works well for many people is the value chain, originally promoted in the early and middle 1980s by Michael Porter and which, as well as being used for general strategic analysis, has been used specifically to show how good information management can give you competitive advantage (See for example: Porter and Millar 1985).

Some experts now discount the value chain on the grounds that it is "old thinking", but there are others who will argue otherwise. One practical viewpoint is that while it is useful, we should continue to use it. Here, it works well for us because it gives us a tool that actually liberates us from thinking solely in terms of the organisation chart. Porter promoted it as a way of seeing the differential between cost and revenue (and therefore the accumulation of profit), but here, we can use it to see how a business works to create value, and where some of the cost drivers and challenges are.

The value chain can be seen as an internal view of a single business (or business *unit* in the case of a large or complex business organisation), or it can be deployed within an industry to see how many businesses work together. The internal value chain shows how the various activities and functions in a business unit contribute to the customer's requirements, and how costs are incurred in so doing. Understanding what is done, how it is done and how business activities are related to customers' needs leads to a better understanding of information and systems opportunities. The value chain helps to get beyond the detail of current arrangements in order to see a bigger picture, in relation to the whole business and (most importantly) the way that customers see it. The original value chain model was based primarily on the arrangements within a manufacturing business, but its structure can be applied to most other types of business with some adaptation, as we shall see. In the first instance, it is only about inputs, processes and outputs, but it puts some useful flesh on those bones.

As can be seen in Fig. 5.2, the value chain identifies two different types of business activity—*primary* and *secondary*—and provides a framework for organising the detail within them. As depicted here, the figure shows a typical view of a value chain structure, with comments explaining each of its ten components. The use of the value chain in strategic analysis is discussed in more detail later (see "Strategic analysis tools"), but for the moment, it simply reminds us that it is the *value* that is seen by key stakeholders (such as customers) that drives a business along; a similar argument applies to organisations in the public sector and in communities in society at large, where there might not be customers but where services are being provided to tax payers and community members who can be seen as "customers" in a context like this one.

Business Process Redesign (BPR)

The value chain gives us an early indication of process thinking by focusing on the five stages of a process that delivers value to customers, and the generic layers of supporting activity that facilitates it (five such layers, as shown in Fig. 5.2, but in the literature, the details of support activities vary and different terms will be found to those that are used here).

Although it was targeted at manufacturing businesses that "make for stock", it is possible, with adaptation, to apply it to a wide variety of business situations, for example for a "make to order" business.[1] However, we must always remind ourselves that it is based on concern for the *customer*. Then, we must ask who else has

[1] In the author's experience it has even been applied to an analysis of committee work with a group of senior civil servants, which then led to revelations about how information technology could make committee activities *very* much more effective!

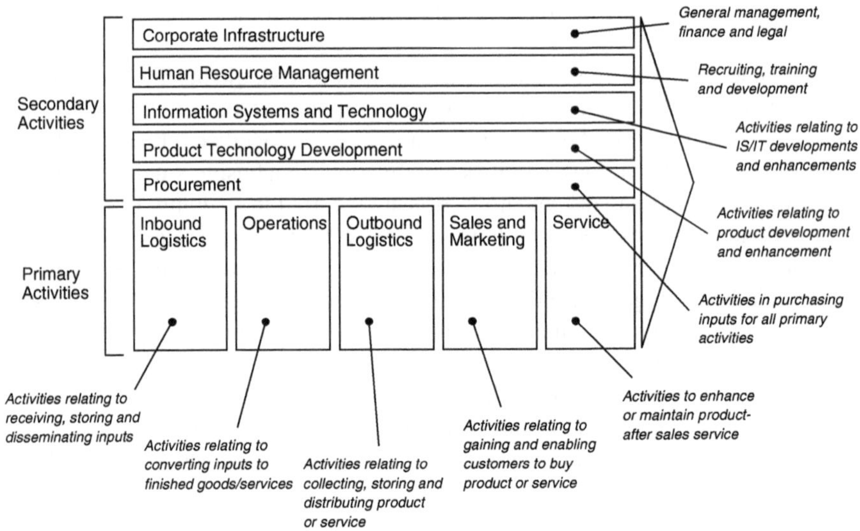

Fig. 5.2 The internal value chain

a view about our business that might affect how we work the business. Is the customer the only stakeholder? No, there are many.

It follows that we need a more general approach to the design of a business as it might be seen through those processes that deliver to customers. The value chain provides a generic process to meet customers' expectations, but what about the shareholder? What about suppliers? What about employees? Typically, there will be some ten or more stakeholder groups, each of which must be served in an appropriate way if a business is to be sustainable. Hence, we must seek out an analytical approach that will deal with all stakeholders and take some account of their relative importance. As one example, it is interesting to note how and when a business or state-owned enterprise is headed for privatisation, the *investor* becomes the critical stakeholder as the management team scrambles to make the profit and loss account look as healthy as possible. In South Africa, the privatisation of the telecommunications industry took the eye of telecommunications management off the customer, and put it firmly on the prospective shareholder; for years, the needs of customers were secondary, as anyone living in South Africa at the time will affirm. There are other examples where the interests of customers as stakeholders have been subjugated in favour of others.

Radical Process Redesign

Partly as an evolution of systems thinking, and partly as a result of the total quality management experience, as experience with business process management accumulated, many progressive businesses took up the idea that business processes can be *radically redesigned*. The argument is that business processes are typically more an accident of serendipity and organisational history than conscious planning and process design, and there must therefore be significant benefits to be gained from a rationalisation and reorganisation of processes through a tested design method.

The Depth and Scope of Change

An age-old question concerns the willingness of organisations to change. We can point to industries where change was very painful but prevailed in the end. For example, the banking and insurance industries were well set in their habits and invested very heavily in the 1970s and 1980s in what we now call legacy systems, only to find that others, more fleet of foot and more imaginative of thought, were able to move in and usurp their market dominance. PayPal and other payment mechanisms come to mind, and in some regions, even airtime on a mobile phone network is used as currency.

But let us go back in time again, for a moment. An excellent example of radical business process design that is worth recounting briefly here is the "**first direct**" story from the United Kingdom (the emboldening and absence of capitalisation in their name is their choice; it is not a typographical error).

The **first direct** story

Before the World Wide Web, before liberation of the telecommunications industry, and before the dramatic expansion of retailer services to include banking, a young man joined the Midland Bank in London and began to promote the idea of a telephone banking service. This does not seem surprising today, but at that time, when we all expected to have to travel to the bank and spend time in queues for any non-trivial operation (such as one could not do at an automatic teller machine, the most recent banking innovation at that time), telephone banking was a dramatically different idea. For three years, he argued his case, until he was finally given approval to launch a new telephone-based bank, with a completely new brand. In fact, the affiliation to the Midland Bank was written so small on all the marketing literature that you would have been hard pressed to spot it, indicating a concern within Midland Bank that should the whole idea go "pear-shaped", the reputation of the host bank would not be too badly affected.

The young man in question found premises, hired a similarly young and unfettered management team, and set about the task. Although the new bank, **first direct**, used the same back office systems as the Midland Bank, a completely new front end was built so that specially trained banking assistants could undertake virtually any transaction on behalf of a customer, on the telephone, in real time. Service quality was the target. At the time, it was amusing to hear the young man say: "I went to a place where they understood service and taught them banking …" (Leeds in Yorkshire, as it happens) "… this was much easier than teaching the bank about service". The new bank was launched in only ten months. Within a further eighteen months, **first direct** was servicing almost half a million accounts with just over one thousand staff—an extraordinary achievement by any measure.

By its development of a front-end system that revolutionised how banks deal with customers, **first direct** provides an excellent example of information management success. At the time, it established an important basic rule of business: *it is easier to start a new business than it is to change an existing one*. This is exemplified by many of today's technology-related business successes such as Amazon and Google, most of which grew from very small beginnings in what we like to call "green fields" (although, more likely a garage or a coffee shop!). Consider how behemoths such as IBM and Microsoft have struggled to deal with change, but remember that both were conceived in the discontent of strong individuals, who decided to make a fresh start (Thomas Watson in the first case, and Bill Gates in the second).

The **first direct** example raises two issues that need to be appreciated by anyone considering their own chances of radical business redesign:

- First, what depth of change can be tolerated in a particular organisation? Is the organisation in a condition to put up with deep, radical change? For **first direct**, the change was deep because it involved a change from over-the-counter to telephone banking, 24 h operation and a completely new approach to customer relations. This challenge was met by the creation of a completely new bank with completely new personnel.
- Second, what scope or breadth of change can we tolerate? Are we trying to change everything that we do, for all our customers? Are we to change all our business activities and reconstruct all processes, or just some? Once other banks saw what **first direct** had been able to achieve, they all followed, but they all had to assess the extent of the required changes within their own structures.

These are different issues, because it is much easier to deal with deep change with a narrow scope, or mild change with a broad scope, than to change the whole of the world within which we work. In the case of **first direct**, the depth was dealt with by creating a new business. The scope was limited to what we would now refer to as "front-end services".

Radical change in an existing, well-established organisation is more difficult. Another short story describes a completely different situation and a different approach to change management.[2]

[2] This story was recounted to your author some time after it happened, and it seems improbable, but my recollection of the details is still very clear.

A brutal approach to radical change

At Angus Fire Services in Oxfordshire in the UK, shortly before Christmas one year, employees arriving early were surprised to find five black luxury BMWs parked in the directors' car parking places.

They were even more surprised to find five men in suits inside the building, rampaging through the offices, pulling out drawers, tipping the contents of files out on the floor, demanding to know what this or that document was and challenging individuals to explain what they did and why they were useful to the business. In one dramatic moment, one of the "suits" pointed to the decorated Christmas tree at the top of the stairs, and cried "Get this f&$%ing tree out of here!". No work was done that day, and people were traumatised.

The five "suits" were representatives of the new business owners—a British holding company that routinely bought up family businesses like Angus Fire Services and "modernised" them.

After the works holiday, the factory and offices were opened again, and employees approached the premises in some trepidation. A new face was standing at the top of the main stairs, with a smile on his face and an outstretched hand, saying, "Good morning, I'm Peter. I am the new Finance Director, who are you?" The nasty guys were gone, Mr "Nice Guy" had arrived.

If you are going to try and inculcate change in a small, stable business like this, then trauma is one way to do it. This is not a story specifically about information, or information management, but it did precede an era when Angus Fire invested heavily in new systems and Website content. Would the family have wanted to invest all that money in new systems for the business?

Depth of Change

There are three levels at which we can approach business processes:

- First, we can simply take stock of business activity generally, because we wish to optimise operational costs on a more informed basis. Should we find that any activities are particularly inefficient or time-consuming, we can explore the application of information technology to their improvement. *This is an approach we can reasonably refer to as "business process improvement", because we are not trying to redesign or radically change anything. We are just trying to make things work a little better. Most pundits would exclude this level from any definition of BPR.*
- Second, we can look at the business more carefully, not just to identify efficiency improvement opportunities but also the way that activities combine into business

processes that are visible in some way to the outside world (to customers and suppliers, as well as other business partners such as banks and transportation service providers); this is the means whereby external stakeholders make judgement about our business performance. In order to gain significant benefits, we further decide to look at the bigger picture and go for wholesale change: elimination of redundant activities, redeployment of inventory, and closer sharing of information with partners. This significantly changes the way the business works, and also the way that our business partners work with us. *This is one view of what most people regard as "business process redesign". We are looking for an overall improvement of* 80 % *here, not just* 10 *or* 20 % *in this department or the other.*

- Third, at the most extreme level, we can try to find completely new business process models from a "clean sheet". This has been rarely referred to in the BPR literature, but it is increasingly evident in practice. For example, a public sector organisation that is asked to go "private" needs to ignore all current thinking about processes because it will be hopelessly bureaucratic and wholly inappropriate to the commercial model that they seek. The challenge in these cases is to find a new process model from first principles. The famously successful Web-based businesses that succeeded, such as Google and Amazon, did so because they completely redefined the way a particular kind of business should work—advertising in the one case, and retail bookselling in the other. *This third level is pure "business process invention", not yet a term that has been widely used. It raises the question: if we have no business at present, or we wish to completely redefine our business, how shall we begin?*

Inevitably, any real case of business change will be something of a mixture of these three levels of approach. Some actions will be as simple as automating current operations to run efficiently; some will involve redesign of business interfaces for more effective operation and services to customers, and some will demand completely new thinking. Look at the Fig 5.3 that uses the value chain as an icon to represent cooperating businesses, and to show where different kinds of change can happen.

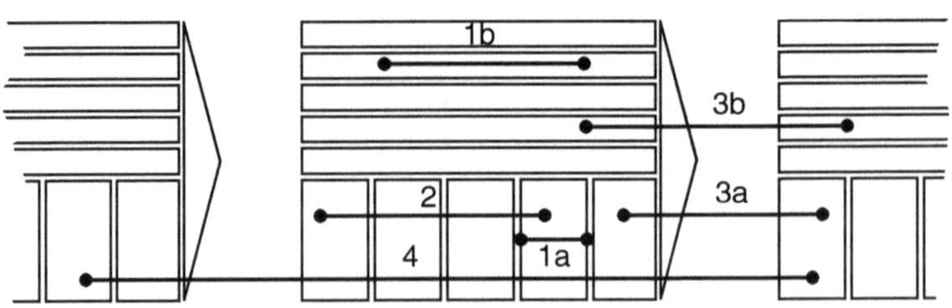

Fig. 5.3 Using the value chain to indicate the scope of change

Scope of Change

In addition to the depth of change, we must decide the scope of change. Are we dealing with one department, with a whole business unit, or with a complete industry?

We can define scope of change at the different levels of local redesign, internal redesign, interface redesign, and industry network redesign. The value chain comes to our assistance here; look at the figure above, where you can see the different kinds of change that might be useful to do:

- **Case 1** is where we are redesigning within a single functional area of our business, either in the value-adding stream (1a) or in the supporting activities (1b). This might be an improvement to a production scheduling system or a new financial management package. *No problem here: change is confined to a single area of management responsibility.*
- **Case 2** is where we are straddling different functional areas of the business in order to achieve improved information flow and tighter integration of activities. This might be a workflow management system or an integrated stock management system. *This gets more difficult. We are touching the domain of control of different managers and we will have to persuade each of them that it is in their interests to cooperate.*
- **Case 3** is where we set out to build links with external parties, in this case with our customer. It might be that we are proposing EDI linking or that they have asked us to participate in their new procurement management system. *This also gets difficult but for different reasons. The strategic significance of an idea like procurement management is different for each of the parties. The timescales involved in external partnerships can be considerably extended, and not all partners will pull with the same enthusiasm.*
- **Case 4** is the most challenging, because our customers and our suppliers have decided to get together and exclude our business altogether from the chain of industry activity. The term that is used to describe this is "disintermediation". *This is the ultimate challenge and requires us to seriously reflect on the contribution that we make to our industry. Agents, distributors and factoring businesses all around the world are in exactly this situation, whether they are in travel, motor spares or any other area where they used to be needed because they had a grip on local demand and sole access to local customers, for example. As is now very evident, these things change.*

The differences are marked, and the managerial approach to each scenario will be completely different. Nevertheless, experts have tried to establish certain principles of business process redesign.

Principles of BPR

The principles of BPR were established in the early literature as follows:

- **Organise around outcomes, not tasks**: a process model must let us see what the outcome is (or will be), and how it is derived.
- **Have those who use the output perform the process**: well-designed information systems can integrate the overall process and—in effect—enable the ultimate users of the output to initiate the production of the outputs themselves.
- **Subsume information processing into the real work**: there is no need to have a separate operation to achieve information processing—technology makes it possible for a workstation to be provided at the point where the real work is done, providing seamless access to all of the information and processing capability that is required.
- **Treat dispersed resources as centralised**: networking technologies make it trivially simple to locate information workers anywhere, while still maintaining central control.
- **Link parallel activities**: Very often, there is duplication of activity; information analysis reveals this duplication and—by understanding the underlying information structure—makes it possible to eliminate it or reduce it.
- **Put the decision point where the work is performed**: too often, work flow is interrupted so that approval can be given by a more senior authority; by making the basis for the decision clear and by making all the requisite information available, the decision point can be removed to the point where the real work is being done.
- **Capture information only once, at source**: the level of duplication of information in most organisations is alarming; for example, one might find many different places where an organisation keeps customers' (or members') names and addresses—my record is a bank (again) where there were 18 places where customers' contact information was kept.

The relevance and contribution of systems thinking to the achievement of business process redesign is quite clear from this set of principles. The tortuous processes that we often find in "ordinary" businesses derive from the historical difficulty in making information quickly and easily available at any location where it might be needed. This is no longer a problem and becomes the seed for new ideas about how businesses can operate differently.

Development of Business Processes

Having a process model of a business is important because it sits between the high- and low-level viewpoints and helps to communicate what is envisioned and what is intended to change. A process model sits comfortably between the new vision (the stimulus to improve a business) and the practical considerations (who does what, when and with what resources). Otherwise, how are we to assure the viability and completeness of our vision for the business? Do we have to wait until our ideas are operational in order to find out that they were inadequate? No we do not, far better to take a methodical approach, embracing both the higher- and the lower-level viewpoints, before we commit to an implementation that might be impractical. We need a model of the business that everybody agrees *is* the business that everyone can study, understand and work with.

Approaches to Business Modelling

As we have already seen, there are different ways to model a business. In addition to the process and information models that were introduced in the previous section of the book, the approach to any model can vary from the purely intuitive (done with a coloured pen, a whiteboard and relying entirely upon what comes to mind at the time) to a tightly specified analytical method (involving many steps and rules at every stage). Different approaches are to be found enshrined in the proprietary methods offered by consulting companies and experts. Some proprietary methods adopt extreme views, some are incomplete, some are largely ineffective because they are badly conceived, and some are only applicable in specific circumstances.

As experience accumulates within a business, it has been found that the most effective approach to strategic business analysis is one which is grown *within the organisation*; it is necessary to understand certain principles of analysis, but beyond that, the best approach is one which is "owned", which is familiar and which deals with the issues as they are seen. Thus, extreme views are neither appropriate nor necessary: what is necessary is to stimulate thinking and to nurture it. Some degree of structure might be helpful to ensure that random thoughts can be organised and interrelated, but it is equally necessary not to constrain thinking, and so if there are rules, they should be applied lightly.

There is one approach to business process analysis that embraces both visionary and operational viewpoints and that provides an informal but structured analytical method that enables reconciliation of these different levels of thinking. It is a top-down approach to business process analysis, but with some attributes of a bottom-up approach in order to ensure balance. It is not intended to be prescriptive, and with familiarity, there is no reason why the sequence of steps presented here should not be taken differently to account for different needs. For example, it might be useful to *iterate* the analysis when there is insufficient clarity or certainty about some aspect of the business. Equally, it might be useful to take more or less account of the business *as it is today*, in order to reflect the depth and scope of change that is sought by the organisation.

The two-pronged approach described here works at two levels that are at the heart of the matter:

- What are we to do as a business, and why?
- How are we to do it?

The analysis method is illustrated here using the example of a zoo—some readers will smile, thinking that yes, the organisation that they work for does resemble a zoo. But that is not the reason a zoo is chosen, it is chosen as a *fresh* example of an information-intensive business that most readers will *not* be familiar with, and it was inspired by the engagement with Malaysian MBA students described earlier.

The example material provided below is only partially developed in order to avoid a large volume of analysis material. Real-world examples will involve a greater volume of detail than is presented here, but the way in which the analytical method works will be the same.

The General Approach

There are five stages in the general approach to business process analysis:

- Develop a VISION: Before we start any detailed analysis, it is necessary to identify what the vision of the business is. This is a question for the top management team to address, before the analysis starts. *In so doing, we must be clear about the scope of the business that we have in mind: in larger organisations, it will be necessary to identify the strategic business unit (SBU) that is to be the basic unit of analysis; in smaller organisations, it is possible that the whole of the business can be treated as one.*
- Determine WHAT must be done: What is to be done is established by the analysis of stakeholders and their expectations. From the agreed expectations, a set of processes is developed which address them, individually or in combination. *The processes will have different significance to the business, one from another. Some will be critical to competitive advantage, and others will not. Some may be more important to the future of the organisation than to its current success.*
- Determine HOW it shall be done: How the business is to run is established initially by an analysis of those things that the management team agrees have to be managed. These might be the obvious tangible things (such as buildings or people), or they might be intangible (such as projects or services), but in all cases, they are the things that are necessary in order to support the reality of the vision. *Here, we will refer to them as the business "components" or business "objects". Each of these components is therefore a target of management attention and will have a life cycle; it is through the analysis of the life cycle that business activities are established. Managerial responsibilities for each activity can be noted and measures proposed for assessing how well they are done.*
- RECONCILE activities with processes: By mapping the activities (from Step 3) into the processes (from Step 2), a view is developed of how the business processes may be operationalised.

- ASSESS current performance: By assessing the current performance of each activity, the sum of achieved performance within the containing processes can be analysed and assessed. Similarly, the sum of achieved performance by management responsibility can be assessed. *These are powerful outputs that give an organisation a very clear indication of the steps that must be taken to achieve process success.*

There are two key results from the analysis. First, it produces a clear view of the processes by which the business will achieve the stakeholders' aims and expectations. Second, it produces an understanding of the relationship between activities and processes, and the way in which processes are operationalised by activities. These two linkages are perhaps the most critical for management to understand if they are to create a business that can successfully address the expectations of stakeholders.

(See Fig. 5.4 for a graphical overview of this approach)

Explanations of terms used:

- **Vision**: An agreed summary of the purpose and direction of the business, including a clear indication of the special attributes of the business that will distinguish it from others of the same kind.
- **Stakeholder**: A type of person (or body of people) that has the power to influence the operation and overall performance of a business.
- **Expectation**: A need or requirement of a stakeholder group that affects perceptions of the success (or failure) achieved by a business and the delight that it creates for stakeholders.
- **Business process**: A logical envelope that coordinates and gives purpose to activities. Processes satisfy the expectations of stakeholders. They normally cross the functional boundaries in the organisation.
- **Business object (component)**: Any "thing" of concern to the board and sufficiently critical to the organisation that it has to be managed. A business object is likely to be resource oriented.
- **Object life cycle**: The main stages through which a business object transits in its lifetime, typically (but not necessarily) specification, acquisition, use and disposal. Each stage in the life cycle indicates the activities that are required to sustain the transition and existence of the object.
- **Business activity**: A mechanism through which the organisation has chosen to operationalise its processes and which uses resources to achieve process goals. Activities add cost to the organisation, and they may cross functional boundaries.

There is sometimes confusion about the differences between "vision" and "mission". A vision is a snapshot that gives a target to aim for, whereas a mission has a much stronger sense of action and will include strong pointers to what must be done. Here, we will not refer to mission explicitly, to develop a mission statement as well as a vision, it would be best done after the process analysis described here, because the means to achieve the vision will then be much clearer.

Examples of all of the above are provided in the pages that follow.

An Analysis Method

Figure 5.4 shows a general scheme of analytical steps that will allow an organisation to work through a process analysis. It is described in more detail in the paragraphs that follow, and the sequence of steps indicated in the figure is followed in the description that follows.

1. **Develop a Vision**

A vision statement must be negotiated with the senior management team. Every word in a written vision statement needs to be evaluated—for its meaning and for the contribution that it makes. Later on, the wording and content of the vision statement will be important in weighting and ranking the detail that comes from the analysis.

A good vision statement sets a target to aim at. It makes clear the principal outcome of all the intentions of the business and qualifies it in a way that makes

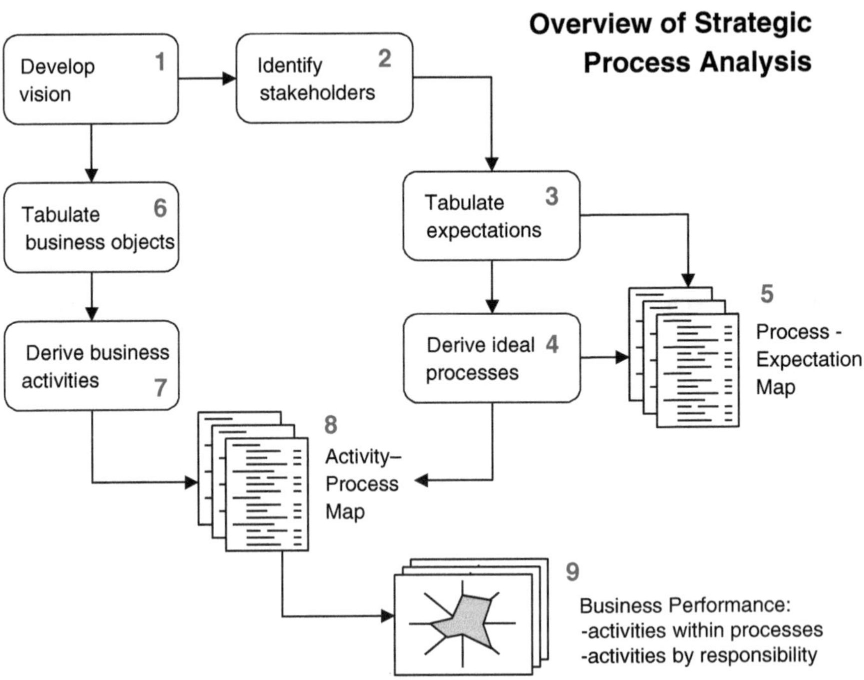

Fig. 5.4 The process of business process analysis

clear the principal objectives or constraints in achieving that outcome (such as ecological constraints, or the intention to provide exceptional levels of quality in products and services, or not). By having a clear statement of the vision, the nuances of organisational capability and competency become clearer, and the specific capabilities the organisation needs to deliver the vision become apparent. A vision is about choices: positioning, scoping and differentiating the business when compared to its peers or its competitors.

As the vision statement begins to stabilise, highlight the words that define or imply the capabilities required and the key entities with which the business will be concerned. If any are missing, decide what words need to be added to focus on precisely where the organisation chooses to operate, and how it defines and differentiates itself.

So, how does it go from there? Taking the example of a zoo, imagine that this is a private zoo with a new management team that is determined to improve its performance and deliver real value to all the stakeholders.

> "I know we need to make a profit but this zoo is going to be guided by proper ethical principles" insisted the new Chief Executive. "I want us to educate and entertain. I want visitors to enjoy themselves with the minimum effort. I want them to have the very best facilities. We'll win by providing really good value for money!"
>
> "Oh yeh?" retorted the Head Keeper. "And who's going to muck out the cages?"

Look carefully at the statement from the new Chief Executive Officer of the zoo, at the right. She is clearly setting lofty targets. At the same time, the Head Keeper (of animals) is determined to maintain a practical viewpoint and to make sure that operational issues are not forgotten.

A suitable vision statement from further discussion between the management team might be[3]:

> The zoo vision
> We wish to be an **ethical** and **profitable** business, and to provide **educational** and entertaining experiences.

2. **Identify stakeholders**

A stakeholder is any identifiable individual or organisation that can influence the course of the business. Stakeholders have differing degrees of importance based

[3] These examples are contrived and not based on any analysis of a "real" Zoo.

Table 5.1 The zoo stakeholders

ID	Stakeholder	Weighting
S1	Visitors	70
S2	Shareholders	15
S3	Government	5
S4	Employees	0
S5	Directors	0
S6	Suppliers	6
S7	Local community	4
Total weighting:		100

upon the extent to which they might apply their influence and the probable consequences of it.

In addition to the traditional stakeholders (shareholders, employees, directors), it is necessary to include those that might not be so obvious but that can affect the operation and direction of the business (such as the government, industry regulator or the local community). The degree to which stakeholders can affect the business will vary, and they should be weighted to represent this variation; a process of discussion and agreement must establish the weighting.

Clearly, we are not the zoo and we cannot easily get around a table with the management team of a zoo, but to illustrate the sort of result at this stage, a representative list of stakeholders for the zoo might be as follows (Table 5.1).

The weightings here are achieved by allocating 100 points across the full list, allocating none at all to those stakeholders who are deemed to have no influence: directors (because they are entirely beholden to shareholders) and employees (because they are entirely beholden to the directors)—of course, this might not actually be the case in a real business, but it does illustrate a point: stakeholders can be excluded if they are, in some sense, of no material significance in shaping and managing the business.

3. **Tabulate stakeholder expectations**

Because stakeholders can influence the business to some degree or another, they must be consulted in order to identify and tabulate their expectations. Different stakeholder groups may share the same expectations (for example, both shareholders and directors will expect healthy revenues), but they are also likely to have conflicting hopes and aspirations (such as the employees' expectation of high salaries and investments in their skills through training, and the shareholders' expectation of economy in operational matters). Although we might be working with only seven stakeholders (as in this case, although we only illustrate the expectations of three of them in Table 5.2), we can see that at this stage the volume of evidence that we are working with really begins to expand.

Table 5.2 Stakeholder expectations at the zoo

ID	Stakeholder	Expectations	Weighting	Measure of expectation
S1	Visitors		70	
	1.1	Safety		Number of injured visitors
	1.2	Entertainment		Length of stay
				Repeat business
'...etc.				
S2	Shareholders		15	
	2.1	Dividend		Yield versus other investments
	2.2	Growth of share value		Growth versus other investments
S3	Government		5	
	3.1	Ethical operation		Bad publicity
				Visitor complaints
'...etc.				

Note that

- There will usually be more than one expectation per stakeholder
- The same expectations might recur from one stakeholder to the next
- Expectations might be in conflict with one another
- For stakeholders with a zero weighting, it is not really necessary to include their expectations, but they need to be consulted
- For stakeholders with a high weighting, additional care must be taken to establish expectations with confidence
- For each expectation, it is necessary to nominate a measure that would indicate the extent of realisation

The question of measures is important, for there is no purpose to an expectation that cannot be measured. As we shall see elsewhere, the means whereby we measure business performance are important, and no measures are more important than those that indicate the delight (or otherwise) delivered to stakeholders. What is the benefit of additional sales in a particular market segment (a low level, activity measure), if we cannot relate that to the expectations of customers (the highest level of measure)? What is the benefit of a lower cost of operation, even across the board, if we cannot relate that to the expectations of shareholders?

At this point, we need to look more carefully at the expectations that have emerged from stakeholders. An analysis of seven or so stakeholders, each having four or five expectations, might lead to a list overall of 30 or 40 expectations in total—that would be typical. It is necessary to review the overall list of expectations and rationalise them where they touch upon identical or similar aspects of success. For example, consider the following partial list in Table 5.3, that gives a few more examples than in the table above.

Table 5.3 More stakeholder expectations at the zoo

Stakeholder	Expectations
Visitors	1.1 Safety
	1.2 Entertainment
	1.3 Education
	1.4 Amenities
Shareholders	2.1 Dividend
	2.2 Growth of share value
	2.3 Ethical operation
Government	3.1 Safety
	3.2 Ethical operation
	3.3 Conformance to regulations
Employees	4.1 Safety
	4.2 Good working conditions
	4.3 Security of future employment
	4.4 Career development

There is evident overlap in these expectations. For example, visitors, government and employees all expect safety. Shareholders and government expect ethical operation. And then, there is potential overlap between the government expectation of conformance to regulations and the employees' expectation of good working conditions. If employees are weighted highly (they are not weighted highly in the example above, as it happens), then one would want to ensure employee working conditions well above the level required by government; as they are not weighted highly, we would decide to work to the level of government regulations only. This is the way in which our early decisions about vision and weighting affect the more detailed organisation of the analysis such as we have here (Table 5.3).

It follows from a rationalisation of expectations that we can now put the stakeholders to one side in our minds, and work with just one consolidated list of all expectations. Note that because employees are not weighted at all (rightly or wrongly—it simply makes a point in this example), all their expectations other than safety, which is shared with others, are eliminated from the list (Table 5.4).

The final list should be presented in ranked order, taking full account of weightings: the perceived importance of each expectation, the stakeholder group from which it was derived and the number of stakeholder groups that held that expectation. In the illustration here, we are supposing that safety was the most important and that other expectations were ranked as shown.

4. **Derive list of ideal processes**

We are now ready to develop our first list of processes. Because we have established a consolidated list of all expectations, of all stakeholders that we have

Table 5.4 Consolidated expectations of all stakeholders

Consolidated and ranked expectations
Safety
Ethical operation
Education
Entertainment
Amenities
Growth of share value
Dividend
Conformance to regulations

decided are significant, we now know everything that we must do to succeed, do we not? We even know what is the most important thing, that we must do first.

Starting with the first expectation, we must ask what kind of process will satisfy the expectation? In the first instance here, we have safety. An appropriate process to ensure safety could be named "manage safety", but the word "manage" is one that can be overworked. What does it mean in this case? Lots of different things come to mind: planning, monitoring and documenting—to mention just three. A better word might be "ensure" because it puts the focus on what is required: to ensure that there are no risks and no accidents to visitors or employees.

Hence, we arrive at **ensure safety** as the first requisite process.

Note the use of the verb–object construct in naming a process: **ensure** (verb) **safety** (object). This helps to highlight the fact that we are nominating a process that will do something, hence the use of a transitive verb. It is good practice to follow this convention, and there are rules for the creation of new processes:

- For the first expectation, create a process that will satisfy it (as we have done above).
- For subsequent expectations, examine whether they will be satisfied by any of the processes so far established. If so, note it and consider whether the relevant processes need adjustments to the name, or redefinition, or adaptation. If an existing process will not satisfy it, then create a new process and add it to the list.
- For any new processes, review their possible contribution to other expectations (already served by an existing process) and note that as appropriate.

5. **Process–expectation map**

In this way, we can build up a matrix showing how each of the processes that have been nominated contributes to each of the expectations from the consolidated list (Table 5.5). The zoo processes might look like Table 5.6:

- Note how most of the processes contribute to more than one expectation. The strength of the contribution could be noted; the strongest contribution in each case is on the diagonal.

Table 5.5 Processes at the zoo

Expectation			Safety	Ethical operation	Education	Entertainment	Amenities	Growth of share value	Dividend	Conformance to regulations
Process										
P1	Ensure	Safety	✓		✓		✓	✓		✓
P2	Look after	Animals		✓				✓		✓
P3	Educate	Visitors	✓	✓	✓			✓		
P4	Entertain	Visitors		✓		✓		✓		
P5	Provide	Amenities				✓	✓	✓		✓
P6	Manage	Finances						✓	✓	✓
P7	Govern	Zoo						✓		✓

Table 5.6 Business objects at the zoo

The zoo business objects
Visitor
Supplier
Food
Animal mix
Visit
Cage
Keeper
Facility
Vet

- Note that all processes are seen as contributing to share value, simply because perceptions are everything when it comes to investor perceptions of value.
- Note that all except two processes contribute to conformance with government regulations. This is because of the pervasive nature of such regulations.

The final form of such a matrix will not evolve through the use of rules, but rather out of the discussion that must accompany the exercise. While you may have the impression that this approach is very deterministic, being based on simple but seemingly quite strict rules, that is not really the case. It should be seen as a vehicle for the whole management team to get a grip on the key issues, to discuss them and to decide how an idealised set of processes (such as those in the table above) might best serve the interests of stakeholders. The analysis should not be done by one person alone.

At the end of the day, processes will be assessed by the extent to which they satisfy expectations and the importance of those expectations according to the mission statement, and according to the weighting originally assigned to each stakeholder. Each process should be thought of as having distinct outcomes that address the requirements of stakeholders.

At this stage, the analysis has established what kind of business is at hand, who might influence its success and why we must do what we must do. This gives us an *idealised* view of the business based on external considerations, but it is not yet complete; we need to think more about how the business will actually work and the practical issues that might affect what we do.

6. Tabulate business objects

Having identified an idealised set of business processes, we need to populate each with the activities (at a lower level) that will "realise" the process. This could be done by brainstorming (involving a group of people who ought to know about these things because it is their area of responsibility) or by reduction (taking a process and breaking it down into parts, and then breaking those parts into subparts and so on). However, this will not necessarily lead to a workable model for the business because many necessary activities will have only an indirect association with business processes and will not be evident in the "what" view: budgeting and cash flow analysis may be examples, when thinking strategically these kinds of activity sometimes fall "under the radar", but exactly what activities might fall into this category depends on the business that is under consideration.

We therefore have to find a more comprehensive way to identify activities, both those that are externally significant because they directly support processes and those that only indirectly support them. In order to do this, we go back to the vision statement and derive from it the primary objects that comprise the essential components or elements of the business.

A business object can be seen as any "thing" that we need to manage: it might be referred to as an entity, or as a component, and we have already noted that entities are "things" about which we need to keep information. The challenge (as we have noted when discussing entity modelling) is to embrace *all* the things that we need to manage, be they animate (customers, employees), inanimate (product, facility) or abstract (project, problem, objective). We do this through a simple two-stage process, but unfortunately, it is confused by the number of objects that we might have to deal with, and the even greater number of activities that will service them.

With the vision statement to hand, the next step is to tabulate and organise a list of the high-level objects in a business—things that the management team agrees will have to be managed and that define the substance of the business. This is easily done by brainstorming but with just a few rules for guidance.

- Always name an entity using a noun, for example "AMENITY", "VISITOR" or "SUPPLIER".
- Stakeholders and the objects already identified in the process names are already candidate objects; it is likely that these will all need managing, but each should be discussed on its merits and given appropriate representation in the tabulation of objects.
- Only include high-level objects that represent key components of the business, and make clear each one's unique nature and structure; avoid becoming consumed with low-level detail. If it is not something that requires management time, then we can ignore it at this stage.

For the zoo, a list of objects would include at least the business objects shown in Table 5.6.

And with such a list, we can get to work on the activities that will support them.

7. **Derive activities using object life cycle analysis**

Each object will have a life cycle. Take suppliers: they have to be selected according to certain criteria and then added to a list. For a period of time, perhaps a long time, they will serve as suppliers to the zoo. However, some will fail to perform or their supplies will be no longer needed, and so we must dispose of them by taking them off the list. Take visitors: they must be persuaded to attend the zoo, to partake of the activities and facilities, and to come again as often as possible.

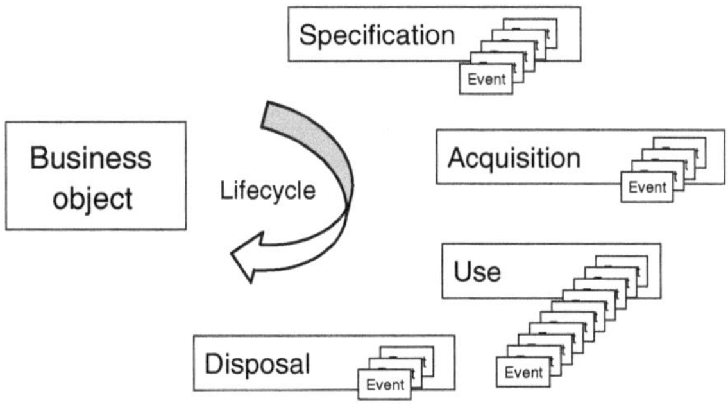

Fig. 5.5 The business object life cycle

Sometimes, visitors may be deemed to be undesirable (because of bad behaviour or for other reasons) or they might die, in which case we must take them off the mailing list. In every case, we can quickly establish a life cycle of involvement with the business objects, and then refine it at our leisure (Fig. 5.5).

In an actual analysis, then, we must discuss and agree the outline of the life cycle for all business objects and then tabulate all the activities within each phase. Typically, four stages are evident, each containing or involving a number of activities:

- **Specification**: activities to identify requirements, analyse and document them, and then to agree on them before embarking on acquisition.
- **Acquisition**: activities involved in identifying sources, eliciting availability and establishing suitability and then actually negotiating terms and taking delivery, thereby concluding the acquisition phase.
- **Use**: all of the activities during the lifetime of usage—possibly very many, and possibly divided into different kinds of activity.
- **Disposal**: those activities involved in assessing the ongoing usefulness of an object and possibly leading to a decision to dispose of it; all of the steps involved in achieving disposition.

However, the actual stages in the life cycle of an object might not fit this strict pattern and some interpretation will be required. A partial view of the zoo activities, derived from life cycle analysis of just three objects, might be as follows (Table 5.7).

In order to further improve the understanding of activities, it might be useful to analyse the ways in which objects interact with each other. For example, how will visitors to the zoo interact with keepers? If they do (for example by constantly asking for directions), then there is a putative activity: something along the lines of "direct visitors around the zoo"). It is possible to do this using a matrix with all objects listed along the top and also listed down the side (a little like those miles-from-town-to-town tables that we used to use to plan our journeys, before GPS systems and maps became available on the World Wide Web). It is only necessary to visit each cell representing the intersection of an entity with another (including itself) and to decide whether or not there is any interaction between them (or with itself) and record it.

Table 5.7 Activities at the zoo

Object	Specification phase	Acquisition phase	Use phase	Disposal phase
Visitor	Advertise to the public	Deal with enquiries	Inform about exhibits	Obtain comments about level of satisfaction and future requirements
	Liaise with schools			
	Market to previous visitors	Provide information about the zoo	Provide refreshment	
			Provide other amenities	
		Take admission moneys		
Supplier	Formulate invitations to tender	Advertise invitations to tender	Place supplier orders	Review supplier performance
		Evaluate tenders	Receive deliveries	Conclude contract of supply
			Check supplier invoices	
			Make supplier payments	
		Award contracts of supply	Monitor supplier performance	
Food	Analyse animal nutritional requirements	Place internal food orders on zoo food store	Prepare animal feed	Clean out animal cages and enclosures
	Publish feeding schedules	Collect food from store	Fulfil animal feeding	
Animal mix	…etc			

8. **Activity–processes map**

With a stable view of the idealised processes, and a reasonably complete view of the activities within the business, we are in a position to test the merits of what we do now against what we should be doing. There are two key questions:

- How do the activities from the object life cycle analysis stack up against the idealised processes? In principle, every activity must contribute to at least one process; otherwise, why are we doing it?
- Are our idealised processes adequately populated with activities? It is conceivable that we are simply not doing all the things that we should be doing, in order to serve the needs of our stakeholders.

So, in order to set about this final mapping, we need to develop the activity—process matrix.

As the identification of activities proceeds, examine each for the contribution that it makes to a process, if any. The relationship may be strong, such as "sales clerk records the details of customer order", which clearly makes a critical contribution to the "fulfil customer orders" process, or it may be less strong. The degree of strength in the relationship can be recorded.

There are a number of possible outcomes:

- Each process has a proportionate number of activities. Typically, if there were 8 identified processes and 160 activities, one would expect that each process would have of the order of 20 activities to operationalise it. In the event, this may be so, but it is not necessary for processes to share activities in a proportionate way—it depends on how complex they are.
- A process may have no activities, or very few. Having just a few activities is not necessarily a problem, although management will clearly want to review things to make sure that nothing has been omitted. In the unlikely case that a process has no supporting activities, it is very likely that significant business components have been missed or that the process analysis is flawed.
- An activity may not be mapped to any process. Any activity that has no role within a process is redundant and should be considered for elimination.

A selection of zoo activities mapped to processes is shown below. This map—the matrix of processes and activities—allows us to assess the completeness of the analysis so far. In order to do this, the matrix can be used to list against each process the activities that contribute to it, equally to list the activities and the extent to which they contribute to processes. From this, judgements can be made. In summary, again:

- Does each process have sufficient "support" in the sense that there are activities making a direct contribution to it?
- Does each activity have sufficient "purpose", in that it makes a sufficient contribution to make it worthwhile?

Clearly, the objective of the analysis and modelling effort is to create a better understanding of what is to be done to fulfil the vision of the business, and to make sure that those working in the organisation can see clearly how the vision is to be operationalised, and where things are done well and where things are not done well. And, of course, to see where we need to bolster operations by the use of appropriate information systems (Table 5.8).

One way to establish a plan of action is to build separate models for the "now" and "future" forms of the business. Here, we have not done that, the illustration being limited to a future model for the business only. However, having created such a detailed view of what the future business must do, it is sensible to assess how evident the required activities are in the current form of the business, and to make a judgement about how well they are done. Even in the case where there is no formal evidence of a new activity (such as "obtain comments about the level of satisfaction

Table 5.8 Activities mapped to processes

Process	Activities
Ensure safety	Provide information about the zoo
	Inform about exhibits
Look after animals	Analyse animal nutritional requirements
	Publish feeding schedules
	Place internal food orders on zoo food store
	Collect food from store
	Prepare animal feed
	Fulfil animal feeding
	Clean out animal cages and enclosures
Entertain visitors	Advertise to the public
	Liaise with schools
	Market to previous visitors
	Deal with enquiries
	Take admission moneys
	Provide refreshment
	Provide other amenities
	Obtain comments about level of satisfaction and future requirements

and future requirements" in the zoo model—because at present there is no documented feedback mechanism), there will often be some kind of surrogate (zoo employees hearing comments from visitors may discuss them, and may even report them to management; management might even do something about them from time to time).

9. **Assess business performance**

Let us remind ourselves that the purpose of this analysis is to find out where the business might benefit from new information systems. We therefore need to know where we are doing well and where we are not. Hence, the next stage in the analysis is to assess current process performance. Let us suppose for the sake of the discussion that we have a complete set of idealised set of processes and a reasonably complete understanding of business activities. We can assess performance at the level of processes by working upwards from activities. Having mapped activities to processes, it is possible to assess the current performance of the business by surveying opinion about how well activities are currently done (if they are done at all) and aggregating these measures under each of the process headings using the process–activity map. If responsibility for activities has also been tabulated (not discussed above, but not difficult to do), it is also possible to aggregate the performance achieved within each area of responsibility.

"Radar charts" have been found to be a convenient means of presenting performance data. In the example below, activities contributing to the "entertain

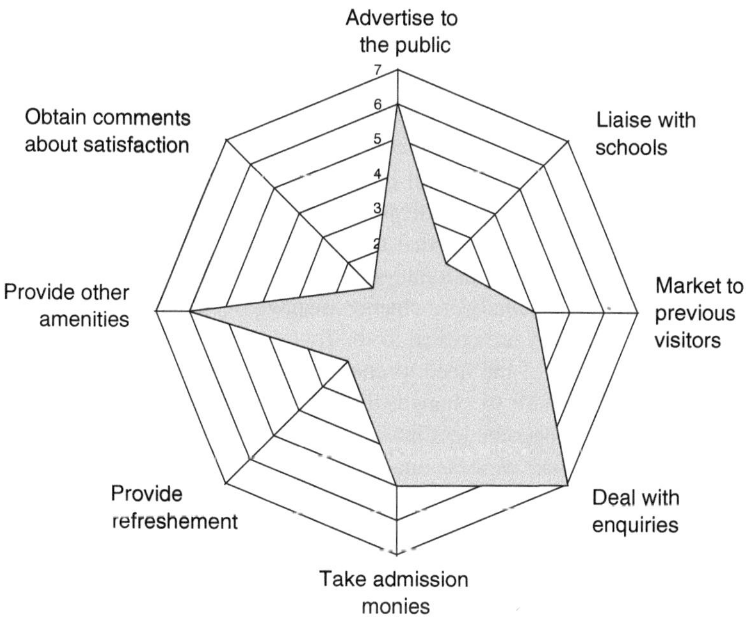

Fig. 5.6 Business performance at the zoo—"entertain visitors"

visitors" process have been assessed and are charted as the radial axes of the chart. It is immediately evident visually how well one activity is undertaken relative to the others. Here, it is immediately evident that the quality of our feedback (from visitors to the zoo) is very poor, although we do deal well with enquiries that come in, advertising is working well, and we are pleased with our amenities. However, we must remember that if this is the *internal* view of how well we are doing, based on the views of management, we must be careful. It is better to base these assessments on what stakeholders actually think, not on what *we* think. Indeed, the data reveal that we know that we are *very bad* at listening to visitor feedback, so what merit is there in these performance figures? The answer is that with a measurement framework such as this, we can take a rational view of the difference between *our* views of business performance and assess it against evidence of what our *stakeholders* think. If we can manage the gap between our view and their view, and ensure that the two views are more or less in accord with each other, then we shall be close to achieving the best possible business result (Fig 5.6).

In general, the performance of each process will be judged according to the performance of the weakest activity contributing to it (so in the example here, we seem to be in bad shape in three important areas!). Then, by comparing one chart with another over time, the differences in process performance can be assessed over time and from one process to another. This is important, because those processes that are "competitive" must be done well (significantly better than they are done by competitors) and their associated activities must be monitored carefully to ensure that none of them is underperforming (see the next section, "Managing business processes", for more detail about the different kinds of process in an organisation).

Other less critical categories of process must also be done well although the criteria by which they are judged will be different—more operational criteria than strategic (they must be done at least as well as competitors, but not necessarily better than them, and well enough that they do not cause problems).

Processes that are transformational—those that actually take the organisation forward through strategic analysis, change management and organisation development—are special. They are critical to the future of an organisation, and so their importance is a function of the need to change, or the desire to change. If there is neither need nor any desire to change, then they become less important, but the business will inevitably become less interesting to work in, it might degenerate, and the very need to undertake process analysis will of course be lessened.

It is also possible to use the radar charts to summarise performance according to the responsibilities held within the business. How well is the Managing Director doing? Is the senior management actually performing well in those areas that are critical to the future of the business, as opposed to those areas that they are comfortable in? What is the actual contribution of the information systems department? Is the future strategy of the organisation really dependent upon the development and delivery of new systems, or are other non-technical factors more important?

Finally, we must take steps to survey the opinion of our stakeholders about business performance, using the expectation measures that we established at the start (in Step 3 of the analysis), and tally the internal view of business performance with the external view.

Managing Business Processes

Let us remember that we are concerned with business processes in order to deliver business performance that is appropriate to the expectations of our stakeholders, and to ensure that we are investing in information technology and systems in the most appropriate areas of activity. But there is one other view: that the processes of an organisation can be the basis of competitive strategy. Not all processes have the same significance, surely? If we are in a traditional manufacturing sector, then perhaps product development is not critical—internal efficiency will be more important to our success. However, if we are in the IT supply industry, then moving new products to market will unquestionably be the most important thing to get right.

We need a way to unravel these differences.

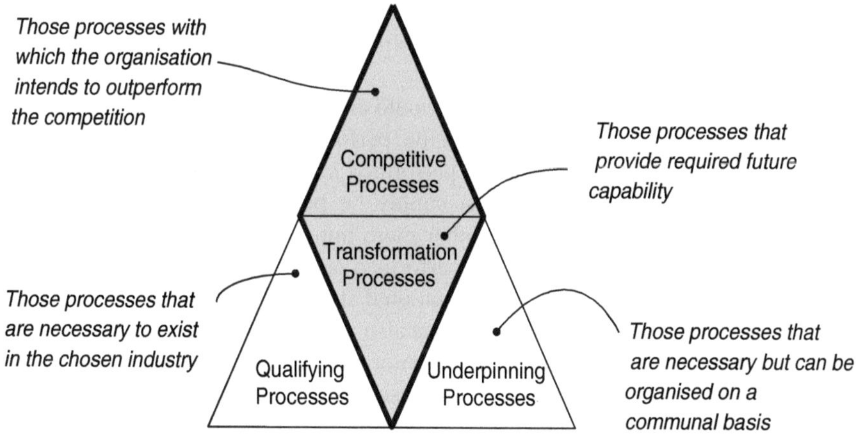

Fig. 5.7 Different categories of processes

The Process Triangle

One way of seeing the differences between different kinds of processes is the "process triangle" (see Fig. 5.7).[4] It is based on four kinds of process significance.

- Some processes are *competitive* and will be the basis of future success; here, we need to outperform the competition.
- Some processes are not competitive, but are absolutely *necessary* if we are to be a credible player in our chosen industry,
- Some processes are important, but are so *pervasive* that they can be organised in our industry on a communal basis.
- Some processes are the basis of *future capability* and will ensure that the organisation moves forward and maintains competencies appropriate to its strategic development ambitions.

These differences between processes are important to understand because they demand different management styles and different approaches to implementation. Without an appreciation of these differences, organisational effort might be dissipated needlessly, doing the wrong things well and failing to recognise the right things that are the ones that really must be done well (generally the competitive and transformational processes). So, the purpose in having this classification is to highlight those processes that are important for different strategic reasons: for

[4] It might be noted that this idea—the process triangle—mirrors the applications portfolio. Similar arguments are used to distinguish at least the three categories: competitive), qualifying (key operational) and underpinning (support). However, it must be remembered that the process triangle is pitched at a much higher level than the applications portfolio. Where there might be hundreds of applications (information systems) there will be only a few processes—perhaps as few as four or five.

competitive reasons (competitive processes), for reasons of operational efficiency (qualifying processes), cost reduction (underpinning) and organisational development (transformation).

This then affects the way in which we would choose to assess the performance of a process. Competitive processes must be performed *better* than others in the industry; qualifying processes must be performed *as well as* others in the industry, whereas underpinning processes must simply be performed well enough not to impact upon the performance of the other more important categories of processes. Transformational processes must be performed at a level that will sustain the evolution and implementation of organisational strategy.

The differences in process characteristics also affect the way we would assess the fulfilment of managerial responsibility. Senior managers must take responsibility for competitive and transformational processes and make sure that they are done well. Operational managers must take responsibility for qualifying processes and ensure that they are done well, according to operational measures of performance. Service managers must take responsibility for underpinning processes and ensure that they are done at the lowest practical cost: there is no purpose in investing heavily in underpinning process activities.

Concluding Comment

This overview of the analysis process has described its sequence and illustrated some of the results that typically come out of it. These results are one of the benefits of such an analysis, but it can also generate a great deal of discussion among those concerned in order to achieve agreement about details on the way through. As with any analysis, the *process* of investigation can be as useful as the *outputs*.

This is not intended to be a precise or deterministic method, and people who have adopted it have almost always adapted the details to suit their own circumstances and their preferences for details. The way in which an analysis is undertaken should recognise this; because of the volume of detail that can arise, any means to minimise the drudgery involved in dealing with large volumes of data are welcome. It will be found that the use of spreadsheets and database tables is helpful in recording the results of the analysis and in reaching appropriate conclusions and in the rapid production of reports in response to the many questions that will occur on the way through. The purpose of a methodical approach such as that presented here is not to make the process mechanistic and precise, but rather to control the volume of analytical evidence and to make the process achievable and manageable where otherwise it would be hopelessly imprecise and difficult to control. Organisations benefit from seeing the connection between their high-level vision and the operational consequences, and the method seems to deliver just the level of detail that is typically needed.

Summary

Managerial Issues in Process Management

As we noted at the start of this discussion of business processes, for a time process management was the subject of unreasonable excitement and later it was the subject of disillusionment. The explanation given here about process analysis should help to explain why people became disillusioned: although the intellectual challenges are not great (there are no complicated ideas involved in the analysis), there is a need to be methodical and the volume of analysis data can become difficult to manage. It also requires that a management team "buys into" the way of thinking about processes in order that productive discussion and agreement can be gained. Herein lies some of the difficulty. It is not easy to persuade managers to follow particular lines of thinking different to what they are used to, especially when they might feel that their future is threatened.

At the heart of process management is the need to see the business in a simple way, through easy-to-understand models, in order to improve it. This gives us a clue as to some of the management issues that still pervade business process management:

Business modelling: By some means, it is necessary to agree how the business is most usefully modelled in order to be able to visualise ideas about processes and negotiate alternatives. Business models need to be owned and nurtured; it is not sufficient to call in consultants and rely entirely upon them. There must be an internal capability and discipline for modelling, even if it is only to maintain lists of processes and activities as in the main illustration of the zoo, as presented here. Graphical techniques might be more insightful and therefore more effective.

Process management: Processes need to be managed, so that it is necessary to have process owners, to record the status and disposition of processes, and to maintain registers of pending problems and opportunities for action. There should be review processes that ensure that thinking about processes is refreshed routinely and that new ideas are able to be incorporated.

Stakeholders: Stakeholders' expectations are critical to the successful development and implementation of strategies, and their hopes and expectations can be used to launch new thinking about how a business should work. Business models should be reviewed by stakeholders and used to elicit stakeholder expectations and refine the details of those models.

Business process outsourcing: In our discussion of information systems, outsourcing emerged as an option within the IT function (for example, crowd-sourced systems design and program coding) and at the operational level (for example the Co-operative Bank, where information technology and other services were outsourced completely, to a range of outsourced services providers). At the higher level of business process outsourcing, it is *critical* that an organisation has the capability to define and then manage the boundary between what an outsourced services provider might do, and what the client organisation must retain to do itself. Without clarity, chaos can easily result as things drop, literally, through gaps in the arrangement and as other things get done twice in two different places.

Change management: Business process-driven change can directly impact the personal domains of senior managers and will usually be seen (in the first instance at least) as a threat to the job security of the workforce. It will make great demands on the ability of an organisation to change, and some would advise organisations with no history of change to not even get started. Happily, as the **first direct** example shows, it is possible to succeed provided that senior management are prepared to listen to the messages that are coming from below.

Some experts are inclined to dismiss the whole idea of business process management as being no more than a repackaging of ideas that have been around for many years. This may be true, but to dismiss it on these grounds is to ignore the fact that despite the early difficulties, it has captured the imagination of progressive organisations more than many other recent management "fads".

Because of its close association with information systems thinking and its reliance on systems in support of change, we can be sure that the general approach to managing business processes will continue to evolve and will be with us for some time to come.

Business Process Management Competencies

Business process management is at the heart of information management, in that here we see how investments in information technology and information systems deliver the efficiency and effectiveness that fulfils our strategic intentions. It is, in the vernacular, "where the rubber hits the road". The fact that the very idea of a business process is alien to traditionally minded workers creates problems and leads to certain competencies and preconditions that must be satisfied, especially in the area of business process modelling:

- Business process modelling describes processes in a comprehensible and purposeful way.
- Information (and data) must be used effectively in processes (and activities).
- All stakeholders need to be able to review business models before decisions are made about them.
- The quality and performance of business processes and business process components must be monitored and sustained.
- A register of problems and opportunities associated with business processes shall be maintained.
- The degree and extent of changes proposed for business processes must be fully analysed, understood and managed.

Research Side Note: Outsourcing Business Processes

Lacity, M.C., Solomon, S., Yan, A. & Willcocks, L.P. (2011) Business process outsourcing studies: a critical review and research directions. Journal of Information Technology, 26 (4), pp. 221–258.

Mary Lacity and her colleagues have undertaken a major review of prior research into business processes and the way in which they are outsourced. Motivation to outsource is based on reducing costs, focusing on core capabilities and filling out other capabilities by accessing the skills of outsourcing suppliers. There are no real surprises so far. But organisations are less likely to outsource business processes that are complex and critical. To make the best of outsourcing, organisations need to have additional skills to deal with contracting, outsourcing supplier performance management, and a compatible culture. These are the things they consider to be comparable to the requirements and consequences of information technology and information systems outsourcing.

Some of the necessary research that they identify includes the following:

- Understanding the innovation that comes from outsourcing.
- Identifying the capabilities that must be retained by the outsourcing client—what do we still have to be able to do for ourselves?
- Investigating how different environments impact on outsourcing—it is not just about us (as clients) and them (as suppliers).
- Assessing other destinations besides India. India has been predominant, but what about other countries and regions?
- Outsourcing suppliers must have special capabilities, but we do not yet understand them.
- Pricing models are changing, from full-time equivalent payments to pay-per-use or transactional methods—what other options are there?
- Organisations are awash with data—how might business analytics services supplement the sort of outsourcing services that are already established?
- What other emerging models and trends are there, for example the emergence of mulitple process outsourcing?

Finally, it is time (they say) that we had a fully developed business process outsourcing theory. We need to gather the constructs and characteristics of outsourcing business processes, and identify and record the patterns that work well or that work badly.

Research Side Note: Seeing Change Happening, From the Bottom-Up

Yoo, Y. (2010) Computing in everyday life: A call for research on experiential computing. MIS Quarterly, 34 (2), pp. 213–231

Youngjin Yoo has written an interesting essay on how everyday experience, with "computing", is changing the way we see information technology and information systems at work. He challenges information systems researchers to go back to basics, and acknowledge that the simple idea of experience is a proper starting point for six new areas of research. It is an excellent paper that is well worth reading, being quite different to some of the dry and (in my view) very shallow research that is published today.

Exploring Business Information

6

What is Business Information?

Business information is derived from the interpretation of data, and it is the basis upon which informed decisions are made.

To the extent that all organisations are concerned to acquire information, to store it, to analyse it in some way and to use it to take decisions about what to do in particular circumstances, information can be seen as the lifeblood of any organisation. It must be seen separately from data, which is merely the *representation* of information, (usually, in the present context, a *digital* representation).

Take for example, the following 13 digits:

8407145125186

These are, as presented above, meaningless ***data***—far from anything that could be considered "information". However, seen in a context, we can guess at their significance (Fig. 6.1).

We now have ***information***—this is clearly an identity number for a "non-South African citizen" (it is invented; it is not a *real* South African ID number, but it follows the formatting rules). You might deduce on close inspection that the first *six* digits of the ID number, taken together, might be birth year, birth month and birth day, and you would be right.

The Nature of Information

This simple example makes the point that data and information are different, and you will already be aware that the structure of numbers like these—such as ISBN numbers for books, article numbers for consumer products and vehicle driver

A. Bytheway, *Investing in Information*,
DOI 10.1007/978-3-319-11909-0_6

I.D.No. 840714 5125 18 6

NIE S.A.BURGER / NON S.A.CITIZEN

Fig. 6.1 Data becomes information

licences the world over—are all laid out in particular ways because the position of the digits is significant, as well as the value.

In South Africa, as in other countries, an ID number is the basis for many different kinds of ***decision***. A citizen of the country gets certain privileges, whereas someone with only residency rights (not full citizenship) does not; hence, the ID number is used to decide whether one can vote or not, whether one qualifies for social security benefits or not and even the nature of your relationship with your bank and permission to bring money in and out of the country. Given its obvious importance in taking decisions in life and in work, it is surprising that the *nature* of information is so often misunderstood.

The above small and simple example—an ID number as data, and then as information, and then as the basis for a decision—makes clearer the difference between data, information and "knowledge". There are much more complex examples to be seen, and already in this example, it is clear that there are different components: the digits of the birthday, a sequential number within that day and a type of ID that probably indicates a foreigner with residential status but not full citizenship.

In line with this simple example, it is often said that

- Data, when they are interpreted, become ***information***
- Information, when it is understood, becomes ***knowledge***
- Knowledge, when it is deployed, becomes ***wisdom***.

Professor Venkatraman, a leading academic working in the United States, challenged this arrangement of ideas at a public seminar some time ago (Venkatraman 1996), and he spoke persuasively about knowledge not as the beginning of wisdom, but as a basis for ***action*** and then about action as something that leads to an intended ***result***. His talk was around an arrangement of ideas that is sometimes referred to as the "DIKAR" model (Fig. 6.2).

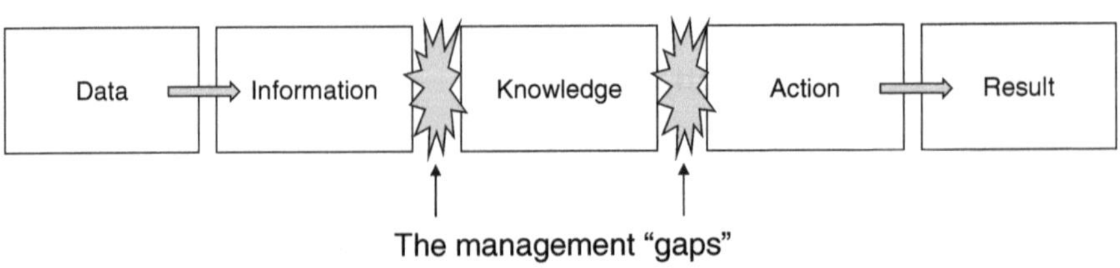

Fig. 6.2 The DIKAR model

He explained that yes, when it is interpreted, data do become information, but *information is merely the basis for an informed decision.* If we are to call this "knowledge", then let us recognise that it is solely intended to lead to well-chosen actions that in turn lead to desired results. At the time, he cautioned that with the thinning down of organisational structures and the elimination of layers of "middle management", seriously problematic gaps were emerging between information and knowledge, and between knowledge and action (see the figure): what he observed was a failure to deploy information correctly in decision-making, and a failure to properly initiate the actions that had been decided. Hence, the potential value from data, in terms of business (or organisational) benefits, was often jeopardised by a manager's inability to work with information well, and to ensure that was needed to be done was actually done.

The DIKAR model is a simple but extremely useful model to have in mind when working with information. It is surprising that it is not more frequently referred to and further developed in the literature of information management research—in the present context, it is (happily) very compatible with the IMBOK, which also strives to encompass raw technology (including databases) at one end, and strategy (and business results) at the other.

Current Issues

Current thinking about information in organisations is increasingly focused on the huge volume of data that become available globally every day, and that might provide a basis for better organisational decisions if only it can be brought under better control. Clearly, the public availability of social media "chit-chat", attributed to specific individuals, is a rich picking for marketing specialists and others who want to be able to understand what people are doing, what they want to spend their money on and what they think about what they have bought and what has happened. One term that is used is "big data"—an odd one in my view, because it could be more accurately termed "voluminous data", but I understand that this alternative does not trip off the tongue so easily as "big data". This phenomenon of voluminous data leads, in turn, to concerns about security.

Hence, there are a number of issues that must be addressed by those who strive to manage the information in organisations in useful and effective ways:

- How can the different kinds of information be seen, understood and managed in appropriate ways?
- When understood, how can information be organised so that it most effectively supports decision-making?
- When organised, how can information be analysed so as to reveal its real significance in managing strategically?

We can deal with these questions, at a managerial level, with another portfolio model.

Understanding Information: A Portfolio Model

Just as we have pondered the qualities and the nature of information systems and business processes, it is of course important to examine the nature of information and the qualities that make some kinds of information different to others.

Working with a group of professional managers, all interested in the nature of information and the potential contribution of good information management to their businesses, a new portfolio model of information was developed that stands as an effective differentiator of different kinds of information and the necessity to manage these kinds of information in different ways; this is working at the same level as the applications portfolio (which differentiates information system and makes clear the different ways that they must be managed, according to their present and future significance), but the information portfolio is a little different. Key questions that the information portfolio addresses include the following:

- How can the actual (and potential) value of information be identified and realised?
- How can we decide whether or not to share information with our business partners?
- What are the risks of losing (or suffering the theft of) information?
- How do different types of information relate to different types of business process, and the successful or unsuccessful outcome of those processes?
- How can information be managed in order to assure its accuracy and availability?
- What kind of infrastructure is best suited to the storage and provision of different kinds of information?

Working with the group of managers, which was diverse, the initial discussion developed a list of about 50 characteristics of information, themselves identified by means of brainstorming with the group. Then, by reviewing, augmenting, consolidating and refining this first rough list of characteristics, it was possible to organise them into higher-level categories and to propose generic attributes that might be incorporated into further information management models. For example, the identification of bipolar (opposing) characteristics begins to establish scales upon which the quality of information could be measured (for example, *agreed* and *contentious*). Where appropriate, opposites were added for those characteristics that did not have them. Some attributes were not of this bipolar nature, being more concerned with the *context* for the information and its potential use (for example, *nature of subject* and *nature of source*). These were dealt with separately.

The pattern that emerged revealed three ways to organise or characterise information, at the highest level:

- First, it might be ***internal*** or ***external*** information.
- Second, it might be ***structured*** or ***unstructured*** information.

In addition, information might be ***valuable*** or ***not valuable*** according to its accessibility inside or outside the organisation, and according to its structure. Structured data within the organisation are more valuable than those which are not structured and not immediately available.

For the record, the 64 resulting attributes are presented (as 32 pairs) in the table that follows. It is an easy but very interesting and revealing exercise to recreate a list such as this, with one's own peers and colleagues (but only reveal the details below when that is done!) (Table 6.1).

The internal–external and structured–not structured typology allows us to develop a portfolio model for information, which could stand as the basis of an information audit within an organisation and certainly reveals important ideas about how information might be migrated around such a portfolio. The concept of value really depends on the location of an instance of information in this space—most valuable when it is internal and structured, and least valuable when it is external and unstructured.

Figure 6.3 is largely self-explanatory, but the way that information moves (or can be moved) around the portfolio bears some discussion and explanation.

Just like the Applications Portfolio, this model gives us insight into the ways that we can optimise our use of information, especially now that there is such a potential torrent of data coming from so many new sources. As Hal Varian (Chief Economist at Google) said to an audience in the USA:

> "What's getting ubiquitous and cheap? Data! And what is complementary to data? Analysis! So my recommendation is to take lots of courses about how to manipulate and analyse data: databases, machine learning, econometrics, statistics, visualisation, and so on." (Varian 2008).

Things certainly have continued to change over the last decade. The Economist newspaper has pointed out that the number of mobile phones and tablets has already surpassed the number of laptops and PCs, in 2011. The number of PCs in use passed 1 billion in 2008, but the number of mobile devices is projected to reach 10 billion by 2020. Use of these mobile devices leaves a stream of evidence in terms of messages, emails, locations, opinions and enquiries that is a potential goldmine of personal and other information for the burgeoning megacompanies that have shown they are able to use it, like Google and Facebook and the world's intelligence and security services, of course. It follows that as well as from the news, the opinionistas and the bloggers of the world there is an impossibly large volume of data emerging from mobile devices and other intelligent sources. It gets worse: consider the potential for telemetry data concerning personal health and wellness that we might, if we can generate it, access it, and harvest it, turn into valuable information about our health.

The information portfolio helps us to deal with these challenges, and it organises the way that we might work around them. The notes that follow relate to the numbered elements of the model as presented in Fig. 6.2.

Table 6.1 The empirically derived characteristics of information

Internal	*External*
Confidential	Public
Exclusive	Not exclusive
Internal	Exchanged externally
Operational/contributory	Legal/regulatory/not contributory
Possessed	Not possessed
Secure	Not secure
Dependent	Independent
Disaggregated	Aggregated
Interactive	Broadcast
Reusable	Disposable
Status giving	Not status giving
Structured	*Unstructured*
Clear	Unclear
Hard (factual material)	Soft (opinion, subjective)
Simple	Complex
Specific	Not specific
Accurate	Inaccurate
Agreed	Contentious
Indicative	Predictive
Sparse	Rich
Valuable	*Not valuable*
Accessible	Not accessible
Purposeful	Just in case
Quickly available	Not quickly available
Relevant	Useless
Reliable (high integrity)	Unreliable (low integrity)
Timely	Not timely
Valuable now	Not valuable now
Valuable in the future	Not valuable in the future
"Comfortable"	Not "Comfortable"
Adaptable	Not adaptable
Current	Historical
Easy to deliver	Difficult to deliver
Transient	Permanent

Stage 1: Taking advantage of public information

The simplest first step in managing with the portfolio is to recognise and adopt well-structured external schemes of reference data, such as postcodes, weather data, GPS positioning data and even travel timetables. It is now routine in the United Kingdom to undertake a Web-based transaction using first your house number and then the postcode—the combination of these seven or eight digits and characters identifies

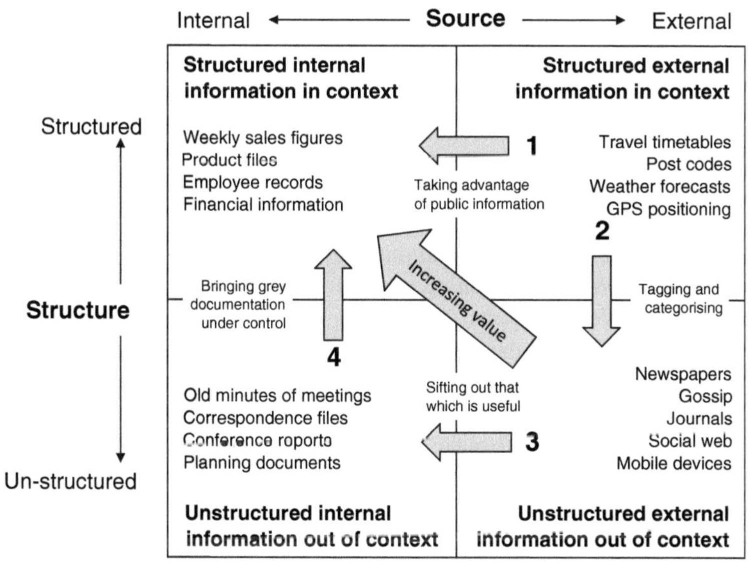

Fig. 6.3 The information portfolio

your full address immediately, without any ambiguity, and the remainder of the order screen is then normally auto-filled from that raw data.

Other administrations elsewhere in the world are not so advanced and not so rigorous with their postcoding schemes that the data are reliable. In South Africa, a new road tolling scheme (at the time of writing) relies on the existing national database of registered road vehicles in order to track down drivers or vehicle owners who have used the tolled roads and not paid. The quality of the vehicle registration data is so poor that some experts think the road tolling scheme will collapse, as revenues are falling far below what is needed to pay for the cost of building and operating the tolling system.

Elsewhere, in education, in health and in general administration, there are many existing schemes that provide perfectly adequate structuring for data, and not choosing them risks serious problems of compatibility in the future; where there are duplicate or overlapping schemes, then we have a problem, of course. The inefficiencies and risks of having to translate one set of external codes (for example, a supplier part number code) into an internal code (for example an internal stock number) can undermine business performance, and lead to a constant struggle to keep things properly lined up and to sort out the avoidable problems that arise. The international effort to organise well-defined structures and codes for illnesses, drugs, educational material, fast-moving consumer goods and even crimes (to mention just a few) are worthwhile and helpful, and should be supported and encouraged.

Stage 2: Tagging the noise on the Web
Outside of the boundaries of any single organisation, there is a constant flow of potentially relevant information that needs to be monitored in case there is something there that is potentially valuable to that organisation. The problem is there is so much of it, mostly on the social pages of the World Wide Web of course.

There are different ways to harvest and organise such data, possibly by using existing schemes such as postcodes and GPS data (already mentioned above) but more typically by adding "tags" or by analysing it and fitting it to a prepared scheme of ideas that we might call an ontological model. This effort to organise the vast content of the Web is happening now, for example in the project that is known as the "semantic Web"; experts are meeting, papers are being written, and conferences are happening (for example: SEMTECHBIZ 2012)—we are (at the time of writing) at a tipping point that will affect life for many years to come in ways that we cannot yet anticipate.

Hence, there are two ways to make sense of the Web. First, it is possible to construct formal ontologies, and second, it is possible to have open-ended tagging schemes—these two approaches lead to quite different results. The ontological approach attempts to be highly structured and rigorous, and the tagging approach tends to be completely open, it is able to be manipulated, and it is potentially highly redundant.

Ontologies are a formalised structuring of the "things" that comprise our "real" world. In a research project, an ontology will identify the entities (and the relationships between them) that are relevant to the research and about which the project wishes to gather and analyse data (we will return to a discussion of entity modelling again, shortly). An ontological model can be developed using the same kinds of rules that are used in the development of entity-relationship models because (as your author sees them) they achieve a very similar thing. Ontology in a research project that is looking at the impact of information technology in education (a relatively new domain of study) might be as shown in Fig. 6.4.

Here, the research is really just about how learning is affected by the introduction of technology, with a particular regard to the kinds of teachers, learners and education managers that are involved (one might suppose that the research anticipates different outcomes according to the experience and motivation of the teachers, the capability of the learners and the degree to which the management interferes). Note that the research has identified that it is the details of specific instances of the *use of technology*, and specific instances of *management* actions, that will have to be captured and analysed in order to make sense of the phenomenon of learning.

The same idea will apply in different situations, for example where a social Website is trying to understand the behaviour of its "members", or a police team is trying to identify a suspected criminal: it is the instance when one person repeatedly talks about one thing on Facebook, or when one criminal is found to repeatedly commit crimes in a certain way that they are "caught". Hence, the key to hiding your personality on Facebook, or escaping the clutches of the law in the world of crime, is to *always do what you do differently*—then, "they" will have much more difficulty in classifying your behaviour to the point that you become "known". This

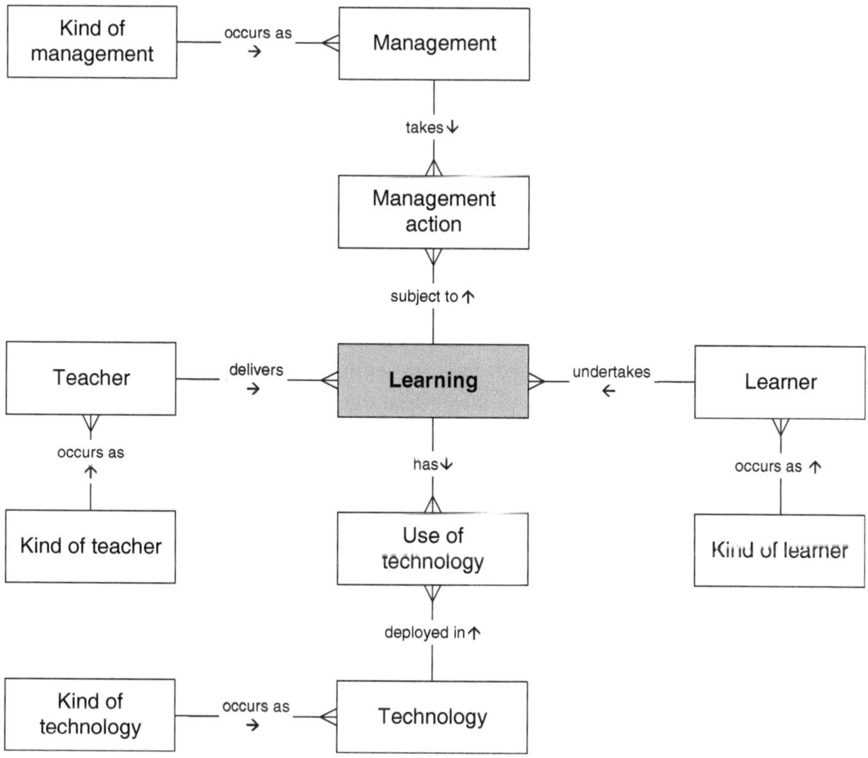

Fig. 6.4 Researching information technology in education: a sample ontology

will be far more effective than adopting five different identities in order to try and hide. Perhaps, of course, you might wish to be "known"?

We cannot afford to become involved in a detailed discussion about data modelling and data design here because we are trying to understand the *management* issues. What managers need is the broad overview, a quick way to check that everything is being attended to and the means to measure the quality of what is being done; for their purposes, high-volume data need to be sifted, selected and analysed.

Stage 3: Sifting and analysing

A research project such as the one above will develop its own ontological view of what it needs to work with, but in the wider world of business the generalised ontologies that are under development extend to hundreds of entities and hundreds of relations between them. They are quite alien to the majority of business people and Web users, who—understandably—prefer to take the line of least difficulty and use the tagging option. It is possible to devise and apply tags to Web content and to other stored data such as photographs and emails, within personal systems or within shared systems, and those tags can be used to quickly select the content relevant to a business issue in a web site, or a photo archive, or a discussion board with tens of thousands of contributions. Exactly how this tagging might actually be done is wide open, and some management will be helpful in avoiding complete chaos, rather have "managed chaos" I think. Individuals work with search engines every day and develop their own lists of tags (or "key words") that work well for them; information consolidators such as the global news providers (many of which simply scour the content of the Web for stories written by others) do this automatically using tags and keywords, with just some human intervention to make sure that the best stories are featured more prominently (but that will always be a *human* judgement, surely?); the sort of face recognition that is now happening (with image management software such as Picasa) is entirely automatic; it uses "tagging" schemes that we do not understand and that are highly complex and embedded in image processing, and at this stage, they are entirely proprietary, it seems.

One might surmise that at this point in time the average business, or government department, or community, will be happy to wait and see what happens with ontologies and with the semantic Web, and go no further than playing with tagging schemes; other progressive businesses and organisations with a special interest in recovering information from raw data will be working closely with these ideas, which are yet to show their true potential in the world of business, in fighting crime, or in manipulating and nurturing groups of people on the social Web.

Stage 4: Structuring and archiving
When it finally comes to organising and structuring information within an organisation, something comparable to the value chain would be useful. A high-level view of the organisation, on just one sheet of paper, with a generic arrangement of ideas that lets us compare out business to the way that other businesses work sounds good.

Organising Information: A Generic Model

Given the importance of information in business today, we might expect that some form of universal or generic information model would be evident in the literature. In fact, few existing authors provide an explicit treatment of information modelling and analysis. Other management literature is equally sparse in this matter, and the treatment of information modelling in the specialist information systems literature is unhelpful to general business managers who have no interest in the deeper theoretical issues. Hence, the principal question addressed here is how can relevant and effective information modelling be rendered meaningful to the non-specialist, especially to managers? This is important to do, because the digital information that is available to managers for decision-making will depend on the design of the databases that contain it, and yet the way that databases are designed is not only difficult for managers to understand, it is also difficult for specialists to understand.

Origins of the Model

As we have noted, experience suggests that most people are quickly able to understand and participate in process modelling, but only a few are able to understand information modelling quickly and easily. In the world of business systems analysis, it is the "entity model" that defines the things about which information is needed, and the "data model" that then defines exactly what data will comprise the basis of that information, in much more detail. Hence, it is the entity model that works at the level that is important to strategic management but is rarely if ever seen in strategic planning documents.

As we shall see shortly, if retail managers do not articulate a need to gather information about customers, then customers will remain invisible except (when they shop) as a few centimetres of "till roll", showing the date, the time, the items purchased, the total costs and possibly the taxes and discounts that were applied. As soon as that data can be related to a known customer, with a known address, the pattern of purchases can be analysed and used to develop bespoke marketing for that customer. It is only a few years since major retailers in Europe, the USA and elsewhere began to issue "loyalty cards" that allowed purchases to be related to customers, and gave the customers the dubious satisfaction of receiving their very own marketing material in the form of discount coupons and suchlike, but it has changed the way that some people shop, and it has changed the informational expectations of managers. But customer information is somewhat external—it is important, but not always as important as the internal organisational requirement for reliable performance information that shows whether organisational performance is meeting the targets set in strategic plans.

We must now ask further questions:

- How can information modelling be made acceptable to management?
- Which high-level entity types are perceived by management to be important?
- How can the impact of strategic change be seen through information models?
- What variety of information is there within a business, and how complete is it?
- What are the key performance indicators that management needs, and where are they to be found in an information model?
- Is it possible to derive a view of the ideal arrangement of business processes, from an alternative starting point?

The value chain has been in use for something like twenty years, and it is well known to many managers. But the value chain is really all about *processes*, not about *information* as such. It is interesting (and puzzling) that the world has never devised and adopted a similar model that provides a generic structure for information in a business, in the same way that the value chain shows a generic model for customer-related processes in a business. However, there is at least one such model that does just this.

But first, we must note again that data and information analysis, being divorced from simple analysis of what people do, is an abstract procedure and people generally find it to be more difficult to understand and internalise than process analysis. However, it can be used to very good effect and it is essential in any business or organisation that is "information intensive", relying on good information management for its success. And while process analysis can take much longer than expected (when the endless detail of low-level commercial activity bogs things down), information analysis can be very rapid indeed. It gets on top of the detail of process thinking, because all that is needed is a vision of what the business is really all *about*, rather than the simpler question of what it *does*.

Clearly, because we are concerned here with information *management*, it is important that we take particular care to understand the information that may prevail in a typical business: this involves an analysis of the *entities* (or, more simply, the "things") with which the business is concerned. As promised, we come back to the question of entity analysis and the rules with which it is done.

An entity has been defined as *anything about which we might wish to keep information*, and so typical entities are "product", "employee", "customer" and "supplier". These are the things about which we must keep information if a typical business is to be able to operate effectively. Untypical businesses such as social networks, police forces and health services have quite different things that they need to worry about, of course. Nevertheless, research has suggested that, in the general case, there are six areas within which we need information about:

- our "marketplace",
- our "products or services",
- the related "procured inputs",
- organisational internal "resources",
- organisational "performance" and
- organisational "processes".

The figure below arranges these six domains of information into a single generic model of the information structure in a typical business, which will be followed by two examples, but first it is informative to explain the background to the development of the generic model. Essentially, it was derived from study of a successful case of information technology and systems investment in a manufacturing company with the direct involvement of the managing director (who had sole personal responsibility for the change programme). By starting with a demonstrably successful case, it was hoped that other (incomplete or potentially less successful) cases could be assisted by a process of comparison.

The business manufactured a range of innovative variable speed electrical drives similar to an electric motor, but the variable speed capability made it suitable for a wide variety of applications in industrial production systems, for example in ventilation and conveyor systems. At the time, turnover was less than £5 million per annum (and falling). The prospects were grim, but the new managing director initiated a major reorientation of the business based upon new product concepts: rather than just making variable speed drives, the business would develop full industrial process control systems—fully engineered solutions to control problems rather than just the basic components.

The approach to the market had to be changed; manufacturing had to take place in clean conditions, and a substantial software development and production capability was needed. Significantly, the workforce had to be replaced (and some retrained) in order to provide the necessary engineering, management and marketing skills. Finally, the company's commercial systems had to be replaced with a modern MRP II system in order to deal with a greatly increased number of procured components, and to provide improved management control. The formulation of the new systems requirements was undertaken using the tools and techniques described here, but with an emphasis on the process analysis perspective rather than the information analysis perspective.

The change programme was a great success. New business followed as the market recognised the merits of the new product range. One early sale was to a regional water utility, providing them with centralised control of remote water distribution plant. Another delivered a new automatically controlled ventilation system for automotive paint-spraying booths. Internally, the MRP II system was installed and implemented ahead of schedule and well within the budget, and delivered the hoped for benefits.

In light of this success, the analysis of the manufacturing business and the approach to the new systems was examined carefully for generic content. By simplification and abstraction, it became evident that there were seven primary domains of management interest, and these became the basis of a new topological framework—a spatial arrangement of high-level concerns, such as "marketplace" and "product", at a somewhat higher level of abstraction than is normally the case with entity modelling.

It was decided to preserve managements' view of the seven domains and use them as an overall framework or topology for the model, and as a way of organising the finer detail that comes from a more typical entity modelling exercise. The risk arises that it might not have been possible to classify the entity types into one or other of these domains, and also that the relationships between them would be so complex as to not fit easily across them. This required some experimentation, but a prototype topology was developed, preserving the domains already identified. Some important steps were taken along the way, which may be interesting to those who need to undertake this kind of analysis.

Activities Were Treated as Entity Types

It can be seen that the seven domains include two that are potentially ambiguous: *commercial activities* and *production activities*. Because of the extent of change to the overall business processes, it was clear that many individual business activities would have to be redefined: there had to be training in the new activities; management wished to be able to assign the workforce to different activities with more precision. This led to the conclusion that activities were things about which it was necessary to keep information, and it was decided that they could be treated as

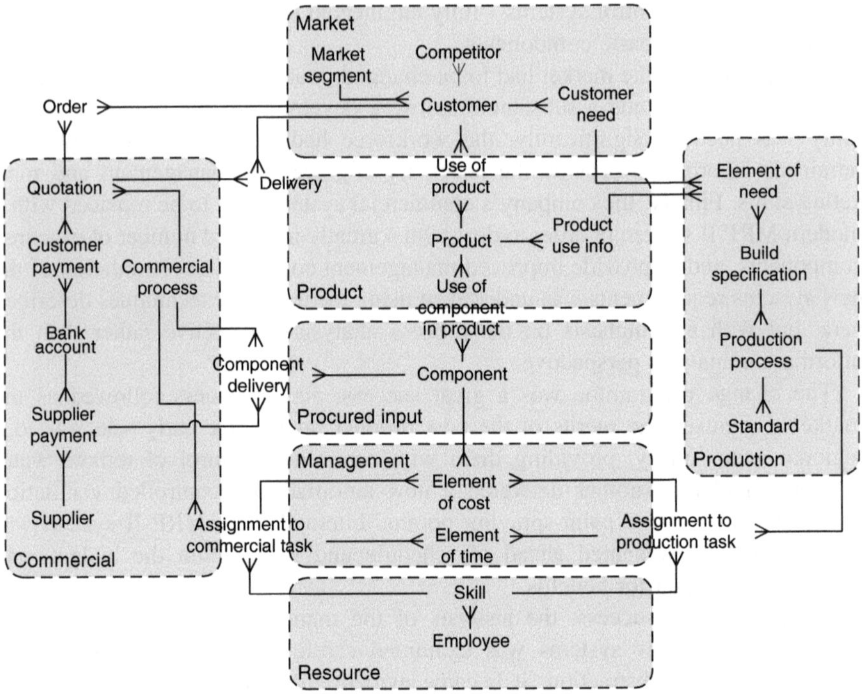

Fig. 6.5 The manufacturing business, as seen by the management (simplified)

entity types. This is a potentially useful idea because it enables us to incorporate the concept of process within the entity model without becoming embroiled in the detail of process modelling (with inputs, outputs, data stores, material stores and so on). It is not often seen in traditional entity models (Fig. 6.5).

Treatment of Associative Entity Types

As soon as any detail is exposed (and sometimes even earlier), the question of associative entity types arises. As we have already noted, these are those entity types that relate two or more primary entity types to each other, resolving a many-to-many relationship.

In the example, the simpler form at the left shows that employees may have many tasks, and a task may be serviced by many employees. This many-to-many relationship would have to be resolved in database design; in this case, the resolution is achieved by the introduction of assignment (at the right side), an entity type that was uppermost in management's mind in this case. Identifying such associative entities can be a critical step, as anyone who has had to deal with data analysis and database design knows.

In working with business models for management, these associative entity types are often identified intuitively. It was decided to pay special attention to these

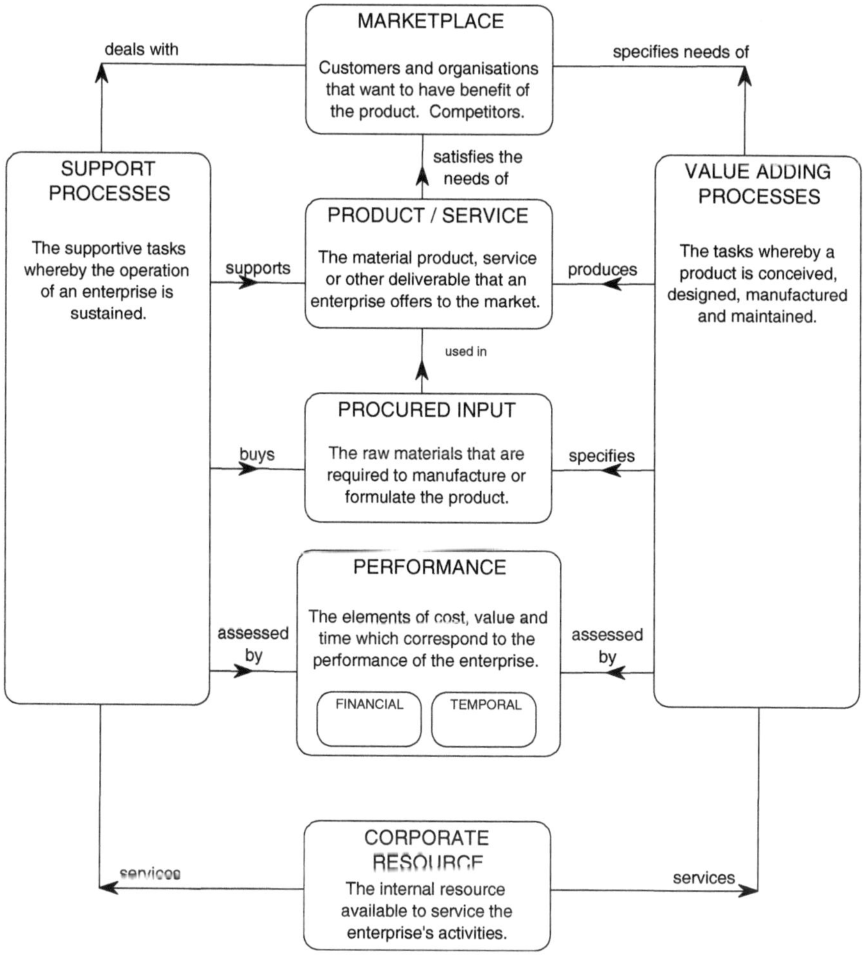

Fig. 6.6 A generic information model for business

associative entity types when they occurred, especially in mapping them to the seven domains.

With some adaptation of the words that are used, this arrangement of ideas can be used to organise a high-level view of information in any kind of organisation. The following paragraphs illustrate the sort of detail that is appropriate to each of these areas in a typical *business* (Fig. 6.6).

Marketplace: Information about the marketplace typically includes details of customers, people and organisations that want to have the benefit of the product, and also, about competitors and the way that their presence impacts on success. *Specifically, we might expect to have information about customers, customer needs,* *market segmentation, market regions and territories, competitors, suppliers and even economic political and social factors in some cases.*

Product: The material product, service, or other "deliverable" that an enterprise offers to the market; its specification, capability, configuration and operational needs. In the case of service operations, the nature of the service and its speed of response; its information content and the timeliness of the information provided. *Specifically, we need product information in terms of price, discount arrangements, inventory levels, availability, packaging requirements, product specification, product make-up and bill of materials, product documentation, applicability, function and performance specification.*

Procured input: The raw materials and inputs that are required to manufacture or formulate the product or service; their sources and the suppliers offering them; their characteristics, such as availability, lead time and cost. In the case of service operations, much of the procured input might be in the form of data, rather than material, taken into the organisation and used to deliver service of some kind to the customer. *Some material examples in this area include procured raw material, components and subassemblies; examples of data might include material classification, specification information, sourcing of material and components, compatibility and allowable substitutions and availability.*

Corporate resource: The available standing corporate resource in terms of people, capital equipment and other assets; and also buildings and property, but not unused inventory (that is better seen as procured input), *for example organisational structure, employee information, skills and disciplines, job descriptions, assignment of employees to jobs and tasks, training courses, capital equipment and corporate assets and allocation of capital equipment to jobs and tasks.*

Corporate performance: This is really management information, probably information about the financial performance of the business and also information about the temporal performance—how quickly and how productively product and service is delivered. Here, we would find the raw input to an executive information system. *Typical management information includes period results, group profitability, product profitability, corporate performance, average time to ship, volume of production and general accounting information.*

Corporate processes: Information about the tasks whereby the operation of an enterprise is sustained: management, financial, administrative and contractual information; information about how sales people are expected to sell, and the procedures whereby a product (or service) is conceived, designed, engineered, manufactured and maintained; information about any aspect of operations that is perceived by the customer as useful, *specifically: sales order processing procedures, purchase ordering procedures, making payments, receiving payments, commercial approval procedures, contract management procedures, cash management procedures, personnel management procedures, corporate management procedures, external commercial procedures, product specification, product development, production engineering, quality control, distribution, installation and commissioning.*

Information about a business process is not the same thing as the process itself. Consider the financial procedures manual in a typical organisation, for example. It tells the workforce how it is to deal with financial procedures such as claiming expenses and invoicing customers. The content of the financial manual is *information about the supporting processes* of the business. Equally, an advanced manufacturing planning system includes information about the routing of work from one point on the factory floor to another, as well as the basic bill of materials—this is *information about the value-adding processes* of the business. This idea that we need information about processes is closely connected with quality management, which is often based on process analysis. Anyone who has been through an ISO 9000 quality management assessment will know what this means: documenting and recording every aspect of how the business works.

However, to someone who is stuck in a business where things "have always been done this way", the idea of organising information about processes will be more difficult to understand, because the information about business processes is vested in the heads of the people who have been doing the work—sometimes in the same way, for years and years. If we are to change the processes within a business, it behoves us to understand and take stock of information about those processes, whether it is written down or simply within the working knowledge of those employed in the business. Until we do this, we will never know what we are trying to deal with.

An Example—Retailing

This is a simplified model drawn from a major retailer in the United Kingdom, developed with the senior management team at the head office ahead of a strategic initiative to introduce loyalty cards.[1] It is actually simpler than would be found for a manufacturing company, but then, some would argue that retailing is a simpler business. There are 15 entity types, located in the seven domains in the generic model presented above, and they clearly display some of the characteristics of traditional retailing (Fig. 6.7).

Some questions arise from study of this model:

- Why is there such a preponderance of information about supply (CONTRACT, information about SOURCE, PURCHASE ORDER, DELIVERY, INVOICE and PAYMENT), and almost none about production? Is this a real reflection of the nature of the business?
- Why do we have so little evidence of MANAGEMENT information? In fact, the performance of individual stores was very closely monitored, but the general visibility of information about corporate performance was limited (especially in comparison with the manufacturing example). What could be done about this?
- Why is the CUSTOMER not within the model? It seems so fundamental to have information about customers within a business, and yet the analysis reveals that

[1] This retailing example has been adapted and condensed from a previous paper by the author, published in the Journal of Applied Management Studies (Bytheway 1996).

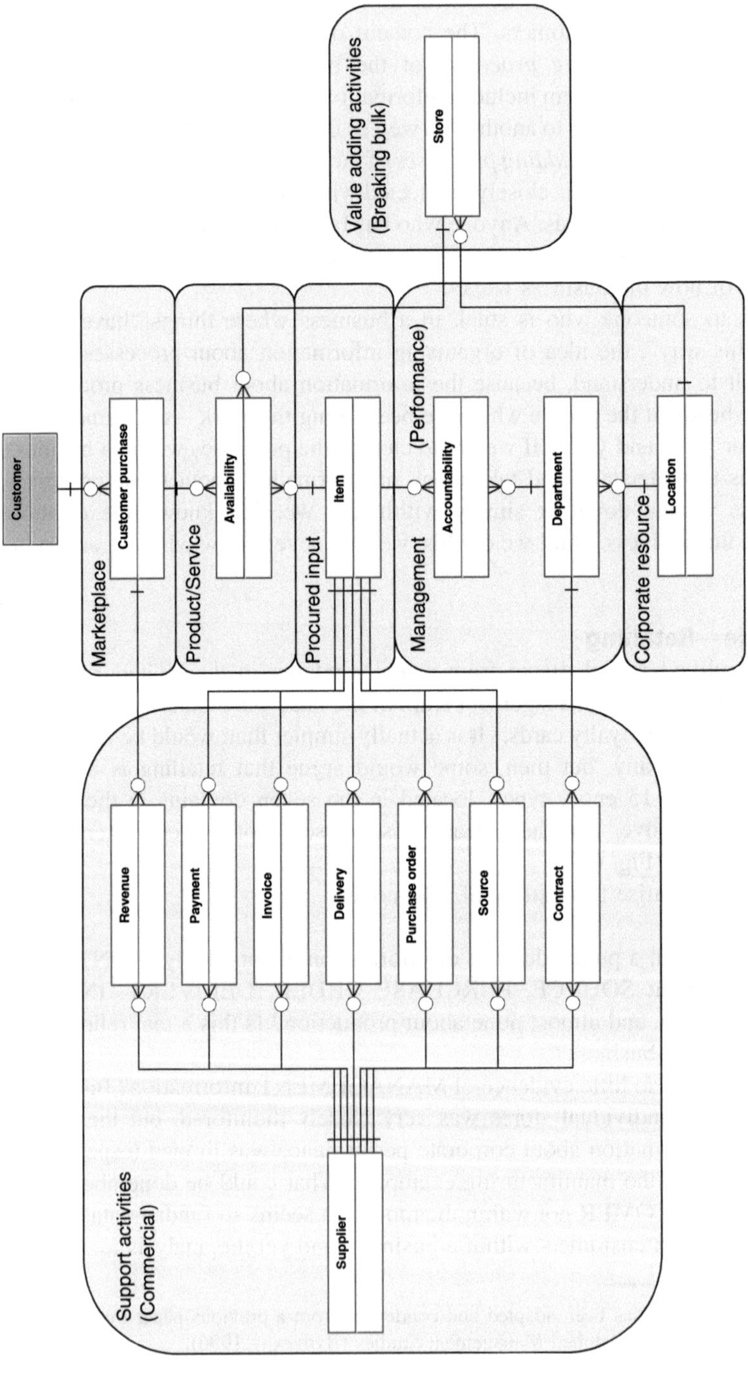

Fig. 6.7 An example of a corporate information model: retailing

there is none in this case. Again one must ask whether this a real reflection of the nature of the business, and whether this is what the management would wish?

- The lack of evident information within the production domain relates to the nature of retailing. We can argue that retailing is really just "bulk-breaking"—goods get into customers' shopping bags by diverse processes involving trunking, regional distribution centres, local distribution and in-store operations. Nothing actually happens to the product, and many customers would as readily buy from the original manufacturer if appropriate packaging quantities were available. As it happens they are not, and so we have to go to the retail store.
- The main "product" of the retailer, as interpreted here, is not the ITEMs which are procured from suppliers but the AVAILABILITY of those items. The role of the retailer is to make available those items that people want, in pack sizes and quantities that suit their needs. This is a well-understood feature of any retail business, and the management of the "availability matrix" in this retail business was the principal means to make sure that the right items were made available in the right stores at the right time.

In reviewing this model with the management steering group, it was found that there is indeed a preponderance of information on the supply side of the business, and a dearth of information about customers' actual needs and local variations in product range. This is a direct result of the intense concern to reduce operational costs and to tighten the relationships with suppliers to the maximum possible degree.

Reorder quantities for stores were provided on-screen to the stores by "the system", but they were overwritten where it was thought appropriate by the staff in the store. For example, if there were a football match scheduled at the weekend, then the quantities for beer would be increased; if there was a seasonal glut of strawberries from local farms, then the quantities for fresh cream would be increased.

This model was used to examine the potential for improved information management, and underpinned a wider study of supply chain performance using an analysis of information right through the supply chain from production through distribution into retailing. Of course, customer information was drawn into the scheme of things and major strategic efforts began in order to deliver customers the best possible value at the lowest cost, and the reputation of this retailer as a low-cost option prevailed for some years until it was taken over by an even larger international operator.

In its execution, this retailing case study showed how, by avoiding immediate development of process models, a business can build firmer foundations for a fresh start. It exercised questions about required competencies and led to thoughts about a competency-based strategy. At a time when the effort and energy of the management team could easily have dissipated its efforts in short-term operational issues, the model provided a means of standing back so as to see the deeper structure of the business and to identify the information hot spots where opportunity lurked.

Using the Model

Stepping back from this specific example, this and other cases have found that information or entity modelling is neither the most frequently used nor the most successful technique, when compared with more easily understood process-oriented techniques. In proprietary analysis methods, the stages and steps concerned with entity type identification and lifecycle analysis are known to be particularly poorly executed in the majority of cases, but this example shows that information modelling can be made acceptable to management. When it is the first step in a strategic analysis of a business, entity modelling has been found to be very rapid and immediately acceptable to senior management.

The generic model provides an easy-to-understand (and easy-to-remember) topology for mapping corporate information models, where these need to be seen by a wide audience, where there is a high level of complexity, or where they need to be compared one with another. This is particularly important in cases such as logistics and supply chain operations where the sharing of information is critical to success.

Further, the generic model is a way of bounding and scoping a business independently of business processes, so that senior management can understand the deeper implications of certain strategic moves, such as the introduction of affinity cards in retailing businesses and the sharing of key operational data with business partners, where there are shared benefits to be achieved. It provides a vehicle for a "stock taking" of the information that is used by an organisation and allows analysis of the potential for information sharing and exchange between different organisations (or within larger organisations comprising many business units where information needs to be integrated). Research has found that the generic model presented in Fig. 6.6.

- stands as a good companion to the value chain
- provides a structure for organising the results of fact finding and interviewing
- has the potential to contribute in other areas.

Where the value chain provides a high-level framework for process modelling, the new framework does the same for information modelling. Anyone who has taken the framework on board as an aid to thinking can use it to formulate ideas "on the fly", and to check the completeness of discussions and presentations. Organisations implementing "activity-based costing" can use it to rigorously map activities to the resource that is consumed according to the activities that are at hand. In marketing, it prepares the ground for a more complete understanding of how products and services really meet customers' needs, and for storing this information in a way that can be accessed and used by those who need it. In engineering and production, it shows how all of the many stages in design, specification and production engineering need to use the same information, and it provides sound foundations for the development of new integrated engineering operations.

Perhaps most important, in this context, is the fact that the generic model provides a sound and tested arrangement of ideas for *structuring* information coming into and going out of the organisation, in a holistic way, thereby making a considerable contribution to the management of information migrating to and from the left and right of the information portfolio in Fig. 6.1. Regrettably, a reading of this chapter of this book will not provide the education and training that is needed in order to do information analysis well, but perhaps it will stimulate enough interest in order that the many other sources available will be availed and used to develop this capability within progressive organisations that depend on good information management.

Summary

Managerial Issues Concerning Business Information

There is a strong preference among most managers (and among many technical specialists) to think about *what they do* with information, rather than *how the design of the information is best conceived, organised and presented.*

I clearly recall presenting an *entity-relationship model* to a technical standards working group in the USA that attempted to show how the information about software engineering and software development work could be organised and arranged for the purposes of standards making; a representative of another working group, who (worryingly) designed software for guided weapon control systems, decried the model stating: "Hey, because you have given us a *process model*, I fail to see how this is going to help with thinking about the *data*". In case you missed something in the preceding pages, an entity-relationship model is *not* a process model—it's the one where everything fits onto *one page*—the process model can require dozens, no, *hundreds of pages*. We should worry about guided weapons, I think.

We can summarise some of the managerial issues concerning business information as follows:

- Thinking abstractly about information is difficult for many people, and those who are able to think about it effectively should be valued.
- Because information models (entity-relationship models) are able to represent the whole of a business on one page, they may be extremely valuable if they are effective in delivering competitive advantage. Careful senior managers in these cases allow sight of their information models on a "need to know" basis.
- The world is generating unimaginable volumes of data in ever new ways, some of which may be important to your business or your organisation, but there is no clarity about how you take full advantage of this. Herein lies a source of real competitive advantage in the near future.
- At the same time, the world is developing schemes and technologies that will tame that data and deliver new streams of information that will be valuable. Remember what Hal Varian said: "*What's getting ubiquitous and cheap? Data!*

And what is complementary to data? Analysis! ". Organisations that are able to harvest data from the Web (and other sources), categorise it and filter it, and then incorporate it into their internal structured databases, will gain huge advantage.

Business Information Management Competencies

- Discussion of business change includes full consideration of the potential for information-related change
- Business models make clear how information (or data) is used in processes (or activities)
- The information (data) components of business models are adequately documented
- The quality of information used in business processes is monitored and managed
- Business processes benefit from adequate information sharing between and within processes
- Information about business performance is made available to those that need it
- Strategies recognise the dependency of the organisation on information, for overall business success
- Discussions about knowledge management are directed to the issue of decision, action and result
- The potential value of external information is recognised and garnered
- The need to categorise and organise unstructured data from within and without the organisation is recognised and nurtured

Research Side Note: Getting a Grip on a Flood of Information

Chen, H., Chiang, R.H. & Storey, V.C. (2012) Business intelligence and analytics: from big data to big impact. MIS Quarterly, 36 (4), pp. 1165–1188.

Hsinchun Chen and colleagues identify three eras within which the world has become awash with information: The first is a data-structured era based on conventional database resources; the second is Web based and acknowledges the availability of vast amounts of business information as well as blogs and social networking sites; the third is perhaps still just on the horizon, where mobile equipment, tags and sensors of all kinds are beginning to originate data that relate to the "Internet of things". They point out that in the third era data are (or will be) "location aware", "person centred" and "context relevant".

This long paper is actually a preamble to a special issue of MISQ, but it is well worth a read if you feel uninformed about big data, business intelligence and business analytics. The papers that follow in the special issue cover marketing, customer satisfaction, strategic decision-making, banking and fraud.

Research Side Note: Does Information Management Contribute to Business Performance?

Mithas, S., Ramasubbu, N. & Sambamurthy, V. (2011) How information management capability influences firm performance. MIS Quarterly, 35 (1), pp. 237–256.

Using a very large archival dataset, and seeking to move from ideas about information technology to information management in organisations, Sunil Mithas and colleagues looked at the ways that information management competencies in organisations affect other functional capabilities. They found that three very important areas are specifically enhanced by good information management: customer management, process management and performance management; these in turn improve organisation performance in four classically important areas: customer service, financial results, human resource effectiveness and overall organisational performance. This paper provides a useful history of previous work and sets out fundamentals that could be the foundations of further work, for example looking at the effects of Sarbanes-Oxley and other international compliance procedures and practitioner-based initiatives such as COBIT.

Research Side Note: You Can Smile But You Can't Hide!

Stone, Z., Zickler, T. & Darrell, T. (2010) Towards large-scale face recognition using social network context. Proceedings of the IEEE, 98 (8), pp. 1408–1415.

Zak Stone and colleagues provide an interesting, short and optimistic (but somewhat mathematical) introduction to issues and methods of face recognition on the social Web. I am not convinced that their positive optimism is warranted; they conclude with this assertion: "Ultimately, the growth of online social networks, the development of improved social tagging systems and the increasing interconnectivity of the Web have the potential to enhance our ability to achieve face recognition at scale. Exploring computational techniques that take advantage of these trends seems a worthwhile endeavor". Really worthwhile? What do you think?

Exploring Business Benefits

7

What is Benefits Management?

> The process of organising and managing, such that the potential and intended benefits of an investment of time, money and effort are actually realised.

Elsewhere in this text, there are many references to the benefits that we might expect from an information systems investment, and there is much evidence of the complications that surround the successful delivery of such benefits. The problem is not so much understanding what a benefit is, rather understanding the *management* processes and activities that will deliver it.

Organisations of different kinds will desire different outcomes from their information technology and systems investments. At an early stage in the life of a business, the critical issues are all about growth and survival: identifying new markets, nurturing relationships with new customers and getting basic capability in place to deliver products or services. The information systems emphasis might be on marketing and sales alone: a simple database to capture information about prospects and to organise information about meetings and orders, an Internet service with which to access the World Wide Web, display basic product and service information and send and receive electronic mail. The benefits here are simple: basic operational capabilities without which the business would simply not be able to operate. In the middle stages of its evolution, the need is to support growth, get costs under control and to develop systems that position the business in its market place. In the mature stages of a business, information systems will be required for corporate governance, for managing the relationship with shareholders, and for managing the performance of a business that might have become complex and unwieldy, none of which is necessarily important to the entrepreneur.

A. Bytheway, *Investing in Information*,
DOI 10.1007/978-3-319-11909-0_7

Understanding where your business (or business unit) actually is, in this cycle of maturity, is important.

Nature of Business Benefits

It has been traditional to undertake "cost-benefit" analysis. Typically, one is expected to estimate and tabulate costs, possibly based on estimates and quotations of cost for acquired items and services, and for the time and effort involved in managing the change. More often than not (in my experience) such figures are often based upon guesswork and are therefore not reliable. Then, one is expected to estimate and tabulate the benefits, in financial terms, and to bring the two views together using a spreadsheet to calculate "net present value" using (for example) discounted cash flow techniques, this allows the balance of estimated short-term expenditure and long-term benefits to be more effectively assessed according to current "rates of return" on investments. Essentially, it allows the benefits to be assessed against alternative investments (e.g. on the money markets), by discounting future savings at a level that reflects the current return on simple deposits in the banks or elsewhere.

A simple analysis might look something like the one below, where the costs are tabulated under six headings and the benefits under three, in each case over 7 years, totalled both ways. Think about what you see in the Fig. 7.1.

The *cost elements* are typical of what can be estimated, with some confidence, from supplier's quotations and from assumptions about the yearly increase in licence costs and the like. However, the benefits are far more dubious. The "head count" saving seems to advance by about 10 % per annum, but who knows what the salary bill will actually be for the next 7 years? The idea that we might increase sales by a similar level each year, with a hefty increase right at the start, is very, very arguable, surely? And what credence can we give to "other cost reductions"? Not much, surely?

	Period							
Costs	1	2	3	4	5	6	7	Totals
Hardware	145,000.00	33,200.00	14,500.00	14,500.00	14,500.00	25,670.00	25,670.00	**273,040.00**
Software	45,578.00	50,135.80	55,149.38	60,664.32	66,730.75	73,403.82	80,744.21	**432,406.28**
Training	65,700.00	6,570.00	6,570.00	6,570.00	6,570.00	6,570.00	6,570.00	**105,120.00**
Operations	0.00	15,700.00	15,700.00	15,700.00	15,700.00	15,700.00	15,700.00	**94,200.00**
Maintenance	0.00	0.00	69,649.38	75,164.32	81,230.75	99,073.82	106,414.21	**431,532.48**
Other licences	134.00	3,459.00	3,459.00	3,459.00	3,459.00	3,459.00	3,459.00	**20,888.00**
Totals	**256,412.00**	**109,064.80**	**165,027.76**	**176,057.64**	**188,190.50**	**223,876.65**	**238,557.41**	1,357,186.76
Benefits								
Reduced head count	34,000.00	37,400.00	41,140.00	45,254.00	49,779.40	54,757.34	60,233.07	**322,563.81**
Increased sales	125,000.00	137,500.00	151,250.00	166,375.00	183,012.50	201,313.75	221,445.13	**1,185,896.38**
Other cost reductions	28,000.00	30,800.00	33,880.00	37,268.00	40,994.80	45,094.28	49,603.71	**265,640.79**
Totals	**187,000.00**	**205,700.00**	**226,270.00**	**248,897.00**	**273,786.70**	**301,165.37**	**331,281.91**	**1,774,100.98**
Benefits over costs	**-69,412.00**	**96,635.20**	**61,242.24**	**72,839.36**	**85,596.20**	**77,288.72**	**92,724.49**	416,914.22
Discounted	**-69,412.00**	**84,072.62**	**45,319.26**	**44,432.01**	**41,086.18**	**27,051.05**	**20,399.39**	192,948.51
Accumualted benefits	-69,412.00	27,223.20	88,465.44	161,304.80	246,901.00	324,189.72	416,914.22	1,195,586.39

Fig. 7.1 Discounted cash flow analysis

Suppose that we are working with dollars. The table shows the simple addition of benefits over costs (over the seven years) as almost $417,000, but when we discount that at 13 % (in the line below), the benefits are more than halved. If we were to find that there was no net increase in the three lines of benefit over time, then the net discounted benefit falls to a negative dis-benefit of −$3,595 (not shown in this example).

The message here is that the numbers game is clearly easy to play, but the *reliability* that we can put on our estimates (even with techniques like discounted cash flow) is very limited indeed. In practice, people do play games with the numbers and, in the worst cases, busy senior managers are cheated by means of complex spreadsheets wherein the contents look impressive and well developed, but are actually based on pure whimsy. Compare this with the strong logic that emerges from critical success factor analysis: if "X" is what we have agreed to do, and if information system "Y" is needed to do it, then we must acquire and deploy information system "Y". End of argument? possibly. At least it is an easier argument than with the numbers.

In the general case, we simply *must have* a negotiated and agreed approach to the definition and management of the expected information systems and technology benefits. As well as getting the justification right, we must follow through with appropriate implementation, thorough requirements analysis, project management, user training and hand-over. And then, we must make sure that the promises that we made right back at the start are actually fulfilled. This cannot be done by the IT department alone, it must be done by those business mangers that are responsible for process management and for the delivery of business performance. On the other side, IT people do need to develop a *service* culture and put *service management* into place, and to understand the total cost of IT operations so that cost analyses can also be reliably fulfilled. The ongoing cost of installed systems usually far exceeds the cost of acquisition and implementation, but the costs of operation are hidden, or not easily related to the cost drivers that caused them, and are therefore difficult to manage. This can make nonsense of any discounted cash flow that was done in order to justify the investment.

The key to success here is to understand users' needs and expectations, undertake competent acquisition, development and deployment of the new information systems and business processes, and then to *proactively manage the delivery of the intended benefits*. Too often, the intended benefits that were so forcefully argued at the start of a project are never delivered in practice. We need to see evidence that business performance has improved in the agreed way, to assess the additional side benefits that were not anticipated but nevertheless delivered, and to feed back the results of improvement initiatives into the next cycle of strategy formulation. Experience with complex systems such as customer relationship management and enterprise resource planning systems suggests that benefits are not just difficult to achieve, they might easily turn into dis-benefits. Many organisations find that business performance actually suffers as a result of new systems, especially at this level of complexity and difficulty, and this must also be fed into the strategic mix.

Benefits and the Applications Portfolio

Benefits can differ markedly in different situations and from different perspectives; yet again, the applications portfolio helps greatly in gaining an understanding of these differences. Many organisations are stuck in the old rut of management thinking, wherein all benefits must be financial, so the portfolio model gives us the best hope that we can pull management thinking out of this rut and persuade them to think more carefully and more strategically about why they are investing in information technology and systems (Fig. 7.2).

In general, we could summarise the benefits that we might expect from information systems as *speed*, *accuracy* and *efficiency* (although there are many more variations, as we shall see). The portfolio once again shows us how the relative importance of these three varies from one quadrant to another.

- *Efficiency* is absolutely critical in the **support** category. This is where we are most concerned to keep costs down. Accuracy is good to have, but a mistake in a support system will not actually bring the business to a halt—that is the sort of thing that happens with key operational systems.
- With **key operational** systems, the focus is on accuracy. If a batch statement production system in a bank makes a mistake, or if a production and stock control system fails to make components and products available when needed, then there will be huge costs for a bank or a manufacturing business. Speed and efficiency are not unimportant, but *accuracy* is the benefit that we seek most of all.
- With **strategic systems,** it is *speed* (of implementation, and benefits delivery) that matters most. Accuracy can be a problem, as the banks found in the early days with their Web-based banking services, but it was the first bank to get a Web banking system up and running reliably that won the plaudits and engaged the customers' interest. Once the new business was won, then it was time to tighten things up because the whole banking industry was following, the window of opportunity was closing, and it was necessary only then to work out the issues of efficiency.

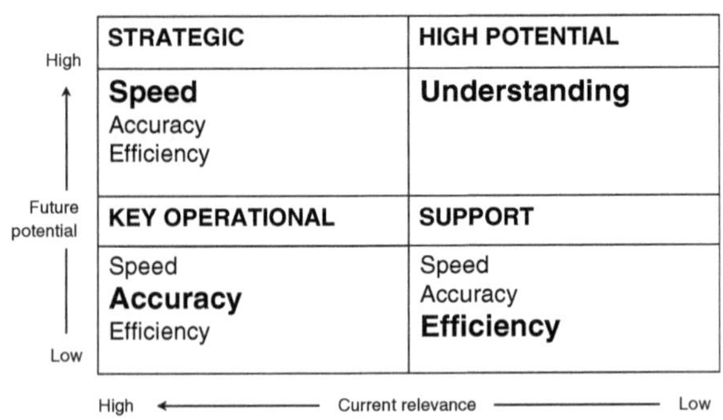

Fig. 7.2 The nature of benefits seen through the applications portfolio

- As is so often the case, the **turnaround system** is a special case. We are not looking for speed, accuracy or efficiency, we are looking for *new understanding*. The organisation that chooses not to encourage turnaround systems investments (or even chooses to prohibit them) will find that it is always a laggard, and it is always following a "me-too" strategy where decisions are taken only because others in the industry have already taken them. Look back at the NCR and STC examples in the chapter on information technology.

In this way, the portfolio keeps us on our toes and reminds us of the subtle but sometimes very important differences between the different kinds of information system, and the consequences of those differences.

So, we might ask, what is actually happening in the world of business management?

A Survey into Benefits Management

Surprising as it may seem, surveys have indicated that almost no organisations make any conscious effort to proactively manage the delivery of the business benefits that are intended to come from information systems investments—fewer than 10 % in some cases. Considering the high cost of IT-related projects, this is indeed surprising. In a survey undertaken some years ago, aimed at finding out what businesses had done to improve the prospects of information systems success:

- 52 % of organisations were found to use formalised analysis methods but were not convinced of the success of this approach.
- 54 % were found to use formalised project managementProject methods, but business managers just acted as "project sponsors" and again the success was very limited.
- 58 % claimed to have an investment justification procedure, but admitted that it is a game they had to play to get proposals through executive committees or past other procedural barriers.
- Only 10 % tried to manage the actual delivery of benefits in a formal way, and yet 76 % believed that there was scope for improvement by managing benefits more effectively.

These are astonishing results that would only be slightly different today. We are talking about very substantial investments, many well over $1,000,000 in value, that are justified based upon inadequate implementation capability and the weakest possible management of actual delivery of benefits. More recent work on benefits management (Ward and Daniel 2005) has generated a great deal of interest amongst senior managers, because it has developed a workable approach to "benefits management" founded on:

- The proper definition, categorisation and structuring of benefits.
- Proper planning to link benefits to process improvement projects.
- The allocation of responsibility for delivering benefits.
- Monitoring and measurement of delivered benefits.
- Seeking out additional benefits that might not have been apparent at the start.

The sections that now follow look at the steps that management can take in order to build a better approach to benefits management.

Managing Benefits in the Modern Context

Two Stages in Achieving Benefits

In an ideal world, business information systems users will have the information that they need at their fingertips; management decisions will be based on timely, accurate and relevant information; new information systems will deliver the negotiated (or promised) benefits through simple return on investment (despite the games that people play with the numbers) or through less tangible outcomes such as we argue with critical success factor analysis; users will be computer literate and well supported by experts; last (but not least), there will be *clear accountability* for the effective exploitation of information systems and technology investments and for assuring that benefits are indeed achieved.

But the world is not ideal. In the real world, the first issue to recognise is that benefits do not come immediately. Research has shown that there are actually two stages: the first is concerned with lower-level learning about how a new system works and the second is then concerned with the incorporation of new behaviours into the ways of working, at the level of the business process, so as to deliver the higher-level benefits not just of efficiency, but also of effectiveness. These two stages can be related to *training*, in the first case, or the very different concept of *education* in the second. It is difficult to move directly to the second stage, but when managers understand the process it can then be managed appropriately, and accelerated. Figure 7.3 summarises some of the issues, looking at the timescales involved. This is a useful model, based on original research by Saroj Patel (Patel 1994), that tells us to plan for *two* stages of benefits delivery, not one.

First, when a system is newly installed, there is the benefit that the users can work the system and (let us say) they can do the work that they are used to doing, but in half the time. This is the point at which people learn to use the menu system and systems features by means of straightforward training, probably based on simple instruction and routine practice. There needs to be clear and helpful documentation to tell people what the system will do and the general level of learning is what we might term "skills development". This stage might take a few days or weeks, and it would be followed by a period of consolidation as user staff become comfortable with the new system and—in the best cases—begin to wonder how they ever used to work without it.

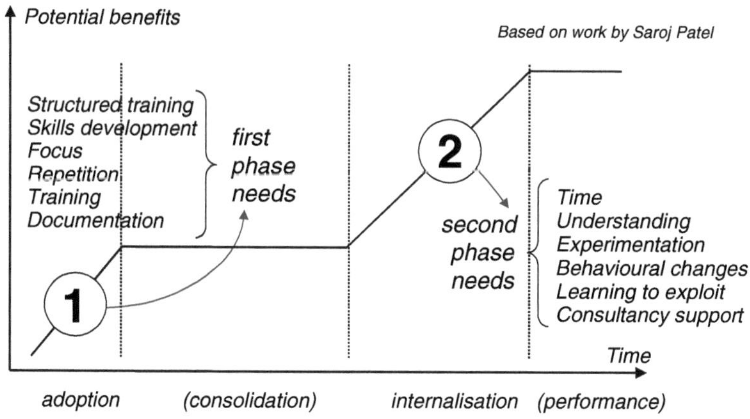

Fig. 7.3 First- and second-stage achievement of benefits

Then, as the system becomes more familiar, user behaviour can change. Although the facilities and functions of the system are exactly the same as when it was delivered, users discover that they can start to change the way that they work and, as well as becoming more efficient, they can become more effective. This is a familiar idea to all of us (think about when you just regarded your cell phone as a replacement for your landline, and then—slowly no doubt—got into the habit of saving your friends phone numbers, noting family birthdays, sending short text messages, taking and managing photographs, accessing the Web, and scanning QR barcodes: that is the sort of shift we are talking about here). This second stage needs us to take a different approach to training and support; rather, we need *education* not training, and we are not working "from the book" any more we are thinking with our heads about how we work and how we can change to become more effective with customers, suppliers, managers and our workmates.

Next, we must acknowledge that benefits are only realised at the level of real business activity where improved business performance can be seen and measured and that the responsibility for delivery of benefits rests with those responsible for the management of business change as much as with the users who will be working with a new system.

Relationship with Process Management and Project Management

Benefits are usually associated with projects, and project management is the mechanism we choose for managing the investment and executing the delivery of new systems. Projects have beginnings, middles and ends—although when the typical project really ends is not always when expected—often, project management is seen as concluding with the "project review", sometimes with the "post-implementation review".

These are actually very different ideas. The *project review* is concerned with whether the project plan worked and what new project skills have been accumulated that could be deployed in future. "On time and on budget" is the hoped-for outcome. People will always have a view about a project, especially those in the project team, and it is also necessary to take time to recognise excellent work, commitment beyond the normal call of duty and also to deal with new problems that must be avoided in the future. But that is not the same as assessing the benefits that were to be delivered. A project review can take place more or less immediately following the conclusion of the project (indeed, it is necessary to do so, before the people involved move away to new projects in new locations).

Because the delivery of benefits can only be judged *much later*, probably some months after implementation, the idea of the *post-implementation review* becomes very important. Tragically, few organisations show the commitment to ensure that these reviews take place at the right time, if at all, and there is a propensity to ignore the management of benefits all together. A part of this problem is that benefits management actually sits "above" project management in the overall hierarchy of things and may not be achievable on a project-by-project basis. Projects deliver new systems that are intended to improve business performance, and these improvements will only be visible at the level of the business process. It is necessary therefore to introduce a new stream of management activity above the level of projects, more closely associated with processes. Sometimes, organisations adopt the idea of *programme management*[1] in situations where there are many projects that all combine to deliver organisational benefits at a higher level. Where process management is not recognised within an organisation but programme management is recognised, it might be possible to pitch benefits management at the level of the programme. It is in any case a good idea to organise projects at the level where there is *certainty*: traditional project management works best in situations where project plans can be laid out with some certainty: no project manager likes to struggle with project plans that cannot be tied down to determinable deliverables, times and costs. It is better to use programme management as the vehicle to manage the uncertainty that is sometimes unavoidable with large projects, and with strategic systems that demand substantial business change (Fig. 7.4).

Hence, here we should see benefits management as a separate management activity that might be strongly associated with projects, but is separate from them and stands above them. It stands as a layer of management activity between project management and process management, and it will be concerned to see that projects deliver the sort of capability that improves business process performance in ways that serve the needs and expectations of stakeholders. For this reason, the benefits management regime needs to straddle the whole spectrum of information management activity, from information technology acquisition through to strategy. If an organisation has adopted *programme* management as an additional step in

[1] In this text, the spelling "program" is used to refer specifically to *computer programs*, as in *program code*; "programme" (the British English spelling) is used elsewhere.

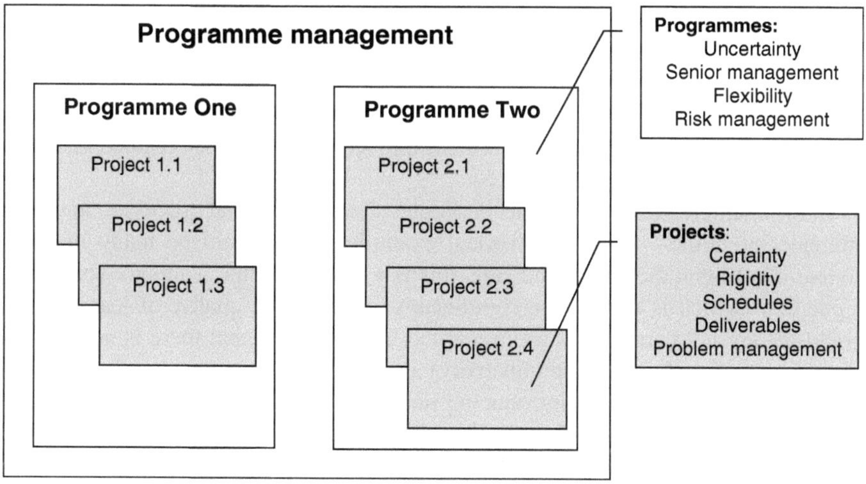

Fig. 7.4 Programme and project management

controlling investments involving business change, then benefits management is probably best set at that level.

Planning the Delivery of Benefits

Given that the early stages of project initiation and requirements analysis can take up to one-third of the total effort in a successful project, it is surprising that so little effort is put into assuring the realisation of benefits. One of the problems is that at the end of a project the team tends to break up, most peoples' attention moves to the next project, wherever that might be, and the users are left swimming in a sea of confusion. The last thing they want to think about is benefits, they simply want to eliminate the confusion and try to get their lives under control again. So at the end of a typical project, the users are just happy to get the project team off their backs. It is enough to have to deal with the new system, without analysing what benefits are emerging from its use.

Therefore, in order to successfully manage the delivery of benefits from information technology and information systems investments, it is important that this cycle of change is understood, that specific responsibility for managing the benefits is placed with an appropriate person, and that primary and secondary benefits are actively sought out and maximised. This requires that we work with benefits at the level of business management and that we set out to proactively manage benefits delivery.

A Simple Example

Look at the figure below, based on information management in a university. It shows how information technology enables systems to contribute to educational and research processes and then how the improved processes are expected to deliver to the institutional strategy (Fig. 7.5).

In the example, there are four technologies, four educational processes, and three strategic intentions—in a fully worked example, there would be many more, of course. Starting at the right-hand side, this is a university that wants to work on its reputation (which is mediocre), significantly improve the quality of learning (the graduates are not particularly well regarded by employers, but there is no shortage of applicants for places at the university) and produce much more research output (the national government is introducing new rewards for successful publication of research outputs in peer-reviewed academic journals).

Perusal of the figure shows how there is interdependency between the features of the model. Electronic whiteboards are not by any means new technology, but there is a new investment being made, so that all teaching rooms and meeting rooms shall have these devices, connected to the university network. This is a highly visible initiative that will *seem* to make a big contribution to all concerned, but in fact we see that it is only expected to contribute to classroom learning, and that this is *presumed* to contribute in turn to better learning and institutional reputation. Something is missing here: exactly *how* will classroom learning (and teaching) improve? Will this really contribute to reputation? Perhaps the outside world will see this as a move to catch up with the general trend, rather than to take a leading role in new educational practice? After all, many primary schools have electronic interactive whiteboards … exactly what aspects of teaching and learning will change, and why will they thereby be improved?

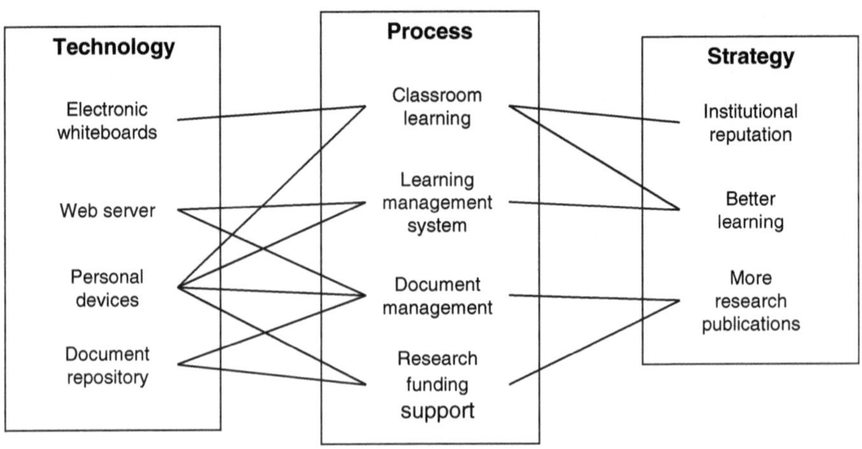

Fig. 7.5 An example of benefits dependency

The issue of personal devices is slightly more interesting, in that this is more likely to be a truly strategic issue. The "smartphone" and the "tablet" are now ubiquitous in developed countries, and becoming so in developing countries (in fact, the penetration of mobile phones in developing countries has been unexpectedly rapid and is seen by many experts as critical to the evolution of educational practice). The analysis in the figure suggests that the contribution of the personal device to educational practice in this university will indeed be pervasive—personal devices are expected to be used in all processes, but the same question arises: precisely *how* will they be used? What changes will be needed to the way we teach, manage material, and undertake research?

And so it goes on—the other features of this example can be debated at length, or a similar analysis can be undertaken for another organisation closer to your interests and needs. The important conclusion that must be drawn at this stage is that although we have identified technologies and organisational processes and keyed them to some aspects of the organisational strategy, something still seems to be missing. The features of an electronic whiteboard are so numerous, and the kinds of teaching and discussion that take place in classrooms and meeting rooms are so varied, that we have only the vaguest view of exactly what will change for the better; equally, there are so many kinds of document, so many stages in the development of good research, and such marked differences in the expectations of academic publications and publishers that we have only the fuzziest idea about how and why our document management processes will actually deliver better facilities to those heavily involved in research. Such high levels of uncertainty represent a real threat to the success of our investment, and yet it is common for organisations to spend very large sums of money on flimsy arguments such as these.

And so we find that benefits are dependent on the way we use technology, but not completely. A more advanced view of the dependencies is needed, that resolves the potential uncertainty in terms of *how technologies will be used to achieve process improvements*, and *how process improvements will contribute to strategic intention*.

In effect, we need to see the resolution of these issues by means of two additional layers in the logic, which is achieved with the IMBOK framework as shown in Fig. 7.6.

In the lower part of the figure are some details of the interdependent components of the electronic whiteboard initiative that provide a much more complete view of what must be done, and what the consequences will be: reading from the left-hand side to the right, we see the components that *enable* the strategic investment objectives, one layer at a time; reading from the right-hand side to the left we see the dependencies that determine whether the strategic investment objectives will be realised. Which way you read it simply depends on your point of view, but at last we see very clearly a framework which allows a complete and coherent discussion between the two communities—the IT specialists at the left and the education specialists at the right—by resolving the differences and dependencies between their different perspectives on the work of the university.

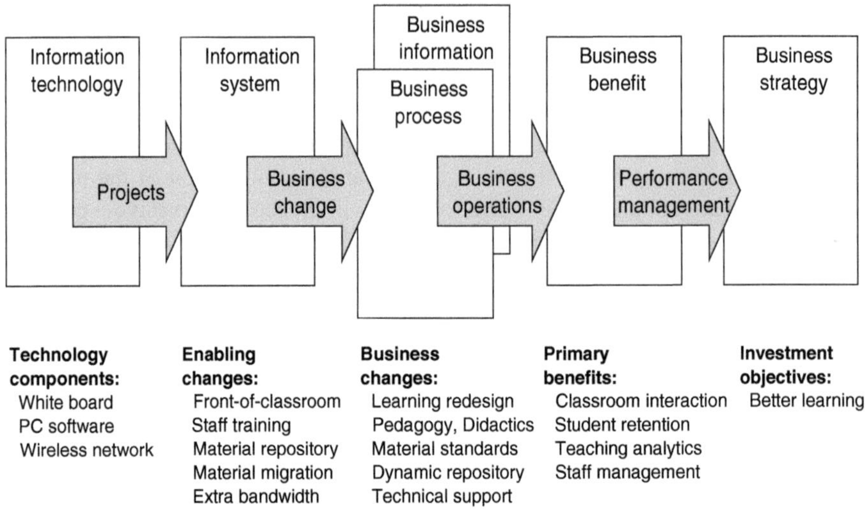

Fig. 7.6 Benefits dependencies in education, seen through the IMBOK

The Benefits Dependency Network—A Business Example

With the IMBOK in mind, we can see that the structuring of benefits is based on a scheme of dependencies (of benefits upon new systems, and of organisational strategy on successful delivery of benefits) that closely parallels the structure of the IMBOK. In the existing literature, this idea is often referred to as the "benefits dependency network" (for an authoritative treatment, see Ward and Daniel 2005). Let us move away from education, and look at a more typical "business" example, using it to examine more carefully how this idea of dependency works.

Suppose that we have the high-level objective to deliver increased sales. This is typical of a strategic remit handed down from the highest level of strategic planning, so that all functional areas must respond and make their contribution to the remit (not just the information technology department, but all areas of business activity). A first attempt at laying out the idea might look like this (Fig. 7.7).

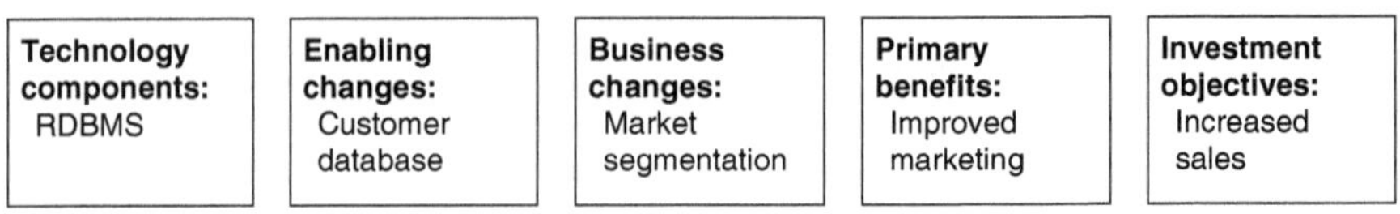

Fig. 7.7 A simple business example

The marketing department will be critically involved in responding to such a remit and will decide that they have to respond with new and more effective procedures for marketing. They may observe that the rate of conversion of sales calls to orders is low compared to their competition and decide that something must be done about it. In discussions, it is realised that sales effort is organised geographically, but the need is to organise it differently. Despite the certainty of increased costs, it is decided to have national sales groups that address different market segments on a specialised basis, so that (for example) there is a banks team that sells to all banks irrespective of where they are located and a manufacturing industry team that sells to manufacturing companies.

This sounds simple, but the problem is that all the information systems were developed with an old-fashioned hierarchical database, organised around sales regions—the "geographical" view. It follows that a new database is needed that is able to support different views of the sales data, and therefore, a relational database management system (RDBMS) must be acquired; let us suppose that it is decided to acquire Oracle in order to achieve this.

In this way, in a few words in a few sentences, we have travelled from purely strategic thinking to a very specific proposal to spend money on a new database regime. By itself the database software will achieve nothing for the business, but incorporated into new systems and populated with the data that describe customers and indicates what they buy, it will support the segmentation of the market into specific types of customer, not just into regions. Now, we have a real chance that we will *only* call on those customers who are legitimate targets for our sales effort, and we will *only* deal with them from a position of understanding about their needs and the ways that they work.

This is a simplified example. We have confined the discussion to just one feature of each step in the dependency, and a moment's thought will raise all sorts of other issues concerning other technology that will be required, the ways in which other areas of the company must assist in this changed approach to marketing, and the consequences for management reporting and decision-making. There will be many interdependencies between five different kinds of component in what we call the *benefits dependency network*:

Investment objectives: Here, we are talking about the few high-level objectives that come from the high level organisational strategy. These objectives will all relate directly to one or more of the key stakeholders in the organisation, and we must expect that they will be directed at meeting stakeholder expectations. Not all of them all of the time; strategic analysis will determine from time to time which are the more important areas of stakeholder concern to address. For example, if a telecommunications business is headed for privatisation, the role of the customer is diminished as management attention is refocused on making the business attractive to investors. "*Increase sales*" is an easy example, others might include "*Reduce costs*" (another easy one!), "*Go international*", or "*Improve corporate governance*". In IMBOK terms, we are working here at the level of *business strategy*.

Primary benefits: Targets to be met by the different functional areas of the business come from the strategy. The HR department may have to recruit more staff, or staff with different skills; they may have to make plans to reduce the workforce through redundancy and retrenchment. The production division might have to retool a production line or even create an entirely new one. The quality control authority might have to redefine QC procedures and drive the organisation through and monitor ISO 9000 inspection and registration. This is the level at which functional directors and senior managers pick up their personal targets that will determine their career futures. In IMBOK terms, we are working here at the level of *business benefits*.

Business change: When senior managers have decided what must be done, they will set to work to change the way their people work or (in the case of service departments like HR and IT) to provide the support that others need. This sounds easy but of course it is not. It is especially difficult to do well when it is allowed to be seen as the role of the IT department. Even a successful IT department with a long history of successful information systems delivery cannot be expected to deliver business change. This is where things usually go wrong. In IMBOK terms, we are working here at the level of *business processes*, *business information* and the lower level business activities that comprise routine business operations.

Enabling change: Support for improved or revised business activity within business processes comes from new information systems. Projects that combine information technology skills with business skills will acquire (or build) new information systems that serve the needs of revised business processes: the conventional information systems project. In IMBOK terms, we are working here at the level of *information systems*.

Technology components: All of the above things are dependent on the availability of appropriate information technology at the level of infrastructure. This includes more than what is sometimes assumed to be the case; we are not talking only about the nuts and bolts (or the operating systems and hardware systems components) but about *electronic commerce*, and *the World Wide Web*. Even at that level, until we have defined business activities that can incorporate electronic commerce and the Web these technologies are useless to us and a huge potential distraction. Worse, if we *fail* to specify how they shall be used we risk extended wastage of time, money and resources trying to build systems from the bottom up. For turnaround systems that might be a useful approach, but in all other cases, the deployment of technology has to be done in the context of defined and agreed business requirements. In IMBOK terms, we are working here at the level of *information technology*.

With all of this in mind, a more careful and detailed analysis of the components of the dependency network, and the specific dependencies between them, might look like this (Fig. 7.8).

Above is a more representative (but still simplified) example taken from a pharmaceutical company that wished to increase the volume of sales and improve the effectiveness of marketing. See how the complexity in the centre of the network reveals the many interdependencies that must be managed. If they are not, if any

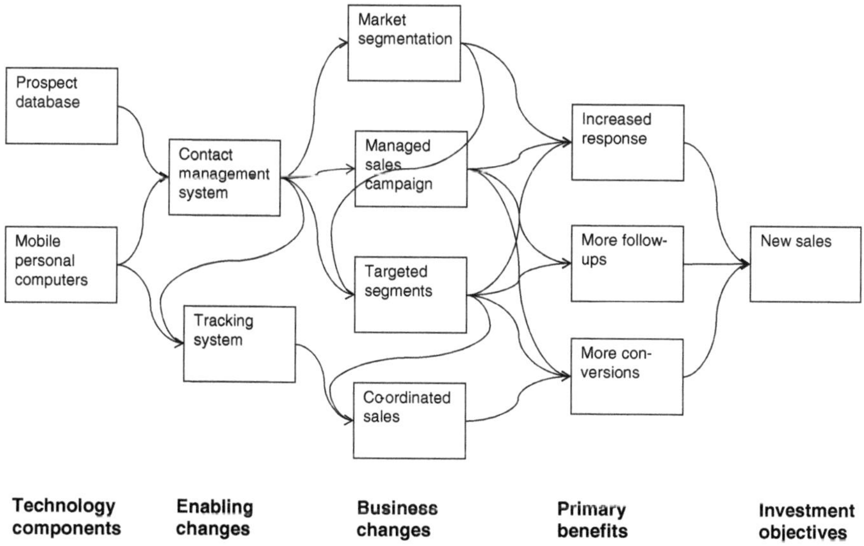

Fig. 7.8 Benefits dependency networks: a simplified example

link is "broken", then there is a real possibility that the investment in new systems to support the necessary business changes will fail. Note also how business changes (in the centre) are in some cases dependent upon themselves—the idea of inter-dependency can be used to further explain how each step in the logic depends on all the others.

In real cases, it is the *development* of the network that is perhaps the most useful thing. As is so often the case, it is not so much the end result as the *process* that brings clarity and understanding to the arguments. Networks such as these should not be developed by "experts" from the "enterprise architecture" department, nor by consultants, nor by committees. They should be developed cooperatively by all involved managers, in workshops that are dedicated to the purpose and supported by appropriate facilities: whiteboards, flip charts, even the traditional "brown paper and sticky yellow notes". Experience has shown that properly motivated management teams can develop these networks in three, four or five working sessions, that the final network might be accommodated on A3-sized paper and that there would typically be 50 or more components spread across all five layers. It is a taxing and challenging process, but the results can be very worthwhile. Without proper attention to each of the five layers of dependency, from technology to strategy and back again, the strength and security of an investment decision will be seriously compromised (Table 7.1).

Table 7.1 A summary of the benefits management cycle

Stage		Actions
1	Identify and structure benefits	Analyse drivers behind investment decisions, and reconcile with stakeholder expectations
		Determine the different types of benefit and how they will be measured
		Establish ownership and agree responsibilities for delivery
		Identify business changes and stakeholder impact.
		Develop and stabilise benefits dependency network
2	Plan benefits realisation	Determine change actions required at the level of enabling changes
		Review with current project activities and map benefits to the projects that will deliver the enabling changes. Revise project plans where necessary
		Finalise and disseminate benefits realisation plan: responsibilities, timetables, measures and targets
3	Execute the plan	Monitor project progress and check against expected business changes and primary benefits
		Review and refine benefits realisation plan as may be necessary.
		Manage the business change programme(s) and organise post-implementation reviews
4	Evaluate and review	Assess achievement of enabling changes, business changes, primary benefits and investment objectives
		Review potential learning arising at all levels: from projects, business change programmes and benefits management
		When done with planned benefits, use the project/programme team to drive through and leverage further potential benefits that could not have been anticipated at the start, based on learning achieved

The Benefits Management Cycle

The benefits dependency network makes clear the logic that connects information technology costs to strategic investment intentions, but that is only part of the story. An approach to benefits management has been devised that organises the necessary activities into a logical sequence. In principle, it is no more than the classic management cycle of "Think, Plan, Act, Check" (refer back to Fig. 1.3); however, some of the specific techniques and ideas are interesting and very specific to the process. Table 7.1 summarises the actions required to achieve the planning and execution of benefits management; the paragraphs that follow examine the stages in more detail.

Stage 1: Identify and Structure Benefits

Building the Network

The first stage is about working through to a dependency network that is stable and agreed by all those concerned. Different techniques will be needed to build a satisfactory view of each of the five "layers". Look at the figure (Fig. 7.9).

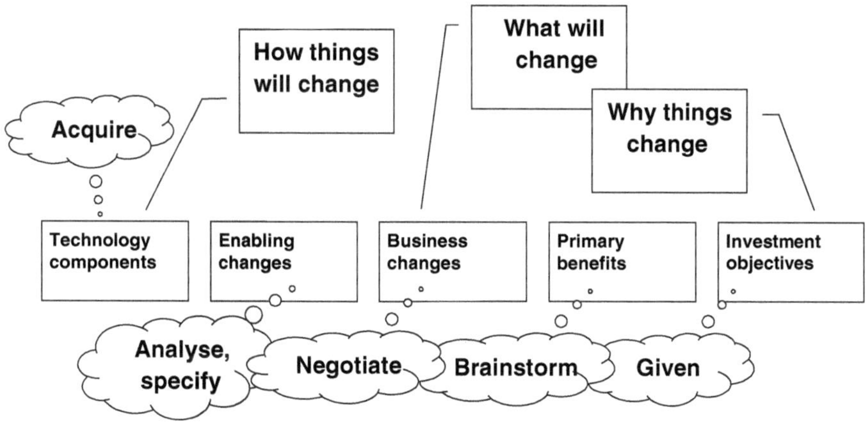

Fig. 7.9 Building the benefits dependency network

Investment objectives are the reasons why things must change and they are *given*, but the translation of those high-level objectives into the specific benefits that divisional directors can commit to might require some brainstorming. There are many choices as to what will change. If the board of directors have decided that we are to go "international" there are many ways to do it—through the use of Web services directly connecting with remote customers, through the use of agents, or through the establishment of overseas offices. In each case, the required consequential changes to the business will be quite different.

When primary benefits are agreed, the related business changes will come from a more careful analysis of requirements and some negotiation of the details with those concerned. Then, we can revert to conventional systems analysis and system design so that we can work through to the question of how things will change and how we will acquire appropriate technologies and build appropriate systems.

Classifying the Benefits

It is possible to take a simple view of the different kinds of benefit that might be sought: "efficiency", "effectiveness" and "evolution" come to mind ... but if we are to *demonstrate* the achievement of these different kinds of benefit, we need indicators:

Efficiency is not really a problem; we can measure throughput and resource consumption and come up with reliable and defensible numbers.

Effectiveness is somewhat more problematic. How do we measure "customer happiness"? If we are trying to reduce the number of warranty claims arising from faults in our products, how reliable is a measure of the number of returns that have been made?

Evolution is really challenging. How do you measure the extent to which a whole business has moved forwards, with new values and a new culture?

There are other problems. At an early stage in the analysis of the benefits that could be achieved, there will be differences of opinion about whether they are actually realistic. So when someone argues for improved customer satisfaction there will be those who agree that it can be measured and those who do not. At the end of the day, it would be good if we were able to turn *all* benefits, even evolutionary ones, into financial returns, but we have already established that this is not easy and may lead to cheating and playing with "the numbers".

The problem of categorising benefits in a way that builds stronger arguments for the board room (which is where decisions have to be made) has been addressed as follows:

- In the beginning, benefits must be regarded as tentative, but must be validated as being realistic targets. *Suppose that our customer base is visibly reducing, and we want to invest in new systems to improve customer satisfaction. We argue that this will reduce the rate at which we are losing customers.*
- Having agreed that a benefit is realistic we must agree that there is the means to *observe* it, only then can we tabulate it with others to gain a complete view. *If our customers are all overseas, and they all speak different languages, how can we possibly observe their level of satisfaction? We would have to deal with this problem before we go any further, for example by investing in specialist help from a market research consultancy.*
- Observation is one thing, but *measurement* is yet another. A benefit may have a measure, but can it be measured? People can be weighed with a weighing machine, but can they be persuaded to stand on it? *Equally, can the customers be persuaded to cooperate with an international survey, and will cultural differences make the results of a survey useless?* We might propose to run the survey periodically, so that in each area of our international operations we can see the difference from one period to the next, notwithstanding any differences in culture and general expectation from one country or region to another.
- Finally, we have to try to turn measured benefits into a *financial* outcome. We can put forward estimates, but at the end of the day when we promise a 20 % rise in profitability, we may only be believed *because we have a track record.* History is important here, and without it, we will have to tread carefully in order to create it.

Benefits Identification Workshop

Getting people together to discuss the potential for benefits and the organisation of them is probably best done through a workshop (or two, or three workshops—it has been found that at least three iterations will be needed to scope out and to stabilise the benefits dependency network). In a typical organisation, such a workshop needs to be open to all and supported by all managerial stakeholders who may be involved in the delivery of improved business performance. The process of discussion and argument, hopefully focused on an emerging benefits dependency network, is a good way to get all those involved thinking along the same lines and committed to the same objectives.

A first workshop will be directed at:

- Identifying the key drivers and objectives out of the organisational strategy and other high-level directives that are evident.
- Identifying stakeholders, of all kinds. Generally, a stakeholder is seen as someone (or some organisation) that has an interest in an organisation and can impact on its performance (those who are interested but cannot impact on performance can be ignored). In this context, it is about those who will be pleased to see their expectations fulfilled but also those who could block our plans and deny the achievement of objectives. So, we must gather our thoughts about the external *and* internal stakeholders who are concerned and make sure that we have at least a preliminary understanding of their current and probable future attitude to the proposals.

With this knowledge at hand, then we can set about the derivation of the dependency network and the structuring of benefits in a way that will suit the presentation of our arguments to all concerned, but especially to the senior management body that will approve the proposals. This means that we must attend to the question of measures, the extent to which the measures can be achieved, and the extent to which they can be translated into financial outcomes.

In this way, the first workshop leads to stakeholder interviews, a deeper analysis and understanding of what is proposed, and—importantly—an understanding through stakeholder analysis of the possible *dis-benefits* that might have to be managed.

Getting Approval

At the end of the day, major decisions about information systems investments will be made in the board room, and the promise of financial results may well be the only argument that will successfully persuade senior management. Where there is no track record of successful delivery, then no subjective argument about quality and probability will be believed and the request will probably be refused. When one reflects on the reliability of the information systems profession, and the relentless failure to bring projects in on time and to budget, it should be no surprise that senior managers are increasingly reluctant to invest on a "wing and a prayer". Reliable performance and delivery to measurable targets is what this is all about.

A proposed benefit that cannot be observed and measured cannot be seriously considered as an argument; one that can, and that can then be turned into a financial outcome, is the best hope for an approval to invest.

Stage 2: Plan Benefits Realisation

Suppose that we have identified, organised and agreed the benefits that we seek, and that we have gained approval to proceed. It is now time to get more involved with the detail and we will wish to move towards implementation, looking at the details of the technologies needed and the probable projects that will deliver the systems that are needed to enable business change.

Benefits Planning Workshop

A further workshop—probably the second—would be directed to the following:

- The refinement of objectives and the ways by which measures will be achieved (this in itself requires that information—and probably information systems—are available to derive and report on the achievement of measured benefits).
- A clearer and more detailed understanding of the business changes that are needed and the identification of enablers at the level of new information systems, or changes to existing systems.
- Finalisation of the benefits plan including targets, responsibilities, timescales, and the resources to be committed to the execution of benefits management and delivery.
- Setting up of actual measurement and tracking of business performance in order to deliver the evidence that is needed (Fig. 7.10).

This is summarised pictorially in Fig. 7.10.

Moving into Action

Thus the second workshop leads to a wider dissemination of plans and to the start of education and change programmes that will support and facilitate the changes that

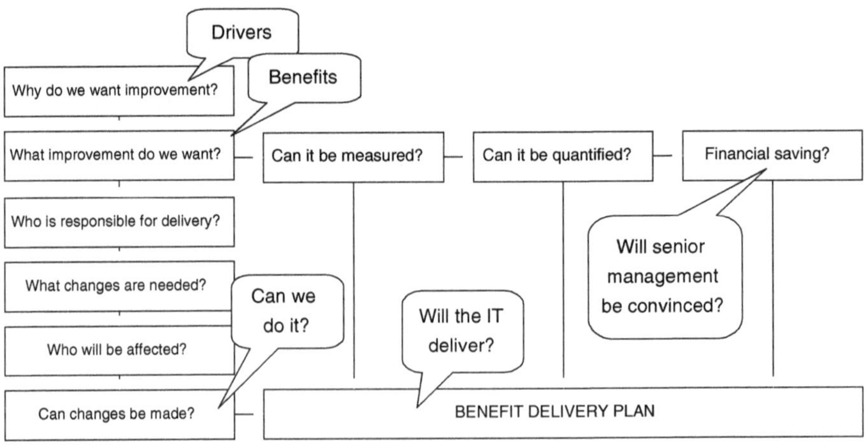

Fig. 7.10 The benefits plan

are necessary. Managing business change is not easy, and within the benefits plan, there must be actions to make sure that all stakeholders are accommodated wherever possible and that contingencies are in place to deal with any difficulties. Periodic reviews of progress will be part of the plan.

Stage 3: Execute Benefits Delivery Plan

Consider the managerial responsibility for projects and benefits. With plans in place, things will proceed at different levels. Project management will look after the specific work that delivers new systems and enhancement to existing systems, and benefits management will oversee all such work and ensure that the best possible chance of success prevails. It is important to recognise the difference between a *project manager* and the *business manager* responsible for benefits delivery. We might term the latter a "business project manager", who

- deals with the investment proposal.
- is the custodian of the benefits management plan.
- convenes benefits review meetings.
- is responsible for delivering the business benefits.
- maintains dialogue with key stakeholders.
- tracks and measures delivery of outputs.

These are not jobs for technically oriented project managers, unless they are experienced in business management and have demonstrated their ability to deal with these things.

Dealing with Stakeholders

As the work proceeds, the potential problems with stakeholders will emerge. There are ways of anticipating and dealing with these. Consider the example that follows, that is drawn from a proposal where an expert system will take over the configuration and specification of computer systems in a computer manufacturing business (Fig. 7.11).

As the detail of the figure shows, the different stakeholder groups have different *current* views about the proposals, and we need them to have different *required* views if the work is to proceed. For example, the sales representatives and manufacturing division are against the plans because in each case, it demands that they change the way they work, and both groups see these changes as problematic. We require the *positive involvement* of the sales representatives, so we have a lot of work to do there; we only need the manufacturing division to *allow* things to happen, and we do not need their active involvement so that will not be so difficult. But in both groups, there is work to be done, as is the case with the sales management and the IT department. There will be no problems with customers, they will be delighted to have a more reliable sales process that delivers what they need

STAKEHOLDER GROUP	PERCEIVED (*DIS*)BENEFITS	CHANGES NEEDED	PERCEIVED RESISTANCE
Customers	Configuration tailored exactly to needs	None	None
Sales & marketing managers	Improved customer service and product quality image	New incentive to get sales reps to use system with customers	Reluctance to change reps reward system
Sales rep	*(extra work in preparing requirements and quotations)*	To use system and improve quality of quotes	No time available to use system. Loss of autonomy
Manufacturing & distribution	Removes need for configuration checking -fewer returns.	Stop current checks -to put onus on reps to get it right	Do not trust sales reps' accuracy in requirements and quotations
IT specialists	New advanced system -old system goes	Skills in expert systems development	None

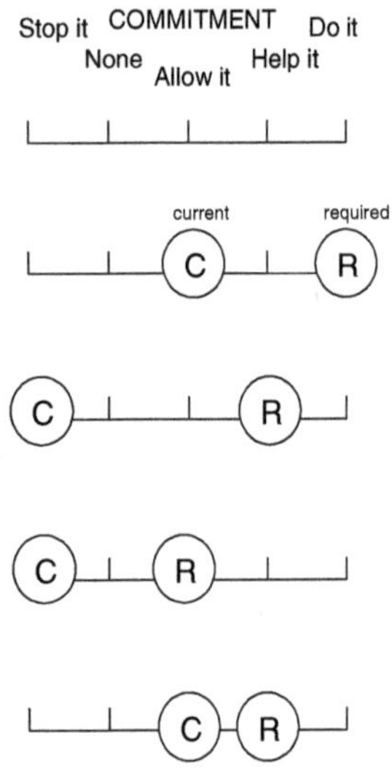

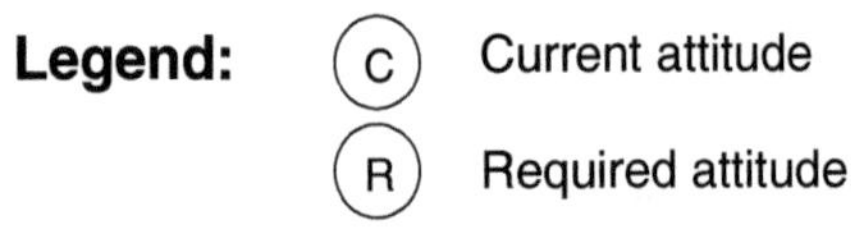

Fig. 7.11 An example stakeholder analysis

with fewer problems, and no interference from sales staff that no longer need to know the technical details that determine configuration needs.

Stage 4: Review, Evaluate and Exploit

When all is done, it is necessary to assess what has been achieved, in a post-implementation review that will occur some time after the technical work and implementation is finished. This requires that all stakeholders come together and look at the latest reports of business performance, assess the success of the projects that delivered new systems, and check things off against the content of the benefits delivery plan that initiated the whole process (Fig. 7.12).

As is the case with any review, it is important to document successes *and* failures, to assign actions arising from the work, and to learn from all that has happened. In most cases, there will be some success and some failure, but happily there are usually some additional benefits apparent at the end of the cycle of work that could not have been anticipated at the start. It is important to pursue them whilst the going is good, so to speak. At this point, we can regard the benefits management cycle as complete.

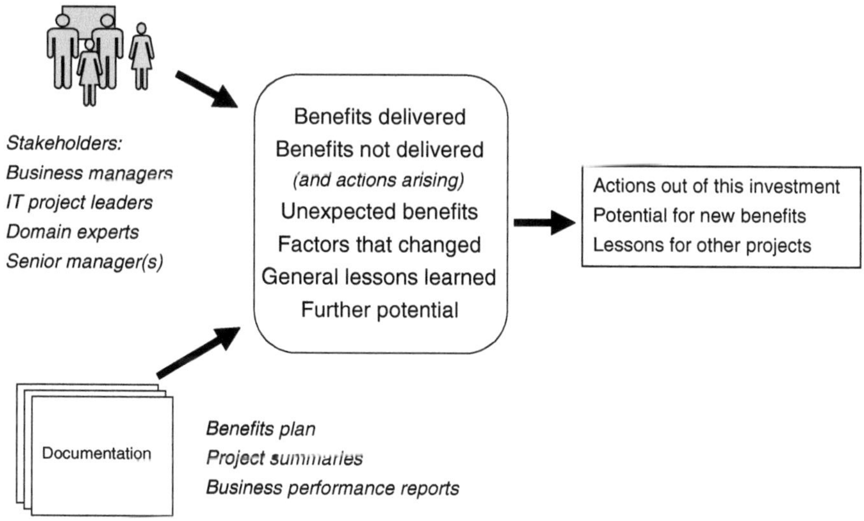

Fig. 7.12 The benefits review

Summary

Managerial Issues in Benefits Management

It is interesting to see how the will to undertake benefits management arises in an organisation. One might imagine that once the merits of the idea are understood, it would be adopted at the start of a major investment cycle, but this is not always what happens. More often, at the end of a particularly difficult project, possibly at a moment of real crisis, management will undertake a post-mortem, determine that things were not done well, and then try to "reverse engineer" benefits management from a situation of potential (or actual) failure. Hence, the initiation of purposeful benefits management cycle might actually only occur at Stage 4, when the degree of difficulty in achieving good results finally becomes clear.

Some of the benefits management issues that must be considered include the following:

- A regime for benefits management requires effort. The reasons for it need to be clear, and the additional work involved needs to be related to the merits of the idea, in particular the prospect of more rewarding investments in information systems. This will require a period of management education and learning.
- Different kinds of business benefits arise from different kinds of information system. These benefits must be used appropriately to justify an investment in information systems-related change. There are qualitative benefits as well as

quantitative ones, but qualitative benefits are more difficult to negotiate and manage.

- In the same way, business benefits can be seen in non-financial as well as in financial terms. But at the end of the day, financial arguments are going to be the most persuasive in the board room. It is possible that successful benefits management will allow non-financial arguments to be more willingly received, as a track record of successful delivery emerges.
- Procedures for reporting the achievement and delivery of business benefits are needed. This might require changes to the management information and reporting systems in an organisation, and it is most useful when the reports of benefits can be set beside reliable reports on costs—then, the net return on investment can be clearly seen.
- Management responsibility must be determined. Responsibility for the delivery of business benefits must be decided in a clear manner and must be willingly accepted by those concerned.
- Risks and dis-benefits are part of the process and must be dealt with. Dis-benefits will be evident in stakeholder analysis, which is an important component of benefits management planning. Benefits sometimes also include stopping doing things that are no longer productive.

Benefits Management Competencies

- Different kinds of business benefits are used to justify investment in IT- and IS-related change
- Business benefits are seen in non-financial as well as in financial terms
- Business benefits are generally seen through quantified measures, rather than by subjective observation
- The variety of business benefits that are sought (and achieved) is appropriate to the business
- The achievement and delivery of business benefits is measured and reported
- Management responsibility for the delivery of business benefits is clear and assumed by those concerned
- Risks and dis-benefits are included in discussion and agreement about benefits management
- There is a regime in place that manages the achievement of business benefits
- There is training in business benefits management related to IT and IS investments
- The outcome of benefits management training is monitored
- Benefits are recognised to include those things that avoid problems as well as those that exploit opportunities
- Benefits can include stopping doing things that are no longer productive

Research Side-Note: IT Capability no Longer Guarantees Business Performance?

Chae, H.-C., Koh, C.E. & Prybutok, V.R. (2014) Information technology capability and firm performance: contradictory findings and their possible causes. MIS Quarterly, 38 (1), pp. 305–326.

Ho-Chang Chae and colleagues have blown a huge hole in the presumption that IT capability guarantees improved firm performance. Contradicting previous research, and reviewing data from over 15 years, they find that the financial performance of a large number of businesses does not relate to IT capability. This result has to be seen in the light of the emergence of Web-based systems, and enterprise-wide systems, many of which obviate the need for internal IT systems development. 2001 seems to be the year when this change in the relationship between performance and IT capability became evident. In their concluding remarks, they note that "the standardisation and homogenisation of IT systems, fuelled by the constantly declining cost of computing, have significantly lowered the barrier of entry to those competitors who could not afford advanced IT systems in the past".

Research Side-Note: A More Optimistic Worked Example Based on Enterprise-wide Systems

Seddon, P.B., Calvert, C. & Yang, S. (2010) A multi-project model of key factors affecting organisational benefits from Enterprise Systems. MIS Quarterly, 34 (2), pp. 305–A11.

This paper looks specifically at enterprise systems, which are an increasingly attractive option at all levels of business. It develops and tests a multi-project model of factors affecting organisational benefits from enterprise systems. It seems to find that the fit of the enterprise system and the commitment of the organisation to undertaking change are both critical in delivering the expected benefits. Secondary factors include integration, process optimisation, improved access to information, and ongoing business improvement projects further enhance benefits on a longer term timeframe, taking a senior management viewpoint.

Exploring Business Strategy

8

What Is Strategy?

Strategy is about change—without change, there is no real need for a strategy. With change in mind, we can argue that the simplest definition of strategy is as follows:

- knowing where you are,
- knowing where you could choose to be, and
- knowing how you intend to get there.

In line with this simple definition, and with basic strategic analysis tools at hand, developing new strategies can seem quite straightforward and fulfilling. But if strategy formulation is relatively simple, *delivering* a strategy is not—it can be a nightmare of confusion and difficulty. There are no tools that will guarantee the easy implementation of a strategy—just persistent efforts to communicate ideas, motivate action and manage change.

Strategy is an integrated set of actions aimed at increasing the long-term well-being and strength of the enterprise, and there is copious literature about strategic management. The tools and techniques presented here summarise some of the best and most useful thinking about the strategic management of information technology and systems; it is shown how systems planning can become more effectively linked to business planning and hence be driven by business management rather than by the IT department alone.

A. Bytheway, *Investing in Information*,
DOI 10.1007/978-3-319-11909-0_8

Nature of Business and Information Systems Strategy

In the past, the information systems strategy of many organisations was essentially the summation of existing activities and plans, which themselves often derived from the bottom-up development of systems rather than a coherent business driven plan. This piecemeal approach to systems resulted in missed opportunities and inefficient use of resources. Perceptions of success or failure were once based on an organisation's ability to deploy technology without regard to business change. This has changed, of course. Most examples of success today are based on significant changes to the way a business works and an ability to manage business change at the same time that new systems are deployed.

There is a clear need to align information systems strategies with the business strategy; hence, in a case where there is no business strategy, the effort to deploy information systems will effectively be piecemeal and frustrated by conflicting interests. Investments in information systems must be in harmony with investments in new product development, human resource development and other strategic areas such as production, marketing and customer relationship management.

Today, investments in systems and technology by those around you—customers, suppliers and competitors—can require you to attend urgently to your own information systems and the way that they are managed. Ignoring such pressures risks significant business disadvantage and so in this way, change is forced upon an organisation. Change must be managed, and the way that we do that is using strategies that are properly formulated and implemented with commitment. Of course, the nature of a strategy can be very different in different kinds of organisation, and in different parts of that organisation, but often there are patterns that can be discerned within industries.

Strategic Contribution of IT

The potential value of good information systems is often not understood. Financial considerations alone are not always sufficient or appropriate because in many circumstances, the benefits of IT-related investments are not financial but still strategically important for other reasons: just having access to information that was previously unavailable is a benefit (especially reliable *management* information, which is notoriously difficult to provide); whether we are thinking about large-scale businesses or the needs of a single individual, enabling actions that were previously impossible might just lift performance above a critical threshold of success.

The ability to take a fully strategic view of information systems is therefore important. The alignment of business and information management strategies requires that managers have the necessary tools. On the one side, technology-related opportunities must be accommodated in strategic thinking; on the other side, appropriate information systems investments must support the realisation of the wider business strategy—it is a combination of seeing opportunity and understanding need. The benefits of information systems implementation can only be achieved with proper planning, based on organisational strategies that are appropriate, agreed and understood.

Consequences of a Lack of Strategy

In all cases, the lack of a coherent strategy for the business at large, and for information systems in particular, can result in any number of the following problems:

- Competitors, suppliers and customers may gain avoidable and undesirable advantages.
- Business goals will become unachievable because of information systems limitations.
- There will be duplication of effort, inaccuracy, delays and poor management information because of a lack of proper systems integration.
- The delivery of information systems will be late and over budget.
- New information systems will fail to deliver the expected benefits because of a lack of clear focus on business needs.
- Priorities and plans will change continually leading to conflict among users and systems staff, and poor productivity all round.
- Technologies will become a constraint to the business because of a failure to maintain compatibility where it is needed.
- Inappropriate systems and technology resource levels will hamper organisational performance.
- A failure to evaluate information systems investments and to set implementation priorities consistently will lead to wasted capital expenditure.

It is very common for information systems to incur a greater expense than is necessary and for benefits to fall well short of expectations. A failure to manage strategically generates organisational conflict and wastes management time; to achieve strategic management, we must learn to manage the demand for information systems in accordance with business needs, and to manage the supply of systems and infrastructure in a coherent way. In the end, we must find the means to *deliver the stated strategic objectives*, perhaps the most difficult thing of all. Experts have argued that project management is the means to deliver corporate strategy (Pellegrinelli and Bowman 1994), but as we learn from the IMBOK, there are many more aspects to successful information management than that alone.

Differences Between Information Systems and Information Technology Strategies

A common question is concerned with understanding the difference between an information systems strategy and an information technology strategy.

Information systems strategies define the information and systems needs for activities within the business. Information systems strategy should define what information systems the business needs for the foreseeable future based on proper analysis of the business, its environment and the general business strategy. The objective is to establish the demand for new systems, aligned closely to plans for the business and its development. A good strategy will make clear who is responsible for the implementation and delivery of new systems and for the benefits that they bring.

Information technology strategies define how system needs will be met and how the information technology that will be required will be acquired, developed and operated so as to support existing and future applications. This involves determining how applications will be delivered and how technology and specialist resources will be acquired, used, controlled and managed. It will describe the activities which need to be undertaken and how they are to be organised, and it will thereby provide foundations for the definition and execution of systems projects that will ultimately deliver benefits and thereby the strategic objectives of the business.

Different Kinds of Organisation

Large, formalised organisations will prefer to strategise in a formalised way, with responsibilities allocated and methods of working prescribed. Smaller organisations might deal with strategy very differently—possible by means of short conversations over lunch or over a weekend. However, both will do better with strategies that are well aligned. Information systems strategies are at particular risk of misalignment because of the nature of systems: they are difficult to visualise and articulate, and the incessant pressure from raw technological innovation has tended to drive information strategies from the bottom up, rather than allowing them to be driven from the top down.

In summary, alignment problems between business and information systems strategies must be addressed. There needs to be an equal interest in both value creation and cost containment, and strategies must recognise and address required resources and risks.

Development of Information Systems Strategies

Systems Strategy in Context

Figure 8.1 shows how the general issues surrounding business strategy combine to make a sensible planning process for information technology and information systems planning. The external business environment typically provides most of the strategic drivers that tell us "why" we must act. External and internal inputs

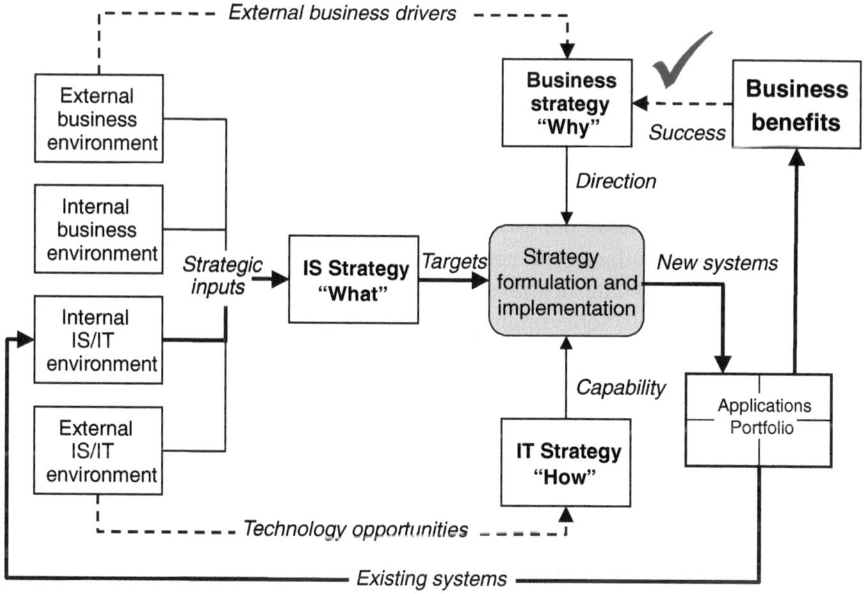

Fig. 8.1 The strategic analysis process

combine to provide us with the "what" must be done. The general technology environment is best seen as generating opportunities, but should only drive thinking if our overall organisational strategy is to be *driven* by information technology developments (as would be the case if we were operating in the software industry, or if we specifically want to be a technology leader in some other context).

At the heart of the figure is strategy formulation and implementation, driven by "why", targeted by "what" and constrained by "how". If all these factors can be taken into account, then the resulting plans for systems implementation should be both viable and appropriate. We can see how the current portfolio of information systems (itself an important input to the question of "what") becomes augmented and enhanced by new information systems that are in accord with business strategy and capability.

Of course, this simple logic is not always reflected in the reality of strategic planning. When the process is driven by technology thinking, it is termed "bottom-up" planning, whereby whimsical technology-based opportunities can determine what will be done. But before you set out to agree that this is a viable approach, reflect for a moment on how much money has been wasted in pursuit of data warehouses, enterprise architectures and other transient thinking over recent years. "Top down" is better than "bottom up", although we must always be cognisant of technology-related opportunities; it is just a question of getting things into perspective and making sure that they are balanced by agreed business needs.

The following notes describe some of the features of the figure in more detail.

The External Business Environment

The external forces bearing down upon a business are complex, and they involve economics, structure and (perhaps most importantly for systems planning) the current basis of competition. The role that information systems and technology play in an industry from time to time needs to be understood.

For example, the increasing power of retailers over manufacturing companies has been enhanced by retail point-of-sale systems and the information these provide for the retailer. Manufacturers need to consider how their systems might be developed to either counter that pressure or perhaps better understand the potential of retail systems to gain some mutual benefit; what some manufacturers have done (particularly in the fast-moving consumer goods sector) is to work with retailers to develop systems that give them moment-by-moment information about sales and then negotiate a sharing of the benefits that arise from improved sales information and reduced stockholdings.

Another example is in the education sector, where the globalisation of educational material and courses proceeds apace. The online delivery *and* assessment of world-class education cause local and regional learning institutions to reflect on where and how (and why) they can be different to this new global competition. A friend told me last week that he is concurrently registered with Harvard University and a Chinese university to learn computer programming using "Java"; he was very clear that there were huge differences between the two (I will spare you the details, and even the conclusion) and he was equally clear that there was no imperative to try and find an alternative programme locally. Better to work in the comfort of his own home in rural South Africa, at his own pace and in his own time. A small story, but very indicative of where education is going.

The business environment will continue to change. In some cases (unlike in education), it will change faster than the lead time necessary to develop new systems, although possibly not faster than the change in base technologies. The speed of change needs to be reflected in reduced systems development lead times that in turn determine many aspects of the systems delivery plans—as we have noted, "agile" development methods have become intensely interesting to progressive, information intensive businesses and organisations.

The Internal Business Environment

An organisation's stated objectives and strategies are sometimes vaguely expressed and not well understood. Unless these are clearly defined, the resulting strategies will be equally vaguely focused and more whimsical than purposeful. Then, there is the question of business operations. It might be surprising to learn that not all managers actually understand how their businesses work. It is sometimes difficult to find a single person (or even a group of people) who can fully explain how an organisation works, in its totality, only within the very shallow scope of their own involvement. If a strategy is to be complete, it is therefore necessary to undertake at least some analysis of what the business does, how it does it, how it is organised and how it is managed.

Such an analysis will take some account of the external business environment (including some kind of stakeholder analysis), and it will be concerned with the business vision, mission, capabilities and structure. It may well reveal weaknesses in the current organisational arrangement of business activity, which could be addressed by better systems, possibly with some degree of organisational change. But, as we have noted, it is important not to become constrained by organisational models if the maximum advantage of information systems investments is to be gained.

At the end of the day, it is about business performance that meets the strategic intentions of the organisation, and only with a proper process is there any basis for performance analysis in terms of resource consumption, cost drivers and value generated; only then, it is possible to identify areas of potential benefit, by the introduction of new or enhanced systems that reduce costs, reduce the demand on resources or increase the added value.

The Internal IS/IT Environment

Existing systems, technology and information resources are the baseline from which a new cycle of investment will be launched. As can be seen from Fig. 8.1, the applications portfolio is perhaps the most important feature of the internal environment and will be the target of our efforts to improve the deployment of information systems.

The current portfolio must be assessed according to its present contribution to the business. The categorisation of information systems into the four quadrants, according to current relevance and future potential, is the best guide to doing this. At the level of information technology operations, IT assets and resources need to be catalogued and examined in order to determine whether current capabilities and infrastructure are adequate for future needs. This is not just an audit of current technology but a review of the people, their skills, how they are managed, and the methods used to develop and support systems and the requisite infrastructure. The IMBOK, with its identification of required competencies and capabilities, helps greatly in this regard.

Implementation difficulties are the main reason why strategies often fail to deliver the changes required. A lack of resources, skills or management process, or any combination, will make it difficult to see the implementation of strategy through to the bitter end. Perhaps the key issues (and the most difficult for the average IT manager to deal with) concern culture and style. The IT department so often seems to be living in a different world from the business and cultural differences run deep. Reconciliation of culture and attitudes is a critical aspect of implementation, and conventionally the most difficult, and it starts at the top. Keith Patching and Robina Chatham undertook a short survey and quickly found that IT managers are not effective players in the boardroom (Chatham and Patching 2000). Things do not seem to have improved since their survey (literally) hit the headlines in the UK technical and business press. Any device or managerial technique that gets technology specialists and business generalists to live and work together will be most welcome.

The External IS/IT Environment

The external environment is constantly revealing new technologies that are first taken up by "early technology adopters" or "technology leaders". For those organisations that do not want to sit on the crest of the wave, it is useful to see how others are using new technology before making any commitment. There will be short-term and long-term implications, and timing is a big factor. If a leader, then there is a need to move quickly. If a lagger, then it is only about how long to wait and what will be the criteria to enable and initiate take-up. All new technologies imply some risk and a learning curve for the business. Early understanding, interpretation and selective use of developing technologies may enable a future advantage to be identified and obtained. A failure to understand will lead to much wasted time and money (as with the early days of the PC, with the World Wide Web, and more recently still with tablets). This is just another strategic decision that has to be taken.

Technology trends and developments need to be evaluated, and there are many ways to appreciate and interpret new developments in information technology. From simply surfing the Web, especially those Websites that specialise in technology watching, right through to attending conferences and purchasing consultancy reports, there are numerous options available. Perhaps the least cost but most effective technique is to choose your friends well and then make a habit of conversing with them in the discretionary time that is available. It is so easy to network today, and so many people are doing it. The use of technology is evident from newspaper reports and through specialist commentators. Knowing how others are employing information technology within your industry, to what purpose and with what success, is a key factor in deciding about strategy. It is important that an organisation understands the business implications of what its competitors, customers and suppliers are doing with information technology and it should not be difficult to find out the details. The more difficult thing is to decide what the specific implications are and what needs to be done.

Summary of Strategic Inputs

The potential impact of new systems on business performance depends not only on what the business wishes to do but what others are already doing. It is the combination of external pressures and internal capabilities that needs to be balanced to ensure proper alignment of systems and business strategies.

The analysis process described here is an adequate guide to achieving viable information systems strategies, provided that agreement is reached as to terminology and process, so that everyone is working on the same basis. Issues and problems will arise, and as the process is exercised, it can be refined to include places where problems can be "parked" pending proper resolution, and where decisions can be recorded so that their significance is not lost. As with other analysis methods and procedures, the figure (Fig. 8.1: the strategic analysis process) makes it look simpler than it is. The volume of strategic data needed can be overwhelming and a proper discipline for document and information management within the strategic process itself will be helpful.

A final comment needs to be made about timescales. On the way through this discussion, we have passingly noted that the timescales for emerging technologies, system development and business change management will certainly all be different. There is a school of thought that says the only viable strategies today are flexible ones; "agility" is the name of the game, and the best strategies are those that work on the basis of constant change. Every organisation needs to think about this, but if there is to be any effective management control of business development, appropriate cycles of strategic planning and management need to be adopted. Let the technologies emerge; if they pass us by today, there will be another one tomorrow, but bring project timescales down so that systems implementation takes no longer than necessary; do not push the business over the edge when it comes to managing the concomitant business change.

The Strategy Process

Current Situation Appraisal: "Where We Are Now?"

First, we must study the competitive and industry forces that are bearing upon the organisation that need to be addressed. Where are the deficiencies in current operations? What new technologies and resources do we have, or could we acquire, that might contribute to business development?

This is the stage at which SWOT (strengths, weaknesses, opportunities and threats) analysis can be used to summarise the internal and external factors that might affect strategic intentions. Strengths and weaknesses are clearly internal in origin, opportunities and threats come from outside, especially from the realm of competition. In the specific area of current operations, business process models at different levels provide a framework for analysing cost and efficiency and the prospects for improving both with new information systems perhaps a simple value chain, perhaps a more detailed model of all key processes and the activities that operationalised them. An assessment of current information technology and capabilities within the organisation will reveal shortfalls (or surpluses) that demand management action.

Opportunity Spotting: "Where We Could Be?"

Based on an analysis of business activities and information-dependent processes, the outcome of situation appraisal will be a number of potential options for information systems investment. There will be an ideal set of options developed with no regard to resource constraints, but then, it will have to be moderated by careful consideration of what will be possible given available resources, and what timescales determine the need for action. Prioritisation will be largely based on those opportunities that will yield the earliest significant benefits.

Scenario planning will be a useful approach that allows discussion—possibly even brainstorming—to work through different scenarios and begin to understand some of the implications and potential benefits. A model of high-level business processes can be reappraised and reconstructed, to see what the consequence might be for organisational structures and for external business partners. Development or reconstruction of a value chain, for example, is a good way of examining options for moving suboptimal activities out to specialist business partners that could undertake them at lower cost and with improved performance.

Decision Time: "Where We Want to Be?"

The final decision about what will be done will be based on a systematic review of business objectives and the information systems dependencies that are critical to achieving them: critical *systems-related* success factors, if you like.

Critical success factor analysis is a popular technique that will lead to a more specific understanding of information needs and areas of business where improved systems will deliver the most benefit. Out of this come the key areas for short- and long-term action: the required plan for information systems development, enhancement and correction. Perhaps some of the ideas from the prior stages will be put on one side and, because they are worth further consideration, then brought out for later review if related factors change.

Summary

We have put forward two related ways of looking at strategy.

- First, the "*Why, What and How*" questions that take us through the logic of strategy: What pressures are there to anything at all? What specifically needs to be done? and how will we do it?
- Second, the "*Where are we now?*", "*Where could we be?*" and "*How shall we get there?*" questions that have a strong sense of project planning. What is the route map from where we are now to where we want to be?

The first has a sense of logic to it—almost a "snapshot" view of the state of the business, arguing from the imperative to act to the "how" question, but with a strong sense of required resources and capabilities; understand the pressures, identify the hot spots and check out that we have the wherewithal. The second has a sense of timing to it—setting out a route map that will take us to our destination; understand our current situation before we do anything, work out the options and set out a plan of action.

These two frames can be used to summarise what we must do. In Table 8.1, the two are set in the rows and columns to provide a final overview of the sort of questions that we can ask. Study the table, and see whether you agree that there is a progression from the top-left corner (embracing just the "what" and "where are we now") as the starting point, to the lower right-hand corner (picking up all remaining cells on the way down in two stages, as indicated).

Summary of Approaches to Strategic Analysis

The framework for strategic analysis presented here gives all management the opportunity (and even the obligation) to involve themselves in the discussion of ideas and the establishment of a demand-driven, opportunity-seeking plan for information systems investment, quite separately from considerations of technology alone.

Implementation of Strategy

A critical issue in strategic planning for new systems is to prioritise the implementation work that comes out of the process. That will come from a number of considerations, but business process analysis (such as we have already explored) will be a large part of the story. It is through an understanding of critical business processes and the current quality of the business activities that support them that we can find the most important areas to work on and invest in. Then, we must make specific plans for each of the emerging projects that will deliver new systems and thereby deliver the hoped for organisational benefits.

It is a corporate responsibility to balance demand and supply issues and to ensure that business plans are achievable. There must be a process that brings together business and systems planning activity and the products that they produce. Too often, planning has been driven in reverse. New systems projects are defined, built up into a plan and presented to management for ratification as a "strategy", but without any reference to the actual business strategy. Informal thinking has dominated systems plans because of a lack of direction and a lack of appropriate analysis tools. On the other hand, informal thinking must not be completely stifled by too rigid a planning process. Much of the competitive advantage that has been won from new systems has its origin in unfettered opportunistic thinking, not always at the highest levels of management.

Table 8.1 Consolidation of approaches to strategy formulation

	Where are we now?	Where could we be?	How will we get there?
Why	What industry forces are bearing upon our business success? What stakeholder pressures should be influencing our thinking? What is the state of customer relations, and what messages are we getting from customers who we work with? **Start here**	What are our competitors doing that set expectations in our industry, that we should try to match or exceed? Do we understand what our customers are hoping that we can do for them, in terms of systems-related products and services?	What do we know about potential industry partners who might already be thinking of working with us? What successes have we had that we can capitalise upon so as to maintain the momentum that we have achieved?
What	What strengths do we have that we are not completely deploying? What deficiencies do we suffer that need to be redressed?	Where are the current hot spots in our kind of business? Are there any specifically interesting technology-related developments that present interesting and synergistic opportunities? What weaknesses have been exposed in our operations that give cause for remedial action? **The middle stages**	What spare capacity do we have that we could redeploy? What changes in organisational structure are in hand, or needed, that might assist or confuse implementation?
How	What are our current systems and infrastructural resources? What capability do we have to acquire systems, or to undertake in-house systems development?	What new capabilities do we have, in information technology areas or elsewhere that we can deploy to improve our prospects? Are there industry or other partners we could approach to find synergistic approaches to implementation issues?	What partnerships do we have that might facilitate new systems? What is our capability to undertake project management and see systems implementation through? What capability do we have to achieve significant business change, and what is the quality of senior management support and commitment? **Finalise planning here**

While senior management will always be involved, it is necessary that line management undertakes the primary responsibility for systems plans and incorporates them into their own functional plans. Business management must drive new developments through to successful achievement of strategic benefits—the IT department cannot do this on their own, nor should they even be involved in all cases. Success will depend upon related business and organisational changes which must be carefully planned and implemented.

Establishing the IS/IT Strategic Planning Process

The planning process must itself be managed, especially in terms of scope and duration. It can (and it must) deliver valuable intermediate results throughout the process, not just at the end. It is therefore a matter of the following:

- what is involved,
- how it is to be achieved and
- what the expected products are to be.

If these things are not agreed at the start, then we are already headed for failure. In smaller businesses, the whole process can be relatively informal and will probably embrace the whole of the business at once. But, as soon as there is more than one "business unit" within the business, we need to be careful.

We generally define a business unit to be a part of a larger business that addresses its own markets. Hence, a business unit:

- has a single identifiable family of products or services
- addresses a single identifiable market and
- has identifiable competition.

Where a large, complex business is not already organised into business units that satisfy these criteria, an arrangement must be made in order to make the strategic analysis "doable" and useful. This might require that the physical business is looked at in a "logical" way in order for the approach that is described here to succeed.

Common Problems

Some of the main reasons why such strategy studies fail are as follows:

- Top management commitment to implementing the plan cannot be obtained.
- The planning exercise takes too long for management to sustain interest—it is also very expensive and takes up too much management time when there are urgent operational issues to be dealt with.
- The process produces an overwhelming volume of detail that is difficult to interpret and understand.
- The resulting plan fails to spell out properly the resourcing and financial implications.

Top management commitment is one of the oldest problems and when you consider the distance between technology as a cost driver, and strategic fulfilment as the realisation of our hopes and dreams (as revealed by the IMBOK), it is not surprising that senior management teams have had increasing difficulty in understanding the arguments to invest in technology and systems.

The timing and management of strategic analysis is also an old problem; the problem of "paralysis by analysis" is a common one and those working on strategy formulation projects must be pushed to deliver in reasonable time frames. Strategy formulation is actually a very elastic process, and to embark on a fixed plan for strategy development involving a long sequence of steps is a mistake. Take the ideas presented here and have a three-hour meeting; see what comes out of it; and then run through the whole sequence again. When some stability in the consensus viewpoint emerges, go for a decision and get on with realisation and implementation.

The problem of voluminous detail is also very common and evident in the size of some of the strategic documents that will be seen in senior management offices. Again, it is worth quoting a specific example of how this problem can be solved. The Chief Information Officer of a large financial services business in Cape Town explained that his IT strategy was just four PowerPoint slides. "Well, four slides out of a total of fifteen" he adds with a grin, "and I *have* presented them more than 52 times". There is something to think about there, surely? Why does strategy have to be more complicated than what can be said on four slides, and what is the consequence of making it so?

Getting Started

For an organisation that has never undertaken a strategic analysis of information systems potential, there is always a first time. We must be mindful that it is important to deliver at least some useful outcome the first time around the cycle; otherwise, the process and the people involved will be discredited.

There are three main approaches adopted for resourcing strategic planning, namely:

- Set up a special IS/IT planning function to carry out the task, located within the IT department, which then owns the strategy.
- Employ consultants to bring in the necessary skills to facilitate the process.
- Set up a task force or steering group to do the job, preferably led by an experienced and respected business manager.

Relying entirely on the IT department is not a good idea. Then, the use of consultants carries large risks: they will typically produce a detailed report but probably fail to cede ownership of the ideas to the client—it is worth negotiating to make sure that there is some provision for "knowledge transfer" from the consulting team to the client. Some consulting companies do this willingly, and others do not.

The third option, the task force, is not the easiest approach but it is by far the best. Not only does the resulting strategy belong to the organisation, but also it is more likely to be truly business driven, to be carried out efficiently and be realisable. This is the approach most likely to succeed.

The Longer Term

Following the first iteration, a longer term approach needs to be established. Ideally, strategic planning for information technology and systems should become an integral part of the overall business planning process and such a strategy should be an appropriate response to the strategic needs of the business. As noted, the strategy formulation and planning activities will themselves need management and the typical arrangement is a management steering committee that will solicit feedback and reconcile the supply and demand issues that will arise from time to time. This may or may not marry well with organisational culture. A committee will not be the best approach in a progressive, process-oriented organisation. There, a process manager (possibly seconded from routine duties on a rotating basis) would be a more appropriate arrangement. Michael Earl provides an early but authoritative and interesting overview of how 27 organisations dealt with this problem of organising the strategic analysis (Earl 1993): he highlights the need for a partnership between the technology and business management and reveals that the organisational approach works best, with less of a focus on methodology (of the strategic analysis itself), more a focus on the need for what he calls a "multi-dimensional" approach with "subtle language". He emphasises the axiomatic need to understand the *value* of the investment, and the overall emphasis is on process, involvement and management understanding.

Setting Priorities

Prioritisation of investments is a challenge. Short-term business pressures change, projects fail to proceed as planned, resources are not be available as expected, new opportunities and requirements emerge. Each of these can change our priorities, and therefore, we must be careful not to over-commit to particular schemes of work. There will always be a need to be flexible to account for shifting needs.

The applications portfolio is a consistent, comprehensible and appropriate way of assessing benefits, as we have already found, and it therefore helps with prioritisation by dealing separately with information systems investments that sit in each of the four segments. But before we get too involved in that, consider the three factors that need to be included in the assessment of priorities:

- **What is most important to do**? Different benefits will determine what comes to the top of the list, in the first instance. Strategic information systems clearly deliver the most *potential* benefits, but key operational systems deliver the most *current* benefits, in terms of revenue generation through efficiency and cost reduction.

- **What is capable of being done**? Resources must be available and where there are special skills needed, or where special infrastructure is needed, it may be necessary to push some options down the list to make way for projects that are doable within shorter time frames. Strategic projects make special demands upon management and upon those directly involved with the project, if only because of the urgency to get them completed and the degree of business change involved. Support projects can be relegated to the department or individuals concerned: if they have no capacity to deliver and implement a new system, then it is probably of little consequence in the wider view. There will be another way to work.

- **What is likely to succeed**? All projects carry risks and checklists of risk factors are readily available. The main risk factors are concerned with project size and duration, business instability, organisational rate of change, the number of parts of the organisation involved and technical factors where new technology is being used. Turnaround projects are especially risky, which is why they need a champion who is willing to put their reputation on the line.

Prioritising Within the Portfolio Segments

As a general rule, the conflict between important substantial activities and urgent small ones is difficult to deal with, but it can be managed. I hesitate to admit how old this idea is, but there is a clue in the words I use: when multi-programming operating systems were first developed, there was an algorithm that was used to share the central processor time among concurrent tasks: I have known it as the "Belady" algorithm. What it says, in my recollection of conversations with operating system specialists, is very clear and simple[1]:

> Give big jobs a low scheduling priority, but when they become scheduled give them high execution priority; small jobs get a high scheduling priority, but can be given a low execution priority.

This idea worked well at the time, and it works well for organisations battling to schedule systems development work. I recommend it. Having said that, the applications portfolio gives us a much more nuanced understanding of prioritising and scheduling work.

Support Systems

Within the support segment, setting priorities should not be too difficult—those with the greatest economic benefit using the least resources should get the highest priority. This will encourage users to express benefits quantitatively and look for resource-efficient solutions, such as packages, to obtain a priority. The main argument for such systems is improving efficiency, which should be possible to quantify and convert into a financial argument for investment.

If a support system requires the use of scarce (central) resources, it is reasonable to adopt the most economical solution in light of the efficiency benefits achievable. If one proposed support system is competing with others for limited resources, then

[1] What we find from a search of the Web today is the "Bélády anomaly" a means to optimise *page swapping* in memory—I have to confess that I cannot relate what I read today precisely to what I have written above, but perhaps I will be forgiven for not going into all the details? The message I give here is clear, and useful.

it must show a good economic return for the allocation of a scarce resource. If, however, the project can be carried out within the user department's control, then it is reasonable that the department should decide and fund the work from their own budget. In this case, the investment is an alternative use of local funds and is not competing for scarce IS/IT resources at the centre.

Key Operational Systems

Key operational systems are not difficult to understand, because they underpin the routine value-generating activities of the organisation that should be its greatest strength. They will normally take a high priority—certainly higher than support and turnaround systems. Setting priorities for key operational systems is more problematic than for support or strategic systems because the rationale is more complex. The arguments for key operational systems will be based on economic considerations, risks to current business operations, the achievement of critical success factors and infrastructure improvement.

Unlike strategic systems, all the costs and benefits of a new key operational system should be well understood and should transform into financial returns, but this may not allow for all the arguments involved. The most economical solution may not be the most effective. Financial benefits are not the only driving force, and a feasibility study should examine the best balance of cost, benefit and risk. If a key operational system fails, then the business will suffer.

It might also be worth exploring more integrated solutions than are first proposed to meet a wider range of needs more effectively. Integration is also an important factor in enabling the development of strategic applications that sometimes feed off high volumes of operational data. In this case, the relationship of a proposed system to others must be evaluated for its contribution to the intangible benefits, those that might most effectively address critical success factors such as customer retention and improved supplier management.

Strategic Systems

Those strategic systems that will contribute most to achieving strategic business objectives and use the least resources should go ahead first. A simple decision table can be useful in assessing the strategic contribution of different systems, expressing each in terms of the critical success factors it addresses. This produces a strategic score, or value, for each application. While critical success factors cannot realistically be weighted (they are critical and are either achieved or not—no shades of grey here), the associated business objectives can be given relative priorities.

Strategic applications are essential to achieving business objectives and strategies. It is important to try to estimate costs and benefits to construct a financial justification, but the main arguments for proceeding are likely to remain intangible:

the critical success factors that the application addresses. This is a situation where a detailed discounted cash flow analysis will make no sense.

Achieving the benefits of strategic applications is partly a question of luck (that the target does not move), partly of judgement (the quality of senior management's business acumen), and partly good management of the application development. The key issues are as follows:

- whether the management team is united in endorsing the project;
- whether the organisation at large has agreed that the investment is worthwhile; and
- whether the implementation can be resourced to achieve its objectives in the expected timescale.

This may need repeated senior management intervention to ensure both business and technical resources are made available.

Turnaround Systems

Like strategic applications, turnaround applications should show a relationship to objectives and critical success factors, albeit one that is less clear. Setting objective priorities on scanty evidence is not a good idea, but if an idea *potentially* addresses many critical success factors, it should be elevated above the general scramble for development resources. Because it is reliant upon the energy and enthusiasm of its champions, the prioritisation and resource used by a turnaround application are in effect self-managing, although essential secondary resources can be a problem. The results will depend not only on the value of the idea, but also on the force with which it is pursued.

The very essence of turnaround projects is that the benefits are unknown: the objective is to clarify them and assess them. It is the "R&D" segment of the applications portfolio model and should be justified on the same basis as any other R&D project. Any funding that is needed should come from a general R&D budget rather than central systems and infrastructure funds: this kind of activity can become a bottomless financial pit if it is not monitored properly, and in the end, it is the energy and commitment of those championing the idea that will win through: the role of the champions is critical here. They can be made responsible for their turnaround projects and given a budget, together with a clear brief to deliver results against strictly fixed timescales.

Evaluation and proving of new ideas are what the turnaround segment is really about—nothing should stay in it too long or have too much money spent on it. When initial allocations are used up, further funding would depend strictly on demonstrated results, not just on a vague hope of eventual success. However, it should be obvious that turnaround projects are a main source of strategic applications, and we are looking for the one idea among many that is what is sometimes called a "killer application". There need to be very clear processes that assess turnaround projects and allow them to be promoted to the strategic quadrant, or (in the majority of cases?) relegated to the scrap heap.

The Question of Infrastructure

Information technology infrastructure is the means whereby systems are both developed and operated. It includes the computer equipment, software, networks and people who are all essential to the delivery of systems capability. It also includes common elements such as standards, quality control and project management.

Some initiatives lead to a direct requirement for new infrastructure, for example, when considering "bring your own device" (BYOD) which takes advantage of our collective personal interest in our personal technologies as a resource for the business. In other cases, it is the sum of several applications that makes an infrastructure investment necessary. For example, a new network that will link all offices and provide a vehicle for different applications to be offered at all of those locations, or a new customer database that will service marketing, sales and customer service applications. Infrastructure is important in developing a coherent systems and data architecture, increasing skills, improving the resilience or flexibility of systems and the technology base. This will both avoid excessive costs in supporting the systems and also provide a firm foundation for strategic developments.

We will therefore become involved with evaluating and prioritising infrastructure projects as well as applications projects. Risk to the current business could be assessed in a similar way by asking "what risks do we run if the infrastructure project does not go ahead?" In general, the priority given to an infrastructure project is influenced by all the applications that it will support or contribute to.

In practice of course, it will be found that no particular part of the business will want to pay for shared infrastructure, but the costs must be shared. That means that generally, there must be central funding for infrastructure and—in those organisations working with cost centres—there must be a charge-back mechanism that relates to infrastructure use. Budgeting for infrastructure is often the source of much contentious argument, and clear policies and firm management are needed.

Summary

Every organisation that wants to benefit from information-technology-related investments needs a strategy to assure success. For different kinds of organisation, the approach to strategy will be different, especially when comparing a small, fast moving business with a large, mature multinational business or a large government agency. Strategies must be driven principally by business requirements not by technology opportunities, they must recognise priorities according to the benefits that each new information system will deliver, and they must be set to appropriate time frames that reflect the business planning horizon—this can be five years or more in a stable business, but may be only one to two years (or even months) in a volatile one. In most businesses, a two- to three-year plan would be most appropriate, but timescales have been shortening as businesses become more adept at managing change.

Strategic Analysis Tools

So, we have looked at the context for strategic planning for information systems, and we have a feeling for the process of analysis, especially in the sense of "*Where are we now?*" "*Where could we be?*" and "*How will we get there?*". The next question that arises is "*How shall we undertake the necessary strategic analysis, in terms of the specific tools and techniques that are available to us?*"

In the notes above, there has been more than a hint of value chain analysis, process analysis and portfolio management. In the notes that follow, a selection of strategic analysis tools is described and explained. Bear in mind that there is a much wider selection of tools than is possible to describe and illustrate here, but these are some that have been found useful and provide more than enough scope to get started. There is copious literature about the general use of strategic analysis tools such as these; our purpose here is to highlight the application of the tools in analysing *information systems* strategies.

Table 8.2 lists the tools and positions them according to where they contribute most to the cycle of analysis and according to the level of application:

- **Strategic drivers**: Here, we need tools to identify the strategic forces that are bearing upon our business.
- **Value analysis**: At the next level, we need to understand the way in which value is delivered in our industry, and in our business.
- **Business modelling**: As we move towards operational considerations, we must understand how the business works and, if at all possible, the extent and the quality of the information that it is working with.

Table 8.2 Strategic tools organised by sequence and level of application

Level	Where are we now?	Where could we be?	How will we get there?
Strategic drivers	SWOT (strengths, weaknesses, opportunities and threats); five forces		Critical success factors
Value analysis	External value chain	External and internal value chain	Internal value chain
Business modelling	Stakeholder analysis (five forces)	Process and information analysis	Programme and project management
Portfolio management	Applications portfolio		
Implementation			

- **Portfolio management**: This gives us a simple but very effective overview of the benefits that will be delivered to the business, with risks and timescales.
- **Implementation**: Finally, we need tools to assist in the planning of implementation.

Generally, we would expect to work from the left of this table to the right (across the columns), but in practice, strategic thinking tends to be somewhat sporadic and we must expect to move from one area of concern to another quite quickly, especially in conversation. Our level of concern (down the rows) will be determined by the role that we fulfil in the organisation as well as the stage that has been reached in the analysis.

SWOT (Strategic Drivers: Where Are We Now? Where Could We Be?)

The analysis of strengths, weaknesses, opportunities and threats is one of the most straightforward and most frequently deployed techniques for strategic analysis. It deals well with the internal issues (strengths and weaknesses) and the external issues (opportunities and threats). For our purposes, the latter (opportunities and threats) is probably the most useful to start with because understanding the external situation gives a context for internal assessment, although it is common to start with the former (strengths and weaknesses) as in the case of the example illustrated below, a SWOT analysis for a South African university. This is a somewhat reduced version of the original, which had more detail and some very specific comments about particular strengths and weaknesses, but it illustrates the sort of results that will come from a SWOT analysis.

Strengths and Weaknesses

The internal view of the business is concerned with what is being done well, and what is being done badly, also with strong capabilities and relevant resources, and those that are absent.

Perhaps the most obvious starting point is to consider the state of the establishment. How well trained are the people who are working for the organisation? Is the average age of employees so high that there will be a problem in maintaining numbers, or does this represent an opportunity to refresh the workforce with some new, young blood? Then, there is the question of the resources that people have to work with. Is the equipment up to date and appropriate, or is it deficient? Do people have the information that they need to do their work effectively, and is there a culture that would welcome change or resist it? Finally, what is the state of corporate policies, procedures and business systems? Are they aiding the organisation to move forwards, or are they a hindrance? Many of the organisations that invested heavily in information systems in the early days, the 1960s and 1970s, find that many of the systems of that time are still working, but nobody can maintain them easily and they are holding back progress (Table 8.3).

Table 8.3 Strategy analysis of a University

SWOT analysis for a University	
Organisational strengths	***Organisational weaknesses***
Pockets of excellence from which comes growth—especially in research	No mechanism to manage growth
Innovative courses that help to redefine our role in the marketplace	Poor library resources, especially in regard to electronic journals and bibliographic services
Potential for growth	Under-investment in research
Foreign liaisons with overseas institutions	Lack of funds for the academic use of information technology
Low-cost options relative to other institutions	Information systems and technologies weaknesses
Information systems and technologies strengths	Ineffective existing systems, especially budgeting and financial management systems
Campus networking king is good	
Potentially useful initiatives for e-learning	IT services are not defined and generally are not the subject of service level agreements
Home grown open source Web-supported learning environment	Systems are outdated, no mechanism to establish users' requirements and deliver solutions
	Few standards and inadequate policies and procedures
	No project management discipline and projects routinely fail to meet deadlines
Organisational opportunities	***Organisational threats***
Adopt a fresh approach to curriculum design, teaching, learning and research	Rise of the private higher education sector in South Africa
Embrace the enthusiasm and energy of students and use it to further the development and improvement of the institution	Emergence of technology-based education products and services Falling supply of suitable applicants and falling pass rates
Broaden the basis of competition (for the best students) on the basis of academic quality and value-added to students	Information systems and technology Further reductions in Government spending
Work academic partnerships more effectively, especially the international ones	Failure of the current school system to qualify candidates
Information systems and technologies opportunities	Information systems and technology threats
Improve organisational performance through the effective deployment of IT	Inadequate progress with technical infrastructure in comparison with other local tertiaries
Rebalance budget allocation to improve systems support for academic activities	Failure to meet the operational standards required by national government
Support and encourage use of in-house open-source learning management system	Failure to meet expected quality standards through a lack of a quality management system

Opportunities and Threats

Table 8.3 shows that there is a range of external factors that bear upon the university, it is not only a question of what can be seen within it. The external view of any business is concerned with competition and industry trends, and with new opportunities that are only just on the horizon but already waiting for a progressive organisation to seize them and make new ground.

There is a specific approach to external analysis that is both popular in its own right (it is not always associated with SWOT analysis) and easy to understand and adopt—it is known as the "five forces" analysis, and it was promoted in the 1980s by Michael Porter (at the same time as the Value Chain idea) as a means of competitive analysis (Porter 1985).

Porter's Five Forces

Michael Porter's approach to the appraisal of competitive forces in an industry is based on five perspectives: the customer, the supplier, the whole of the existing industry, and the possibility of new entrants or substitutes (Fig. 8.2).

New entrants are those businesses that have not previously been operating in the industry (or in the particular market segment in question) but choose to make an entry as direct competitors. An example is the case of retail petroleum sales in the United Kingdom, where the major retail groups all moved to start selling petroleum at their major stores, at a lower price than at the traditional petrol service stations.

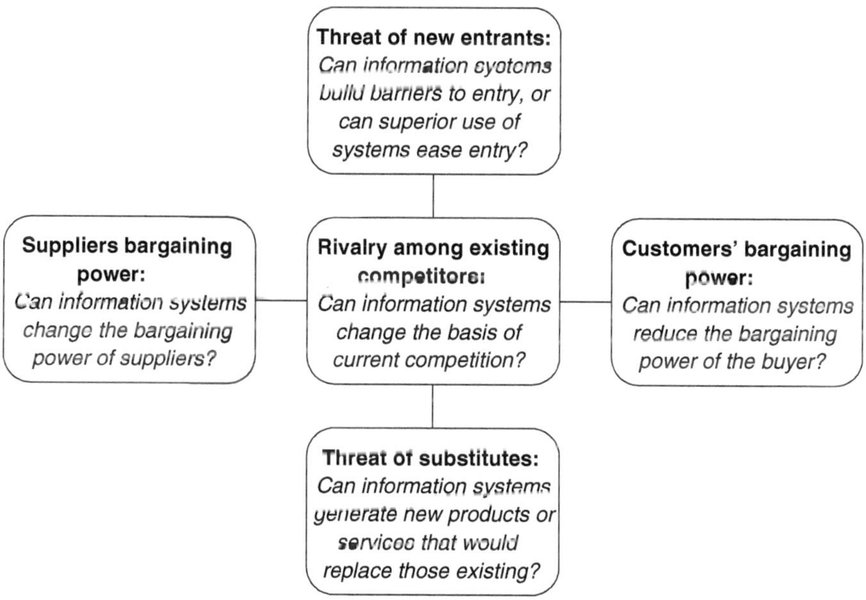

Fig. 8.2 Michael Porter's five forces

They did it very well: huge buying power, general retailing competencies and the combination of weekly grocery shopping with "filling the tank" made a lot of sense to the motorist and to the motorist's family.

Substitutes are different, where a completely different product or service is successful as a substitute for an existing one. An example here might be the widespread adoption of data projectors as a replacement for overhead projectors, already mentioned earlier. Let us summarise that story again: although the purchase price of a data projector is much higher, the cost of producing quality acetates over a long period of time, compared with the convenience of producing and showing educational material electronically, probably successfully made the argument to buy data projectors for most organisations that had some cash at hand to make the initial investment. Suddenly, we have the opportunity to manage teaching and learning material in a quite different way—it can be shared and maintained in a centralised library far more easily than ever before.

Obviously, information systems investments are only one of many ways of dealing with the issues that arise from this kind of competitive analysis. Having ranked competitive forces in terms of intensity of impact and immediacy of threat, the most critical can then be considered in terms of how new systems ideas (perhaps in conjunction with other developments) could be used to gain advantage or avoid disadvantage. As is made evident in the figure, this requires that the capabilities and plans of customers, suppliers and competitors are all known and that a watch is maintained on the horizon of competition and innovation.

The action required may involve two or more of the forces. For example, establishing barriers to entry might combine with increasing customer loyalty, increased switching costs and tying suppliers in more closely. This then makes entry more difficult. Note also that the relationship between a business and its suppliers and its customers is dealt with in detail through value chain analysis.

Threat of New Entrants

When new entrants threaten that additional capacity will be introduced into an industry, then the basis of competition may change and in the short term, at least, prices will be reduced. This can be counteracted in a number of ways by IS investments:

- Better control of distribution and supply channels to limit access.
- Segmenting the market to match the products of the business more accurately and providing a more complex target for the new entrants.
- Exploiting existing economies of scale more effectively to reduce costs in anticipation of a price war.
- Increasing the rate of new product innovation and development and/or differentiating existing products on quality or service.

In all these areas, information systems can help by providing better information, greater efficiency and an ability to react faster, for example by the use of computer-aided design in product design and automated production control methods in manufacturing. The cost of the investment in systems will increase the entry threshold, as has happened over recent years in grocery retailing, travel and financial services.

Threat of Substitute Products or Services

The substitute may be a direct replacement (such as the data projector for an overhead projector), or an indirect replacement in terms of customer preference (such as the choice of a holiday or a new hi-fi, in the personal context). In either case, the threat of substitution will take the market into decline and produce more intense price competition, especially where fixed costs are high. Again, information systems can be used in a number of ways to counteract the threat including the following:

- Redefining market segments and products to match changing preferences and retain profitable areas.
- Improving the rate of product innovation to recapture preferences.
- Enhancing the products with new services to increase their perceived value.
- Improving the price/performance of the existing product by cost reduction.
- Identifying other new customer needs that can be satisfied, thereby exploiting the existing customer base to develop new products.

Of course, it would always be better to stay one step ahead by using the information available to identify changes in customer needs, to be proactive in developing new products or services and to increase the breadth and depth of the product portfolio.

Rivalry Among Existing Competitors

Where rivalry among existing competitors is intense, generally in mature and declining markets, the consequences are likely to be fierce price competition, increasing buyer power, more rapid product enhancement, and distribution and customer service levels becoming critical. These produce an obvious conflict in terms of cutting costs and increasing service levels. Without effective information systems, costs can easily increase in such circumstances and service levels can decline—the wrong product available at the wrong time, at the wrong place and at the wrong price. Whatever system is used, it must be deployed in support of the chosen business strategy—low cost, differentiation or niche marketing—in order to enhance that strategy effectively. For example:

- Identifying how IS can be used to reduce real costs across the board, in relation to competitors, in all activities and relationships in the business.
- Identifying how IS can enhance the type of differentiation sought, whether that be image, product quality, services provided—as perceived by the customer and end consumer.

- Getting close to the end consumer as well as the immediate buyer is important in order to understand their requirements and increase their loyalty and/or fear of buying less good products elsewhere.

Many retailers in highly competitive markets, such as clothing and DIY, have realised that product range, quality and convenience no longer provide sufficient differentiation to induce customer loyalty. Hence, they have added further services to induce the customer to stay with them. Some of these, such as discount cards and personal financial services, are wholly dependent on the availability of information systems and information about the customers: where they live, who they are, what they buy and when.

Bargaining Power of Buyers and Suppliers

Information systems can be used to improve the balance of power with buyers and suppliers in favour of the business.

When a supplier is in a strong position due to its size, or the scarcity of what it provides, it can obviously increase prices, reduce the quality of what is supplied and make it less readily available. At best, this causes uncertainty, and at worst, it causes an inability to satisfy one's own customers profitably. Equally, when buyer power is high due to size, lack of differentiation in available products or over-supply, prices will be forced down at the same time that a higher quality of product and service is being demanded by customers.

One approach is to make it easier for the buyer, by reducing the cost of buying rather than the price of the product—thereby generating mutual benefit. Value chain analysis is used to explore these ideas more thoroughly and is described later in this chapter. Equally, there is merit in making it easier for one's own suppliers; the idea that one can gain from being a good customer is not familiar to all businesses, but when supply-side partnerships deliver advantage to both parties, information systems and information management will be part of the story.

Critical Success Factor Analysis

Critical success factors (CSFs) are those things that *must* go right if strategic objectives are to be achieved. As we move towards completion of a high-level strategic analysis, we will have a view as to where we are and where we want to be, and therefore, the question of what is critical to its achievement should come easily.

Supposing that we have decided to differentiate competitively through a high level of customer intimacy: it will be critical to success that we have an effective customer information management system with appropriate database capability and operational procedures. These requirements can be embodied in critical success factors:

- Customer information must be acquired and managed.
- Supporting customer databases and systems functionality must be in place.

And so on, there may be other critical success factors that derive from other requirements. The important thing to realise (and one of the original considerations that led to the development of critical success factor management techniques) is that these requirements are generally seen to stand above financial arguments. If improved customer relationship management is what we have decided to do, then *it shall be done*, and requisite supporting actions must be taken. There is no attempt to make a financial case. The strategic investment is justified through simple logic, not by arguing that within seven years, at a fixed rate of return, there will be a net positive financial outcome. Organisations that insist on a financial case for investment will always lag behind organisations that have found a way to make strategic investments independently of financial returns, and the use of critical success factors is one way to achieve this.

An Example

From each of the general strategic objectives that are agreed, specific critical success factors can be developed. For example, in the case of a petroleum company that wishes to be a leading retailer of petroleum products and aims to share the rewards with shareholders, employees and customers, it might have objectives such as:

- to achieve 2 % improvement in market share;
- to extend outlet coverage in defined geographical areas;
- to increase sales of non-oil products in existing outlets; and
- to reduce costs of distribution by 5 %.

Following through the example, critical success factors for the first objective (2 % improvement in market share) might be the following:

- effective regional and local pricing;
- increase consumers' brand awareness and loyalty;
- improve non-oil product range to attract customers;
- review all sites in terms of performance and productivity; and
- ensure lead-free petrol demand is matched by supplies at outlets.

Critical success factors must be derived from the agreed objectives, and then they must be used to identify the key actions required and to set targets. There should not be too many for each objective; otherwise, the objective is effectively unachievable (five to eight critical success factors per objective would be typical). Note also that critical success factors can recur across objectives, thus giving them a heavier weighting and requiring that critical success factors across all objectives be consolidated.

Implications for Information Systems

Having established critical success factors, there are consequences for information systems.

First, all critical success factors will require measures to be implemented within the management information system, to monitor their achievement. If something is critical to success, then management will require feedback on progress towards its successful achievement. This requires management information systems.

Second, critical success factors may also require systems enhancements or completely new systems. For instance, given the seventh critical success factor in the illustrative list above (improve non-oil product range to attract customers), it is necessary that sales of non-oil products be recorded and analysed in a consistent way. A new system will be needed to achieve this.

Once defined, critical success factors may also be mapped to the activities in the business. Hence, in conjunction with other techniques, critical success factor analysis can help to focus attention on the information systems contribution. A high-cost activity in the internal value chain that adds considerable value *and* addresses many critical success factors is more critical than a low-cost, low-value-added, "critical-success-factor-free" activities. It therefore qualifies for higher priority information systems investment.

Other Notes on Critical Success Factors

Note that in large organisations, there can be a cascading relationship between objectives and CSFs. Corporate objectives will have certain related CSFs, which may in turn be the source of some business unit objectives, which produce CSFs, which drive functional and departmental objectives. Ultimately, operational objectives at all levels determine critical (career) success factors for employees.

As the business objectives change over time, so will the critical success factors and hence information systems needs and priorities. The analysis can be revisited regularly, and existing priorities can be reconsidered if any of the critical success factors change for any reason. This provides a useful way of stimulating the evolution of information systems strategy from a business perspective and makes systems-related decisions more reliable.

Value Chain Analysis

Value chain analysis helps to analyse the role of information in a business and in the industry within which it works. It can reveal important aspects of relationships between organisations and within the business itself, identifying information that is needed, where it might come from, and also how information systems might affect the competitive positioning of one organisation or another. It helps to establish a position relative to customers, suppliers and competitors and how that position can be enhanced and sustained within the industry structure.

In its earliest form, value chain analysis was intended to help define business strategies in terms of how a business adds value and how it incurs cost. It was seen at first as applicable to just one organisation but later the idea of *industry* value chain analysis emerged. The organisations involved in an industry value chain each consume different resources to produce value; however, this value is only realised when the evolving product or service is acquired by the organisation at the next stage in the chain. The difference between realised values and actual costs is the margin of profit.

Internal Value Chain

The internal value chain shows how the various activities and functions in a business unit contribute to the customer's requirements, and how costs are incurred in so doing. Understanding what is done, how it is done and how business activities are related all leads to a better understanding of information and systems needs and opportunities. The value chain helps to get beyond the detail of current arrangements in order to see the bigger picture in relation to the whole business and the way that customers see it. The original value chain model was based primarily on manufacturing business, but its structure can be applied to most other types of business with a degree of adaptation. The model identifies two different types of business activity—primary and secondary (or support)—and provides a framework for organising the detail within them.

Primary activities: In the lower half of the figures (Fig. 8.3), the primary activities fulfil the *value-adding* role of a business. These primary activities must each be optimised individually, and the whole linked together if the best overall business performance is to be achieved. They occur in five groups, generally considered in a sequence from the supply side (at the left) to the customer side (at the right):

Inbound logistics: Obtaining, receiving, storing and provisioning key inputs and resources required by the central operations of the business. This can include recruiting staff, buying materials and services, and dealing with subcontractors.

Operations: Transforming inputs of all types into the products or services to meet customer requirements. This involves bringing together the requisite materials, resources and assets to produce the right quantity and quality of products or

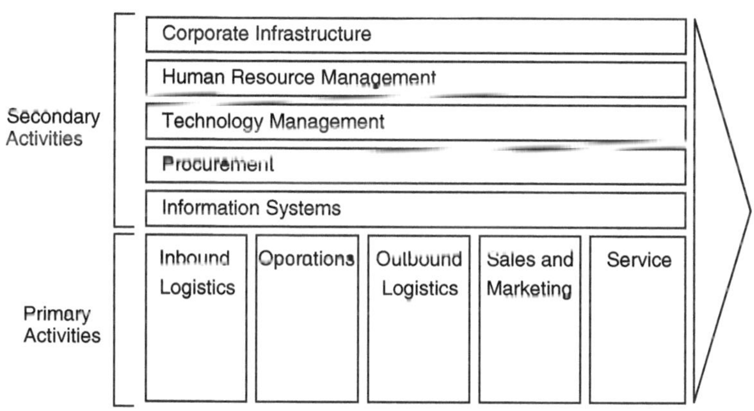

Fig. 8.3 The simple, original form of the value chain

services—for instance in a university, delivering the courses in the prospectus and examining the students.

Outbound logistics: Distributing the products or services to the place of sale, or to customers directly, using channels of distribution by which the customer can obtain the product or service and pay for it.

Sales and marketing: Making customers and consumers aware of the product or service and how they can obtain it; promoting the products in a way that persuades the customer that it satisfies a need at an appropriate price.

Services: Adding additional value for the customer at the time of sale or afterwards, for example, by means of financial services, user training and warranty claims processing.

Secondary activities: These are those required to control and develop the business over time, and to facilitate the working of the primary activities. They do not add value directly but only through the enabling of primary activities. Examples are accounting, personnel, information systems, research and development, property management and legal services.

Use of the Internal Value Chain

In the simple case, a business does not always have much choice over what its actual primary activities are, since they are heavily influenced by the nature of the products, customers and suppliers in its industry. What is critical is how well it carries out each activity and how it links the activities together, so as to maximise the margin between value-added and costs incurred. Information intensive activities such as forecasting, capacity planning, scheduling, pricing and costing must be linked throughout the chain if each stage in the internal value is to make the best contribution to the overall result and must be served by effective information systems.

On the other hand, a business *does* have control over how it carries out its support activities. They can be shared centralised services used by all business units or delegated activities within each of the units. It is a matter of choice, bearing in mind the need for managerial consistency across the units, and the particular business situation and unique aspects of each unit. Either way, the support activities have two main contributions to make the following:

- To enable the primary activities to be carried out at optimum performance levels, for example by providing required services or by the development of new products, technologies or resources to meet current and future business needs.
- To enable the business to be controlled and developed successfully over time, principally through support for the management and through improved methods of planning and control.

Support activities that are not well managed themselves can actually disrupt the smooth running of the business by spreading their tentacles of control throughout the primary activities—marketing people have been heard referring to the “sales prevention system", and no doubt in other business areas similar remarks might be heard. Good information systems to serve the value-adding and supporting activities of a business are what this is all about—not localised systems that serve the needs of a single department or division. The value chain helps us to see the big picture.

As noted above, Porter conceived the value chain in the context of manufacturing industry. It is surprising that the literature has tended to ignore its adaptation and application to other industries. In the service industries, the key value-adding operations may be less obvious, but it is therefore even more important to reveal them. In a home loans operation, for instance, customer savings and mortgage lending can be seen as different businesses that relate to each other only through the use of available funds. On the other hand, savings can be seen as inbound logistics (getting the money in) and mortgages as outbound (putting the money to work), while funds management constitutes the central core activity. In a more modern, progressive, financial services operation where the service is total asset management, the inbound logistic becomes something else altogether: information about the client and the profile of investment needs that the client desires; the outbound logistic is a personalised portfolio of investments that will deliver the right balance of income and capital growth, and the right balance between risk and return.

It is important to understand the cost drivers in a business and why and how they are managed. The value chain model offers a useful way of identifying these drivers and allocating all the real costs in order to identify where savings can be made, and where performance needs to be improved. Continuing investment in one area (e.g., manufacturing productivity) is pointless unless other areas are improved (such as sales forecasting and inventory management). All costs derive from activity of some kind and every activity should be adding value, either directly or indirectly; if it is not, then it should be eliminated, not computerised.

From an information systems perspective, the internal value chain is a valuable way of identifying where better information and systems are needed, especially to show where integration through linked systems could provide potential advantage over competitors (or reduce current disadvantages). A logical approach to identifying how IS can improve the business is as follows:

- Improving relationships with customers and suppliers in all aspects of their interface with the organisation (e.g., through better integration of customer information).
- Improving the critical information flows through the primary activities, removing bottlenecks and delays, and ensuring the accuracy and consistency of information used (e.g., total stock management, customer service monitoring).
- Improving the systems within each primary activity to achieve local improvements in efficiency (e.g., warehouse control, fleet management).
- Improving the way support systems can best assist the primary activities, as well as meeting central requirements (e.g., budgetary control, personnel data).
- Improving efficiency within the support activities by means of localised systems investments (e.g., financial consolidation, asset management).

This may sound perfectly logical because it is driven from the outside of the business and it deals with the *critical* parts of the business before the *non-critical*, but it is almost completely the reverse of the approach that has been taken over the last thirty years. The result is that small armies of people (often 10–20 % of all the "white collar" people employed) sit at the boundaries between business activities and systems operations, reconciling information and analysing the differences between the two. This is not conducive to improved business performance; there is scope in most organisations to radically improve these interfaces by using more appropriate information flows and by redefining the ownership and use of information. This will not only save money, but also it will improve the ability to add value.

Using value chain analysis will assist management to ask searching questions about the strengths and weaknesses of existing systems. It will identify key areas for future investment, especially by the integration of organisational activity. Key aspects of the method of analysis are as follows:

- It reinforces the business unit approach to assessing business requirements and therefore makes better links to business strategy.
- It is independent of the current organisation structure and clearly separates primary and support activities in terms of criticality of systems needs.
- It concentrates on why the business is there—to add value to satisfy the customer—and this enables more focused questions to be asked about the activities and systems, such as how can it be done better, or cheaper, or both? Do we need to do it at all?

By considering the way information flows through and is used by the business, and having regard to the external industry value chain, an organisation can identify those parts of the business and its external relationships that can be improved by better information systems.

This is a high level of analysis that helps to avoid irrelevant details and maintains a view of the wider picture. Without this "big picture", we can be certain that lower level analysis in confined areas of the business will only provide partial solutions, suboptimisation and an ineffective use of analysis time. With the "big picture" to hand, however, we can direct detailed analysis more effectively and maintain the coherency and completeness of our business models at all levels.

An Example

The adaptation of the generic value chain to show the specific detail of a typical DIY retailing organisation is shown in Fig. 8.4.

Figure 8.4 shows how the generic groups can be reinterpreted and redefined to provide a specific model of a non-manufacturing business.

Deciding whether to view the primary parts of a business separately or together can be assisted by value chain analysis, but it will not "automatically" produce a

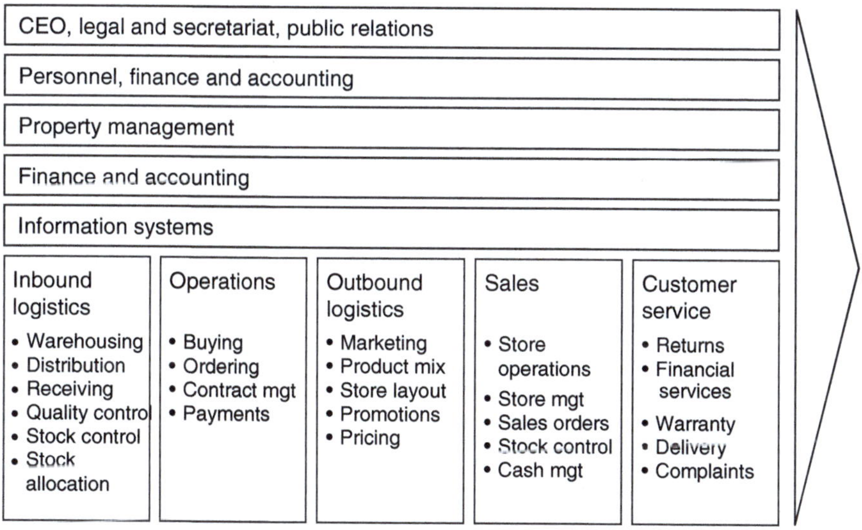

Fig. 8.4 The value chain interpreted for a DIY retailing business

result. The value chain is just a vehicle for exploring options and understanding consequences: it helps to shape a discussion rather than prescribe a solution.

Industry Value Chains

For every industry, there is a value chain that shows how an end product (or service) required at the consumer level is developed from raw inputs. The chain is a series of industrial stages, such as raw material extraction, processing, manufacturing, distribution and retailing. Each stage adds value but incurs cost, and the *difference* between value and cost is the focus of our attention in the simple case. Wherever there is a stage or an activity where cost exceeds value added, management needs to ask whether costs could be reduced or whether a third party with a lower cost base needs to be brought in because they have economies of scale or scarce skills that are not locally available. Transportation is a good example. At one time, many businesses maintained their own fleets of trucks but had to suffer low levels of utilisation and high fixed costs. Over recent years, there has been a general move to employ the services of external trucking businesses where loads are managed more effectively because of the dispersed, high levels of demand that arise from a combination of trucking requirements. Some of those trucking businesses have even been persuaded to have their vehicles carry the livery of a manufacturing company, irrespective of what was being carried in the trucks.

Supply Chain as an Example

See Fig. 8.5. This is a simple representation of a three-stage industry value chain where a major chemicals company provides the key requirements for the manufacture of household cleaning products; in its turn, the manufacturer supplies a

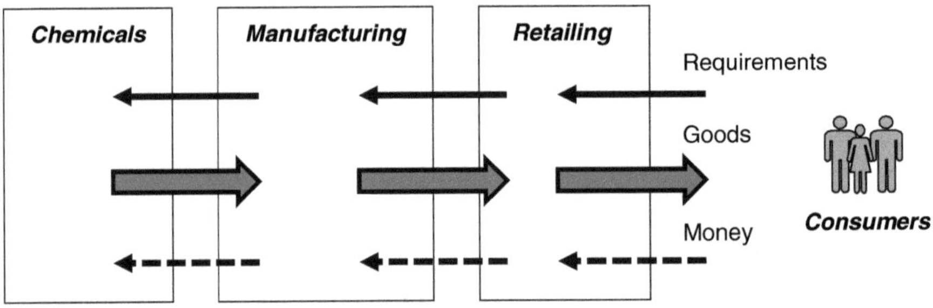

Fig. 8.5 A simple representation of a supply chain

retailer who supplies the general public. As we shall see, this is a dramatically simplified view of something that is actually much more complicated, but we can use this figure to make a simple point. Demand is generated at the consumer level and is communicated down the supply chain (from the right to the left) in different ways—the retailer will issue replenishment orders and the manufacturer will issue raw material orders; stock will move in the opposite direction (from left to right) to fulfil demand.

Finally, (and this is a feature of supply chain management that is often ignored) payment must be made for goods and services rendered, so that money flows back down the supply chain (from right to left) to reward all those involved in the delivery of value, of any kind. In this way, every supply chain involves the movement of information, goods (or services) and money. It is the balance between these three, as seen at each interface, which must be understood and managed well.

Supply and demand must be matched at each stage of a value chain in order to provide the required product or service at an appropriate cost. Within any industry, there is a finite demand in terms of how much of the product is required and how much will be paid for it, and also at any time, there is a finite supply of materials and resources to produce the product or service. Organisations compete not only with companies doing much the same thing but also with others along the chain for a share of the revenue and overall profit available within the industry. That overall profit can be increased if demand and supply can be matched more accurately throughout the chain. Any business that operates at some distance from the final consumer demand, or from the supply of key resources, has to deal with considerable uncertainties and will find it difficult to optimise its performance. If relative to its competitors, it can capture better information about supply and demand, and it can optimise its performance more effectively than its competitors, who will face greater uncertainties.

This industry-level view of information highlights the key flows of information that the business needs to intercept and influence. It provides a basis from which internal information systems needs can be assessed and defined in more detail, but complexity can be a major issue. Many industry value chains are very complex and involve manufacturers, distributors, service providers, sources of skilled staff and capital as well as resources such as equipment and buildings. It is not necessary that

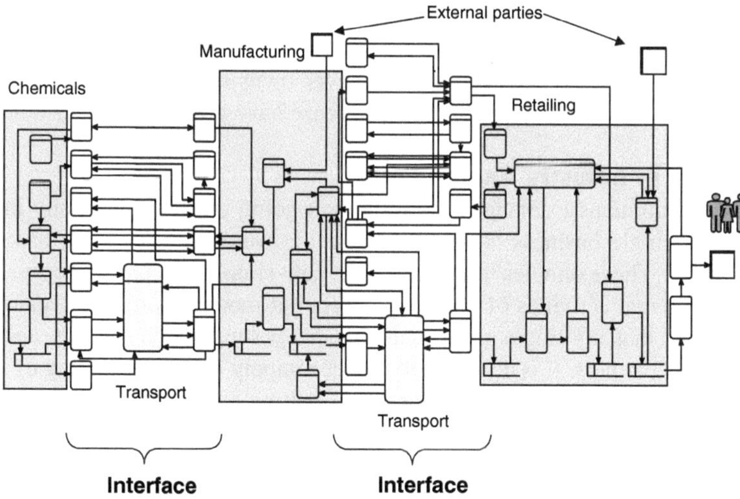

Fig. 8.6 Information in the supply chain—form and just a hint of function

a detailed model of all elements is produced but an appropriate level of working must be found. At the industry level, the activities that actually link one business to another must be identified but the internal activities might be ignored.

See the more detailed model of the supply of household cleaner shown here. No attempt is made here to identify every one of the activities and information flows involved, but it gives a visual impression of the two key interfaces and the complexities involved (Fig. 8.6).

What was learnt from the full analysis of this case study was as follows.

- For each movement of goods, there are about eleven movements of information, each movement costing real money.
- There are seven points at which the raw materials or the goods come to rest, awaiting a management decision or other action.
- The cost of administering the two interfaces was of the same order of magnitude as the profit margin available to be shared between the three players.
- A 25 % reduction in costs was immediately available by simplification of information handling procedures between the three players and the introduction of appropriate information systems (principally in this case for electronic data interchange—essentially doing business the same way but more efficiently: eliminating errors, queries and other exceptional activities).
- A further reduction in costs of 20 % was available through redesign of the interfaces (changing business practices to incorporate automatic replenishment, automatic payments and so on)

A major reconstruction of the supply chain in accordance with progressive thinking at the time brought administration costs to under half of the existing level and allowed much more effective stock management and faster stock turn. This third stage of improvement was based on the manufacturer retaining ownership of the stock right through to the point of sale. The retailer never owns the stock, and many of the business activities and costs that would otherwise have prevailed simply fell away.

Complexity in Industry Value Chains

There is a continuous exchange of information going on throughout any industry chain, but a single business is only a part of the whole and therefore has only a limited view. The examples presented here are simplified, partly because they ignore the internal activities of industry players but more importantly because they ignore the fact that any single player will have *many* supply-side partners, and *many* customer-side partners. It is common to depict a supply chain as a "string of beads" suggesting singularity all along the line, and omitting altogether the critical flow of information and money that must accompany the movement of goods. Supply chains are complex, and over-simplification is a dangerous practice.

A large corporation may own businesses in more than one part of the chain—clearly such an organisation has major opportunities to gain advantages over more focused rivals by sharing information or by developing effective intercompany trading systems. However, in large corporations that are managed on profit-centre lines, the links between divisions within a single firm are often considered to be external and this makes it harder to implement integrated systems. In other cases, unitary companies work strenuously to develop close partnerships with their partners because they know that there are significant mutual advantages to be gained by firms linking their information and systems throughout the chain, irrespective of ownership.

Potential Benefits of Management of the Value Chain

A number of long-term benefits arise from careful attention to the management of the value chain. Given that at any time the industry can generate a certain amount of net profit, that profit can be shared advantageously among the various organisations in the chain. The advantage will most likely accrue to the organisation that pays most careful attention to the way that the industry value chain works. Where demand and supply can be matched more accurately through appropriate information exchange or sharing, interorganisational systems have a special contribution to make to overall efficiency and effectiveness, and the potential for profit sharing increases proportionately.

Clearly, there are different kinds of relationship that might prevail, from raw adversarialism (where industry players fight only for self-interest) through to heavyweight risk- and profit sharing, where two or more players work together very closely to understand and optimise a more holistic view of the value chain. In between, the cooperation of suppliers or customers to provide information in exchange for some benefits allows different levels of partnership, possibly including transportation service providers and banks (where they are substantially involved, and where potential efficiencies are evident).

Where rival firms are competing for the same suppliers, customers and industry resources, their position will be weaker. Suppliers prefer to sell through a partnership where there is some assurance of continuity of demand and more profit, even if discounts have been negotiated. Prices in rival firms will have to increase or service levels will reduce if they are to achieve the new level of profit available to a closely negotiated partnership. Equally, customers will prefer to buy from a negotiated partnership because of the lower overall cost of purchasing and will begin to demand lower priced products and better service levels from those rival companies that they still trade with.

In the best case, the net result is that rivals face increased costs, poorer supply-side service levels and lower sales revenue, at the same time that their customers demand higher service levels. This leads to a long-term, sustained disadvantage for those outside partnership arrangements.

Gaining the Benefits of Information Systems in the Value Chain

Consider the following further examples of industry level cooperation that delivered real benefits:

- DIY retailers have adopted joint stock planning and optimised delivery logistics with their suppliers. Suppliers who cannot or will not cooperate have to find other outlets for their products.
- A major oil company operates a joint stock management system with its main steel supplier at its North Sea depots. The stock belongs to the supplier, but is used as and when required by the oil company and paid for as used—forecasts of demand enable the steel company to maintain appropriate stock levels at the depots.
- Retailers have installed point-of-sale systems that monitor exactly what is bought and when, enabling them to hold the ideal range and quantities, and demand just-in-time replenishment by suppliers. Some of the information is of course extremely valuable for market forecasting purposes and can be sold to intermediaries who specialise in forecasting services.
- Where at one time, a disappointed customer would simply walk out of a shop frustrated, (leaving behind a frustrated sales assistant) online cataloguing systems let retailers find out directly about customer requirements. Web-based sales systems can monitor demand independently of actual stock availability and identify the unfulfilled demand (or "lost sales") that they need to know about as market trends shift.
- A kitchen manufacturer built excellent internal systems that enabled it to outperform its rivals in terms of internal efficiency. However, consumers had to deal with retailers who worked through distributors, that in turn bought from the manufacturer and the advantages of internal efficiency did not materialise until retailers could place orders direct with the factory using additional systems facilities.

- A European timber importer found that the number of housing starts in the United States (mainly timber-framed houses) determined demand (and therefore prices) for Canadian timber. A model was built which monitored the number of housing starts in the United States and successfully forecast likely timber prices several months ahead, giving the importer a distinct advantage when negotiating supplies.
- A lighting company provides architects an information system to help design lighting systems. Architects do not buy the lighting systems of course, but influence contractors who buy from wholesalers, who in turn buy from the manufacturer. By providing the new system, the lighting company can ensure that its latest products are specified and thereby tightens up the whole chain in its favour.

The benefits of information systems investments can be seen clearly in the context of the industry value chain by consideration of any one interface between two of the main players in the chain. The basic relationship is that of buyer and seller: placing orders, taking delivery, checking details, raising and dealing with queries, and financial settlement. Some information exchange is clearly essential, but there is in practice a great deal of ineffective information exchange. Where inaccuracy creeps in, or where information is not available when it is needed, decisions may have to be made that are inappropriate. When goods are ordered that are not actually available, or when goods are delivered that were not actually ordered, the cost of correction can be many times the cost of doing business competently and accurately.

Costs can be reduced by doing business effectively (doing the right thing) and by doing business efficiently (doing things right). The trend towards information systems with broader scope and more significant benefits, through industry level cooperation and information sharing, has led to dramatically reduced operating costs and much wider choice (at the end of the day) for consumers. Consider that twenty years ago, consumers would typically have called in at five or six shops each of which might offer some hundreds of stock items, now they can call at one large-scale supermarket that offers in excess of 30,000 stock items, or log onto the Web and see millions from around the world. This huge choice would simply not be possible without shared systems, electronic data interchange technologies and supply chain optimisation on a wide scale. In this way, significant costs can be taken out of the industry value chain and each partner is able to perform more effectively than previously. The benefits are mutual, in the most literal sense of the word.

Application to Non-profit Organisations

In non-profit making organisations such as public bodies and NGOs, the direct relationship between revenue and cost may not be evident. Income is probably indirect, through donations or taxation. However, there is still a value chain and the organisation's costs must be contained within the funds available. It may not compete for customers, but it does compete for available resources, and the way in which information systems can assist through the improvement of value delivered is just as applicable.

Business Modelling

In general, strategic analysis tools such as the value chain and critical success factors produce a high-level picture of key strategic aspects of the business. Before the need for information systems, investment can be fully resolved a more detailed analysis of *business processes* and *business information* is needed—hence, techniques for business modelling fall into two main categories: process analysis and information analysis. This will identify where information originates (whether inside or outside the business) and help to determine who should be responsible for its management and use. A sample of both is given here, based upon a retailing business. Process modelling is generally more easily understood and will be illustrated first.

Process Analysis

It is possible to start with the value chain, which as a business model in its own right is probably the most useful starting point because it identifies the very high-level processes that constitute all of a business—input, process, output, sales and service (and supporting secondary activities). External data requirements and relationships with suppliers and customers can be addressed first, followed by analysis of the linkages within the primary value chain and its primary and secondary activities. Using the value chain, the information requirements of each of the main business activities can be analysed within the overall context: primary activities with a view to improving value creation and secondary activities with a view to cost reduction and enabling.

Figure 8.8 shows a high-level view of the activities in a retailing business in the form of a value chain, but this time with clearly identified movements of information and goods between the main activities, and at a finer level of detail than is found in the original value chain. Note that in terms of stakeholder-based process analysis described elsewhere, the model here represents the process that serves the needs and expectations of the *customer*—that is what the value chain is intended to do. Other process models might show the activities directed at employees, shareholders and stakeholders other than the customer.

In Fig. 8.7, the thicker lines indicate the movement of goods, and the thinner lines indicate the movement of information. Inspection of this detail helps us to see (in this example) such things as follows:

- The different ways in which we deal with direct store deliveries and deliveries to RDCs (warehouses, often referred to as "regional distribution centres").
- The specific movements of information between primary and supporting activities.
- The different points at which inventory is held: the warehouse and the sales area of the store itself.
- The places where we hold key information, such as contracts with suppliers.
- The lack of any significant activity after the customer sale has taken place.

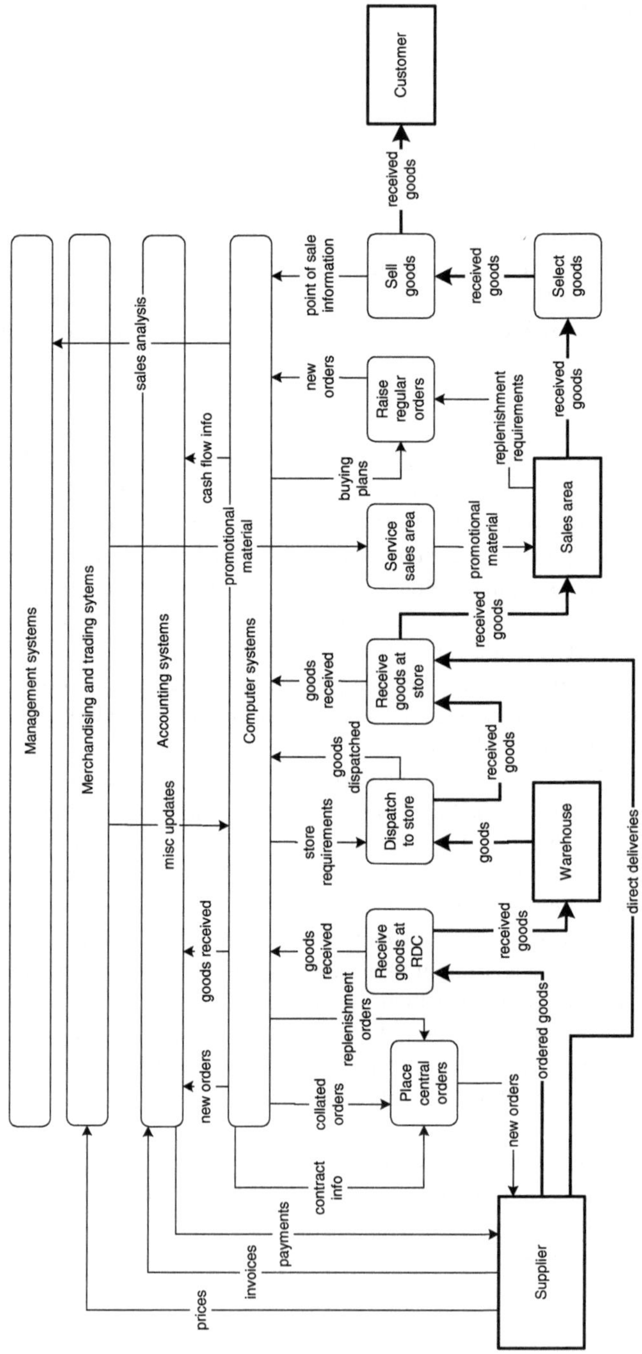

Fig. 8.7 A model for a retail business, in the form of a value chain

It is impossible to show all the detail at this high level but it *is* possible to agree an overall framework within which more detailed models will be used. The consistency between this high-level viewpoint (appropriate to the needs of management) and more detailed models (appropriate to the needs of systems development projects) can always be checked by mapping the one to the other. In this way, the parts of the overall business activity that are to be automated can be clearly positioned and the boundary between systems and clerical activities can be incorporated into the high- and low-level models.

Information Analysis

We have already looked at an "information" equivalent of the value chain that lays out a generic arrangement of information such as will typically be found in a business (See Fig. 6.6: A generic information model for business). Figure 8.8 shows a high-level entity model for the same retailing business for which we saw a process model, laid out in the form of the generic information model. It illustrates the way in which the results of this kind of analysis can be presented.

An information model (based on entities, as this one is) shows the key things about which we choose to keep information, and the relationships between them. For example, Fig. 8.8 shows that there is something known as a "responsible

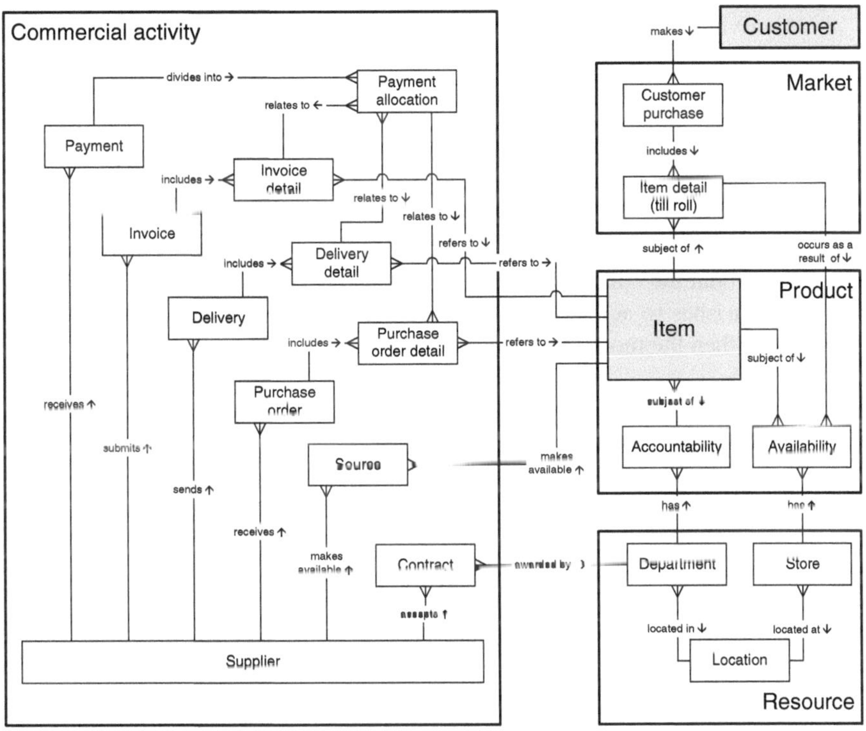

Fig. 8.8 A sample retailing information model (before loyalty cards)

department" which is accountable for every "item" that is sold, through something called "accountability". This tells us that if we have free access to the information used in the business, we could call up (on our computer screen) a list of all "items" that are sold; we could then pick one and ask for its "accountability" which would be a reference to the "department" or perhaps the individuals who are responsible; we could then ask for the details of that "department" including its "location" and what "contracts" it has awarded for other "items".

In this way, the entity model can be seen as a "navigation" map that tells the reader how it is possible to move from consideration of one aspect of the business to another. However, when fully developed such a model leads to database designs that ensure that the business will have the detailed data that are needed and the means to look at it in different ways. The example given leads to a number of observations about the retailing business, having in mind the six different areas mentioned earlier and the need for data in the business. It is followed by some comments that reveal the paucity of information in this business:

- There is little evidence of management information here, and therefore, it is unlikely that information systems based on this model would provide management with what they need.
- There is a good deal of information about supply activities: letting contracts of supply, placing orders, taking delivery, issuing invoices and receiving payments; these activities are all to do with support, and there is no evidence of information about customer-side activities.
- Despite this focus on the supply side, there is no explicit evidence about supplier performance (although it might be "contained within" the supplier entity or derived from operational data about orders and deliveries as and when it is needed). We could choose to extend the model to achieve this.
- There is information about retail stores and their location, but nothing about employees and the skills and capabilities that they have. In a business that does not care about the contribution that employees make this is appropriate, but if a business wishes to actively manage employees and use information systems in so doing, then the model needs to be extended to include employees and related entities.
- Most interestingly, the customer is not actually within the scope of the model. This business has no explicit information about customers. It is only be possible to "see" them through the individual purchases made within the information on the till roll, which does not identify the customer (other than by means of a credit card number, perhaps?).
- The reader may be aware that many retailers have addressed the problem of customer information by providing machine-readable cards that are used to identify customers effortlessly at the time of purchase—loyalty cards. These cards can also enable customer account facilities by allowing purchases to be charged upon presentation of the card.

One benefit of information analysis is to find unrealised potential in existing systems and data, in the context of the future business needs. Weaknesses are to be expected but strengths are also sometimes revealed. In one organisation, a system deemed to be virtually useless was realised to have new potential uses. The problem was that over time, the knowledge of what the system did had decayed, and only one person was still using all of its features. By this person retraining the others, and developing better user documentation, a major redevelopment was avoided and benefits were achieved very quickly.

A Glimpse into the Future

Having said all of the above (about conventional modelling and the organisation of data), we are all aware of the extraordinary strength of Web information retrieval systems such as Google. I was able recently to discuss the ways in which Google works, with someone who knows. I have always had images of the most refined entity models, endless tables associating everything with everything else and exquisitely engineered databases. But this is not the case. The method that is used to manage these huge tracts of data is not a relational database system, it is built on the "map-reduce" system (Google measures data in *petabytes*, where a petabyte is 1,000,000,000,000,000 bytes, or one "quadrillion" bytes—as long ago as 2009, it was reported that Google was processing about 24 PB of data per day). Despite the huge numbers involved, when the explanations were complete and my head was spinning wildly, I decided that the map-reduce method is somewhat akin to "shoe box accounting", where everything is thrown into one place and then recovered according to heuristic patterns ("No, Susan, it's the broken box file with the purple label on the back saying 'old invoices'—yes, I know it is actually the customer complaints file, but I know where it is so why can't you find it?"). Something like that, anyway. Oh, and yes, you might have guessed, there are currently heated arguments among experts as to which is actually the best way to manage huge volumes of data. Here, we will dig no further! The interested reader will no doubt go and google about this. One of the best and simplest explanations available (at the time of writing) was actually a Google research paper.

Summary of Business Modelling

- Information analysis can establish the "information boundaries" of the business and show how they can be extended, so as to extend the influence of the business with its partners
- Conceptual models such as the value chain can be augmented with the key processes and information movements, so as to begin understanding the operational aspects of new business ideas.
- Entity modelling can be used to avoid the common fixation on business processes and to seek out new ideas for business development that are not constrained by process thinking.
- When the formal information systems development process begins, outline process and entity models are used as the basis for much more detailed business modelling with operational management and staff.

- From this level, more specific models are developed to specify the detail of business activities and the means to automate them, and the detail of data models that specify the content of databases.
- The future may well be different, and map-reduce methods originating in the theories and practice of "functional programming" may comprise the new way of dealing with vast volumes of data.

A danger with business modelling is the large volume of information associated with the models when the *full detail* is addressed. It is important that the modelling is undertaken progressively from *the top down*; otherwise, the key requirements will be lost in a mass of impossible detail.

High-level models such as we have looked at may have a long life but detailed models need to be maintained regularly. Entity models should be particularly enduring, and in times of operational change, they can offer a stable foundation for employees to hang on to. This idea comes through in different ways, and not always in an information technology context. At a time of radical change in a construction company, the deputy managing director issued a memorandum which basically said: "This is going to be a very difficult time, but don't ever forget that this business is still about contracts, projects, plant, subcontractors ....", and so on. A clear statement of the *key entities* in the business, if ever there was one.

The final comment on information analysis has to be about documentation. In the final analysis, successful information systems will always depend on our ability to do information analysis and to document our ideas without ambiguity and equivocation. Poor documentation of systems has led to enormous and unnecessary costs over the last thirty years. Worse, poor structuring and poor documentation of the business's information resource not only produces high costs but also leads to lost future opportunities. The lack of reliable documentation is said to be one of the disadvantages of the agile methods, but on the other hand, the development and maintenance of documentation is an unwelcome burden for the technical staff. Systems development environments that include documentation by automatic means are worth serious consideration.

Boston Box

One of the favourite tools of people in marketing management is the "Boston box". This is another of those 2x2 matrices that allows us to explore the differences between current and future potential. The idea of the Boston box itself originates from the realm of marketing, where for many years there have been models that highlight the differences between products at the early, middle and late stages of their effective lives. It originated in the Boston Consulting Group, hence the name by which it is known. It is the foundation for the ideas behind the applications portfolio, and it is worth looking at the basics of the idea again.

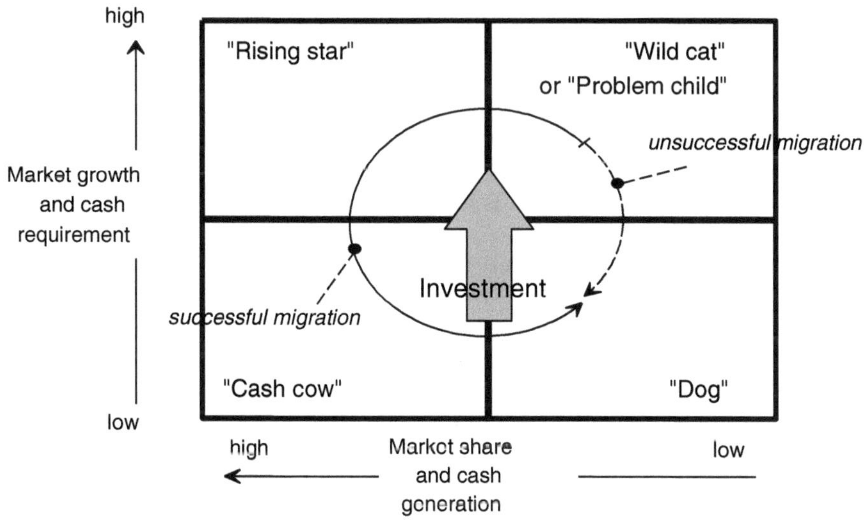

Fig. 8.9 The Boston box

Consider the differences between blackboards and whiteboards. At the time that whiteboards were introduced, just imagine the disbelief that would have accompanied the early estimates of the cost of whiteboard pens, compared with chalk. "*It will never catch on*" people would have said—but look at the situation now. Consider the even greater differences between overhead projectors (average cost, $100?) and data projectors (in the region of $1,000, for the very cheapest?). Who would have imagined, when the cost was not ten but nearer *one hundred* times greater, that data projectors would ever be so commonplace?

What we learn is that there is a life cycle of product evolution that often starts with high costs and disbelief about practicalities, but migrates to market dominance and huge rewards for the manufacturer and patent holder. Ultimately, products that were once innovative become obsolete but might still have to be maintained (while one customer, somewhere, is still using one).

The world of marketing deals with this using the "Boston box"[2] (See Fig. 8.9). The four quadrants are based on two criteria:

- What is the growth potential and potential cash requirement to market the product?
- What is the current market share and how much cash is the product generating?

[2] Reference can be made to the marketing literature for more information about the way that the Boston box is used—it goes a long way further than this.

The four quadrants are then named with terms that have become established in the commonly used business vocabulary:

- The **wild cat** is a product that is new, untried, but full of future potential.
- The **rising star** is a product that has been launched, which is winning market share successfully, but still requires investment to sustain the momentum.
- The **cash cow** is a product that is working well in an established market and is generating cash well.
- The **dog** is a product past its best that might most usefully be retired.

Note the two migration paths in Fig. 8.9 (the thin circular arrows). Generally, products are conceived and introduced in the "wild cat" quadrant. If successful, then they migrate around in an anticlockwise manner until they are retired as dogs. If they do not succeed, there is a very real risk that they default to "dog" status in short order, as shown by the clockwise "unsuccessful migration" in the figure. What is so interesting to us is the significance of this model to the management of information systems. The types of information and systems required in support of products will change during their life cycle, and the nature of the required support at each stage will differ.

Consider some of the implications. The types of system and information management needed at the different stages of the product life cycle are quite different:

Emergence: With new or emerging products, demand is very uncertain and the market is ill-defined. Customer requirements need to be identified and matched with product attributes, and new channels of distribution may have to be developed. The information management focus will be on market research and support for product development.

Growth: In growing markets, information needs will change as demand ceases to exceed supply and competitive pressures increase. In the Boston box, the "stars" will have a quite different look and feel from the others, even from the information management perspective. Stars need major investment to meet the growth in demand, for instance, in marketing capability, production capacity, new distribution channels and renegotiated supplier relationships; these areas of concern must all be supported using appropriate information systems. Information about costs and contribution to profit, changing customer preferences, service expectations and competitor activity will become important as the market begins to mature and patterns that were not possible to anticipate begin to stabilise and become understood. Satisfying demand is more critical than beating specific competitors in the beginning—competition comes later. Systems must support growth and must not inhibit the ability to satisfy demand; systems can also create barriers to entry by tying in customers and suppliers, and by making successful entry to the market dependent on the availability of these systems.

Maturity: In mature markets, competitive rivalry will be intense and supply will gradually exceed demand. The primary objective is to retain market share and "milk" the cash cow: the profits can be reinvested in new areas of product or market development. This implies a more defensive investment strategy, and IS can support this by enabling more accurate market segmentation, increasing productivity and optimising working capital requirements (such as inventories) to match anticipated demand. Important considerations are as follows:

- being more efficient and effective in using resources;
- better management of supply and distribution channels;
- building up customer switching costs; and
- an understanding of specific competitors' products, performance, strengths and weaknesses.

Pricing policies will become more aggressive and critical, and these need to be based on good market and cost information. In general, much more detailed control and planning is required. In many companies, while the marketing and other business issues resulting from the product life cycle are well understood, the means to translate them into appropriate, sustainable, information systems is less well appreciated. Many companies try to force-fit existing systems to the high growth areas but they do not work well, because they were designed for mature products. Force-fitting systems from another part of the product portfolio reduce effectiveness and is all too common.

Decline: At the other extreme, in a declining market, supply will be greater than demand. The nature of the market and the nature of competition will be well understood, and the general business objective will be to achieve cost-effectiveness, or perhaps to be selective and serve profitable niche areas of the market as the profit margin is squeezed by the actions of competitors and the maturity of the market. The information required will be very detailed: demand forecasts, profitability analyses (of customers and products) and cost management (both direct and indirect costs). This will be necessary to maintain profitability and to release resources to invest elsewhere in the business.

Summary

Managerial Issues in Strategic Management

A proper appreciation of how business and systems strategies can be aligned is still one of the most critical issues of the day. For more than 30 years, information systems investments have continued to be risky and have frequently failed to deliver benefits; in the worst cases, they deliver distinct *dis benefits* and can even bring a business to its knees. Investment decisions are typically taken without due regard to the benefits that are expected and that can be delivered. The way to ensure that these benefits are properly understood is to know what the business is trying to achieve at the strategic level and then to serve those needs through appropriate information systems investments that are managed according to the nature of benefit and risk.

The portfolio model is, without question, the most successful single device for engaging management's attention and providing a means for productive discussion about benefits and management style. Taken with the other strategic analysis tools and applied with information systems potential and impacts in mind, the portfolio is really the window through which management debate can move from the world of the business to the world of technology, and back again.

A summary of some of the key management issues concerning strategy is as follows:

- **Strategic alignment**: Ensuring that there is a credible business strategy and then setting well aligned information systems strategies in place that recognise the dependency of the organisation on information for overall business success and that anticipate future circumstances. This is a much more complex process than many people seem to understand—the IMBOK is one way of rendering the problem manageable.
- **Analysis tools**: Choosing and successfully applying appropriate tools for analysing, formulating and refining information system strategies, and ensuring the quality of those strategies.
- **Balance**: Maintaining a balance between the internal and external strategic drivers that bear upon the organisation and determine the actual requirement of strategic management.
- **Ownership and responsibility**: Placing ownership and responsibility for information systems strategies appropriately, and clearly articulating appropriate targets that indicate the success or failure of those strategies.
- **Business units**: Recognising the need for different strategies in individual business units and business functions, and ensuring adequate documentation, dissemination and understanding of strategic plans.

Finally, it is interesting to reflect on the nature of strategy. It is about planning for necessary business change, and therefore, one could argue that where there is no need for change, there is no need for a strategy. However, in studies, it has been found that more than one half of what actually happens in the life of an organisation *could not have been anticipated* even by the most exhaustive strategic planning process. This is a very telling outcome of recent research and needs to be understood. It means that *flexibility* must be built into strategic planning and that the planning horizon must be set at a sensible point in time. There is no advantage to planning for the next five years, when most of what happens in the five months cannot be anticipated.

Strategy Management Competencies

- Appropriate tools are used in analysing, formulating and refining business strategy
- Appropriate tools are used in analysing, formulating and refining IS and IT strategies
- IS and IT strategies are in place and are well aligned with business strategy
- Strategies generally anticipate future circumstances well and account for most eventualities
- We understand enough about strategic management to make it work
- The external environment is monitored and analysed for its strategic significance
- IT- and IS-related opportunities are monitored and analysed for their strategic significance
- Our strategies are of adequate quality for the intended purpose
- Ownership and responsibility for strategies are clear and widely recognised
- Business strategy formulation is adequately supported by appropriate inputs
- Strategies include appropriate goals and objectives, related to IS and IT where appropriate
- Strategic goals and objectives are balanced in terms of current and future requirements
- Strategic goals and objectives are balanced in terms of internal and external imperatives
- Strategies are appropriately comprised of lower level components, where needed
- Strategies are adequately documented and disseminated
- Individual business functions have adequate strategies in place, and they are effective
- Lower level functional strategies are properly aligned with high-level organisational strategies
- Strategies include appropriate measures that indicate the achievement of goals and objectives
- Strategies include appropriate targets that indicate success or failure
- Strategies recognise the dependency of the organisation on information, for overall business success.

Research Side Note: Strategic Beginnings

Earl, M.J. (1993) Experiences in strategic information systems planning. MIS Quarterly, pp. 1–24.

This article is mentioned elsewhere, and although it is old now I am shameless in the way that I refer to this kind of seminal work that actually brings us timeless messages. Earl looks critically at 27 organisations that were willing to share their experiences with strategic information systems planning, and he identifies five generic approaches: Business-Led, Method-driven, Administrative, Technological and Organisational (you will have to go read the article to see the details, it is quite widely available in the usual places). He concludes that the organisational approach is the most effective, essentially that means the whole organisation taking responsibility, working together, and avoiding the sort of methodological paralysis that sometimes ensues. Today, we would say that the trick is to "hang loose ..."

Research Side Note: Have We Grown up yet?

Luftman, J. (2000) Assessing Business-IT alignment maturity. Communications of the Association for Information Systems, 4 (Article 14), pp. 1–51.

This is a classic "maturity model" (there are many of them) that goes into very useful detail about the stages of maturity that organisations need to go through in their efforts to align business and IT strategies. As we continue to face new challenges from the social web, from endless technology advancement, and from globalisation of everything, Luftman's ideas need to be kept in mind as a means of constantly keep ourselves alert to our ability to deal with these things.

Research Side Note: What Managers Should Do

Yayla, A. & Hu, Q. (2009) Antecedents and drivers of IT-Business Strategic Alignment: Empirical validation of a theoretical model. In: Proc 17th European Conference on Information Systems. Verona Italy.

Yayla and Hu concludes that business and IT managers need to do certain things to get things working properly: Business managers should reconsider strategising processes and keep integration of planning as one of their primary goals; they should seek opportunities to increase their level of communication with IT managers and negotiate the responsibilities of IT and business units. IT executives should be more proactive so as to increase the visibility of their unit's success and make sure that they deliver on their promises.

This sounds obvious, but it does not hurt to be reminded from time to time.

Part III
Operationalising Information Management

This book provides a very broad overview of many aspects of managing information in organisations. The reader is presumed to be, in all probability, either a working manager who is dependent on information in his or her work, or a senior student who is intending to graduate in business or information systems studies.

The purpose of these supplementary chapters is to provide some initial guidance in operationalising the ideas that are provided here.

- In working organisations, the critical first step is to establish how confident the organisation is to deploy competencies across all domains of the IMBOK, and this can be done at two levels: a simple, preliminary survey based on just a few questions, or a much more in-depth survey that deploys more than 100 statements with which respondents are asked to agree or disagree. Details of these survey instruments will be found following publication of this book at the companion web site: http://www.imbok.org.
- Research students may flounder when they read previously published work, much of which has informed this book. This is because there are at least four distinctly different philosophical approaches to research, depending on whether the key variables are known and how formalised and structured the researcher prefers to be. This quick overview cuts through the complicated verbiage of academic research and presents clear guidelines that will assist in taking the right research design decision.
- For those readers who want to see more evidence of the origins of the IMBOK, and alternative schemes that deal with alignment issues, the third supplementary chapter reviews the history of models and frameworks like the IMBOK that set out to deal with the alignment problems, and justifies the design of the IMBOK as it now stands.

Assessing Information Management Capability

9

Managers considering the merits of the IMBOK and the specific ways in which it might assist their information technology and systems planning have many tools and techniques to choose from, but the most pressing question right at the start is: how well are we actually doing?

The success of business and information systems strategies has to be judged by the *benefits* that are obtained but that is entirely dependent on the capability of the organisation to undertake the necessary analytical and remedial work. The IMBOK provides a structured means to assess capability and performance, using specific criteria that break down the management domains[1] and the four process interfaces into *statements* that can be deployed in surveys.[2]

This surveying has already been undertaken at two levels, using two separate survey instruments, garnering a large number of responses from a range of organisations.

The Survey Instruments

The two survey instruments work at different levels:

- The first, with 144 statements each representing one of the 144 competencies; this is referred to as the "**micro**" level of working.
- The second, with a simplified form using just nine statements to represent each of the nine groups of competencies; this is referred to as the "**macro**" level of working.

[1] We will treat *business process* and *business information* as one management domain for the present purpose—the survey data that is summarised here pre-dates the division of the central domain into two parts for process and information.

[2] Rob Lambert (a sometime member of faculty at the Cranfield School of Management) was the originator of much of what emerged in the survey instruments, and his insight and perseverance is acknowledged.

A. Bytheway, *Investing in Information*,
DOI 10.1007/978-3-319-11909-0_9

They are used in Likert-scale worksheets, each statement representing one competency; respondents are asked to "agree/disagree" with the statements in order to indicate their *perceptions* of the competency of their organisation to do things well. All statements are phrased in a positive sense, so that "agreement" is good news and "disagreement" is bad news. The focus on perceptions, as opposed to any absolute measure (such as might be found in using COBIT or ITIL) helps to take more careful account of people's feelings and emotions. Most previous thinking has revolved around structured, rational, right-brained thinking, but management is as much concerned with perceptions as with absolutes.

The Micro Level

Working at the micro level is potentially difficult because nobody will willingly respond to 144 individual statements in what will not be a quick survey. A technique has been used whereby worksheets were prepared using randomly selected statements from the total set of 144, but only 20 statements at a time.

Experience at this low level of detail soon indicated that there was a need for a shorter, simpler but compatible approach. This was undertaken at what is called the *macro* level.

The Macro Level

The simplified macro-level worksheet has just nine statements, one for each of the five original domains and one for each of the four interfaces. Two additions were made: an additional statement concerning *culture* for change was included, and a rating of importance of each of the statements (high–low) was included so as to gather data about the relative importance of the different domains.

Four Cases Assessed

The survey has been deployed in four cases, resulting in some thousands of individual opinions:

- A random sample of different businesses (and other organisations) in Cape Town, undertaken at the micro level and referred to here as the "reference sample".
- A purposeful sample of South African Chief Information Officers, also at the micro level.
- A purposeful sample of staff in all departments of a real estate agent, also at the micro level.
- A representative sample of staff working in a large financial services company, this time at the macro level.

The results provide an interesting insight into the perceptions of different stakeholder groups: IT specialists, business specialists, administrative staff, management and others. For example, it is found that IT specialists often under-estimate their capability and fail to realise that their work is actually quite highly valued by others. In other cases senior management have a poor view of organisational ability to manage IT-specific issues such as technology acquisition, IT projects, and business change management.

The analysis uses simple, descriptive statistical methods, directed at the production of "radar charts". It has been found that radar charts are an effective way of presenting complex data to managers, and because the arrangement of summary measures around the circle is fixed, the audience for the results becomes used to the shapes that arise, indicating problems and opportunities. The radar charts (see below) have ten spokes, or axes, as follows:

IT	The **information technology** management domain
IT-IS	*The implementation of information systems*
IS	The **information systems** management domain
IS-BP	*The implementation of business change arising from new systems*
BP	The **business process** management domain (inclusive of what is now the business information)
BP-BB	*The delivery of business benefits from improved business processes*
BB	The **business benefit** management domain
BB-BS	*The fulfilment of business strategy through performance*
BS	The **business strategy** management domain

(The five principal domains of the IMBOK are written in **bold** text, the four interfaces in *italics*).

The tenth vertical "null" axis is reserved for "culture" measures—there was no data for that measure at this stage in the work.

The Reference Sample

As indicated above, the reference sample included a range of responses (1,076 in total) from many different kinds of respondents. Within those responses, were two subsets of *educators* and *government employees*. The results for each are given below, to indicate the beginnings of interesting differences. The red line marks the overall result for the whole reference sample, and the feint blue lines mark the results for the two subsets (Fig. 9.1).

There are significant differences between these results: education is strong on strategy, but government is very weak; government considers its IT management to be strong but education does not. The perceived benefits to education are extremely poor, perhaps because of the strength of the strategic vision and the weakness of the management of the technology that should assist in its realisation; the ability of government to see benefits coming out of routine business activity (in the business

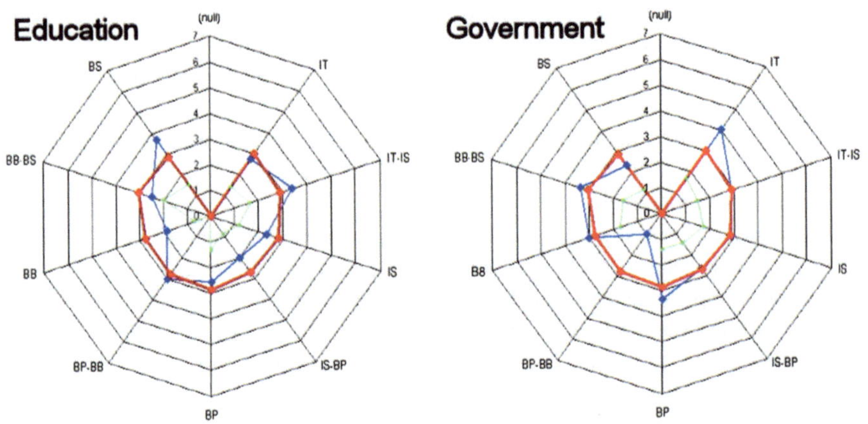

Fig. 9.1 "Education" and "Government" capability compared

processes) is extremely poor. Already we have the beginnings of a much better understanding of significantly different perceptions of competence and capability.

Chief Information Officers

At a workshop in Cape Town, about 20 CIOs were asked to assist by completing worksheets at the micro level (Fig. 9.2).

Fig. 9.2 Results for chief information officers

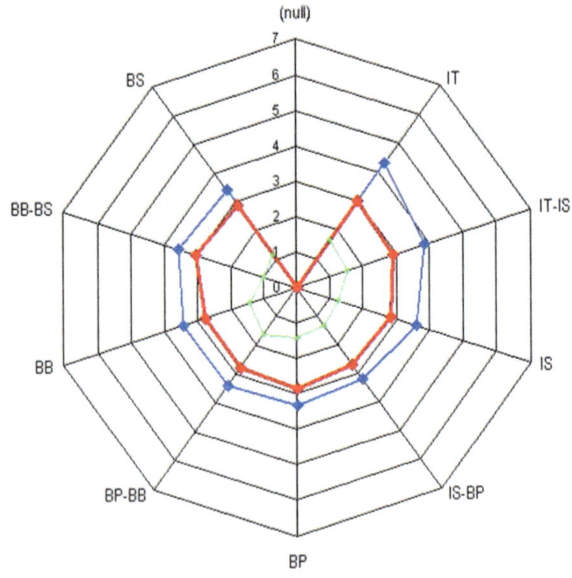

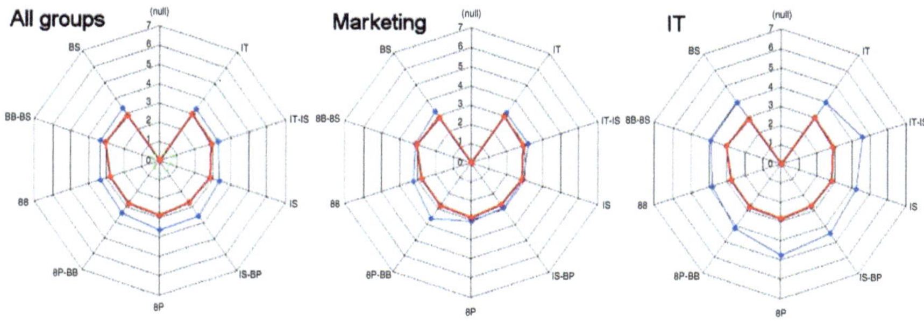

Fig. 9.3 Results from a real estate business

The results show a distinct optimism. Perhaps this is not surprising, a CIO should feel optimistic about the merits of his or her work (but it would be a shock if this optimism was in distinct disagreement with the opinions of others in their organisations).

Real Estate Agent

The first in-company assessment that was undertaken concerned about 80 employees in a real estate agency, where the different views of the different groups proved to be equally interesting (Fig. 9.3).

Perhaps this is a typical result for a typical organisation, where overall there is a positive and optimistic view of information management (compared with the reference dataset). After all, real estate sales and management is an information intensive industry and it is therefore critical to manage information well. This data was gathered at a time when there was a major upgrade taking place on the company web site, and it is interesting to see more optimism in the IT department than in the marketing department. When this analysis was made available to the management, it was possible to work to restore the balance. This is a marketing-led business, where it is essential that marketing staff share the general confidence in getting the technology to work well and deliver the benefits.

Financial Services Company

Because of the large number of potential respondents in this large financial services company, and because of the need to undertake the analysis quickly, this was the first application of the "simple" version of the survey instrument (the macro level). The analysis package being used was further developed, and so this data was more exhaustively analysed than before. The enhanced analyser allows for the selection of different departments and job levels, and it presents averages and standard deviations in detail for both capability and importance.

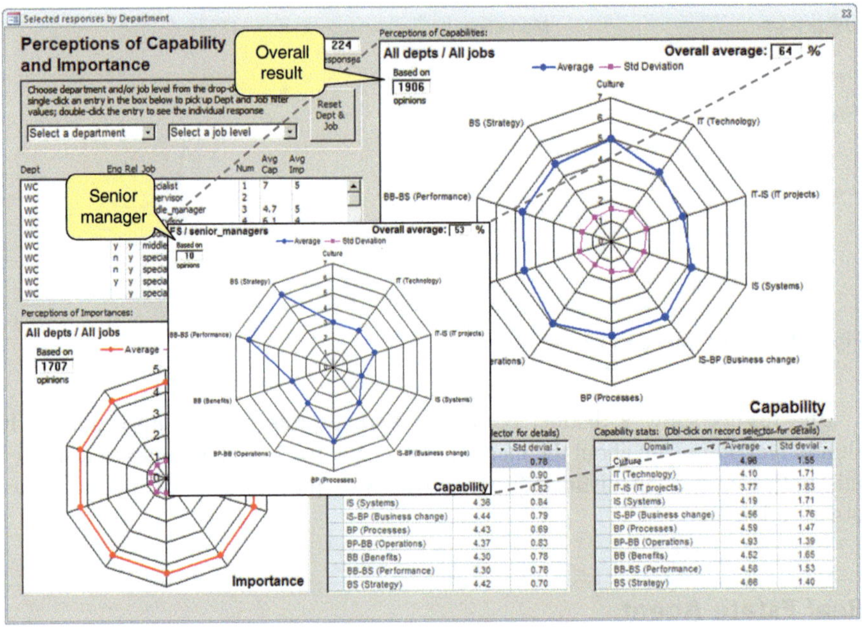

Fig. 9.4 Analysis of macro data from a financial services business

Just two analyses are presented below: in the main image are the results of the whole set of 224 responses (1,906 opinions); overlaid at left-centre are the results for one senior manager who has quite different views than the overall average.

The overall results show that there is broad concern about the level of capability to deal with IT, systems, and systems development. The results are less levelled than in the reference dataset. Given the large number of responses, this is a result that needs further examination. The senior manager has deep concerns about technology and systems capabilities (this is typical of other senior managers in this survey) and it was probably time that something was done to redress this concern. Having said all that, it is interesting that when compared with the reference dataset, the general results for this financial services business are good, averaging something between four and five (compared with <3 in the reference dataset).

When presented with this data, the CIO of the financial services business was pleased, and indicated that more detailed results would be needed in order to guide management actions intended to improve information management capability (Fig. 9.4).

Summary

It is found that the IMBOK deals with the complexities of information management in an effective and comprehensible way. It also confirms that there is no such thing as "alignment of IT and business strategies", it is necessary to align at *four critical interfaces* between *five (now six) domains of management*. Further, the IMBOK provides a means to communicate effectively with senior management without technical terms, just a clear indication of the dependencies that justify the cost drivers (principally the acquisition of information technology and services) in light of the systems needed, the improvements to business processes, and the fulfilment of organisational strategy through appropriate benefits.

Readers who wish to pursue the idea of surveying perceptions of competency should go to the IMBOK community web site and examine the current state of things; the format of the survey instruments is stable and usable, but it is necessary to do further work on the micro survey, so that respondents can provide some contextual and demographic data (about their specific circumstances and their work), whereby an appropriate sub-set of the total set of statements can be extracted and presented for ranking. Putting review procedures into place based on this kind of survey, and establishing a performance management regime, is exactly what is needed to bring problems to the fore, to applaud where good work is being done, and to benchmark information management competencies with peer organisations.

Researching Information Management 10

It is expected that apart from working managers, a significant number of readers of this book will be advanced students, at tertiary level. While some of the material is already migrating down into business studies at school, the scope of what we have here and the quite detailed level of much of the treatment are well beyond the interest and capability of the average school learner. This second supplementary chapter reflects on the state of information systems research, for the benefit of senior students undertaking research into information systems and related matters.

The study of information systems is no longer a new area for study, but there is still debate about the best way to design *research* into information systems issues. The positioning of your ideas and justifying the approach to your research design could be based on any one of hundreds of expert opinions, frameworks, and even vocabularies. This short note attempts to cut through some of the complexity of abstract thinking and semantics that is so often seen, and it lays out a few basic guidelines that will help to get a good research project started.

Epistemology

Epistemology is one of those words we tend to slide over, in a search for a word that is more familiar, and yet it is a word that is fundamental to understanding research. It simply means understanding "the way that we know what we know", or, in our present context, what will be the philosophical approach that we will take to our research? Are we guessing? Will we just talk to people? Will we write things down? Shall we gather some numbers that we can work with statistically?

In the specific context of information-management-related research, the epistemological approach that you choose is likely to be one of four kinds:

- Positivist,
- Interpretivist,

A. Bytheway, *Investing in Information*,
DOI 10.1007/978-3-319-11909-0_10

- Critical or
- Pragmatic.

The paragraphs that follow examine the differences between these four approaches to research.

Positivist and Interpretive Research

Most information systems research is positivist. This means (putting it *very* simply) that you are "positive" you know what needs to be measured, and commonly you would choose to undertake the measurements by means of a survey.

For example, if you are one of the many people who are studying the TAM model concerning the acceptance of information technology by individuals and organisations, a stream of work that was started by Fred Davis in the 1980s, then you will quickly realise that the two principal variables that you need to measure are "*perceived usefulness*" and "*perceived ease of use*" (Davis 1989); the many published papers that follow Davis's early work provide a wide range of examinations, definitions and extensions of these variables and you will have no problem seeing how other people have approached this kind of research. With that understanding in place, you can undertake your own survey that provides the data you need to garner measurements of the variables (that you are now positive that you need to measure).

However, if you think you have found an area for research that is new, then there may be no prior work that guides you as to what you could or should measure, and your only choice is to go and talk to people to find out what they think. Let us suppose that there is no existing research into how people search the Internet for information about household maintenance, and how useful they find different approaches—how to fix a light switch, how to change a tap washer and so on. We do not know how people will search, nor how they will judge the usefulness of such guidance as they find—let us suppose that the guys and gals at Google will not tell us.[1] We have to go and talk with householders, in order to find out how they searched and what problems they faced, in order to discover the patterns of behaviour (if there are any) that begin to indicate *what the variables are*.

In the first case, you are *positive* that you understand the variables you must measure, and so you are approaching your research as a *positivist*. In the second case, you want to *find out* what might be the variables and you want to see, hear and understand what people do, and so you are approaching your research as an *interpretivist*. Positivist research is often undertaken using question-and-answer surveys that produce statistical data that are then subjected to *statistical analysis*; interpretive research is often undertaken using interviews that produce textual data that are then subjected to *content analysis*.

[1] Although this is not certain, one of my students was recently given permission (willingly) to use the copious data on tripadvisor.com, in order to flesh out a survey on hotel guest satisfaction and management communications within hotels.

But this simple summary masks the subtlety that you will find in actual research, and anyone who knows research methods well protests that there is a third approach: "critical research".

Critical Research

It was in 1991 that Orlikowski and Baroudi published their study and summary of 155 prior papers dealing with information systems research, which revealed that 150 were "positivist", 5 were "interpretive", and none at all were "critical" (Orlikowski and Baroudi 1991). This tendency of the majority of researchers to adopt the positivist tradition has continued, particularly in the United States.

Others have looked in other directions. Both Myers and Klein have a long history of thinking about and writing about research methods, and in 2011, they revisited the question of how information systems research is typically done and focused on critical research in order to find out whether it is really different and whether it has qualities that make it worthwhile (Myers and Klein 2011). They examined a small selection of published critical research papers and developed a set of principles that they consider characterises such research. They wanted to encourage researchers to give more consideration to critical methods, which other experts have argued are no more than a variation on interpretive methods.

In order to explain how critical research can be seen to be different to interpretive methods, they point out that it is necessary to understand something about how research works: it can work with ideas that are well established before the research starts, or it may develop new ideas "on the fly" as the research proceeds. The first is described as *a priori* research, meaning that the things one is looking for are defined at the start; the second is defined as *a posteriori* research, because the things that we are looking for emerge during the study.

With this in mind, Myers and Klein find three important characteristics of critical research:

- First, critical research tends to work a priori because it takes a critical view of existing theories, sometimes from other domains of study, in order to test them in the current domain of study; interpretive research is more likely to be developing a new theory than testing "old" ones.
- Second, critical research often sets out to find out how to remove constraints and transform the way things are, in order to make them better. Interpretive research usually does not, it simply sets out to understand something that might be good or might be bad. Reflection on how things might usefully be changed is left for others to decide about.
- Third, critical research tends to be more varied in its detail and in its execution. Whereas the "rules" for interpretive research are quite clear and quite forcefully articulated by its promoters, critical research is a slippery thing that is not so easily characterised.

In this way, critical research *challenges* the things that we otherwise take for granted, and it uses the principle of *value* to decide what transformation if any is needed, thereby bringing us close to *action research*, and at the same time, it can reveal *further meaning* from research data such as might be elicited through interpretive research (Fig. 10.1).

The 2011 paper by Myers and Klein is strongly recommended to anyone who would like to study a clear and authoritative history of information-systems-related research and leading expert opinion about what the differences between positivist, interpretive and critical research are. Michael Myers also has Web pages that are frequently cited as a source of further information.[2]

Pragmatic Research

Another fourth stream of thinking about research needs to be acknowledged: some 30 years ago, Richard Daft published an interesting paper that rebuts the presumed need for *any* formalised decision about research when looking at how organisations work (as much information systems and information management research naturally will). He argues that research needs to be *crafted*; he focuses particularly on the potential problems with formalised survey-based research:

> "What troubles me is that many of us seem never to have discovered or acknowledged the craft aspects of scholarship. Formal techniques and methods dominate in most manuscripts and journal articles that I read. The authors act as if there is only a single approach, which includes measurement precision, perfect prediction, dispassionate analysis, and many variables. Authors often eschew real organisations, storytelling and common sense … A great scholar such as Kurt Lewin used apprenticeship to pass the research craft to his students. By showing students how to design studies on the basis of anticipated surprise, beauty, first-hand experience, emotion, and storytelling, we can be role models for the kinds of things that go into significant research. (Daft 1983, p. 545)

While this can be seen as an argument for interpretive research as much as an argument for research "craft", the appeal to step away from presumptive rules and prescribed methods is very inviting. Perhaps we have lost something in the 30 years that have passed since Daft wrote this. With the dramatic increase in the number of people doing research in this time, perhaps it was inevitable that structure and techniques would dominate, in order to render research "teachable" to larger classes of postgraduate students. However, what Daft was arguing still finds traction today:

[2] See http://www.qual.auckland.ac.nz for Michael Myers' interesting material on qualitative research methods.

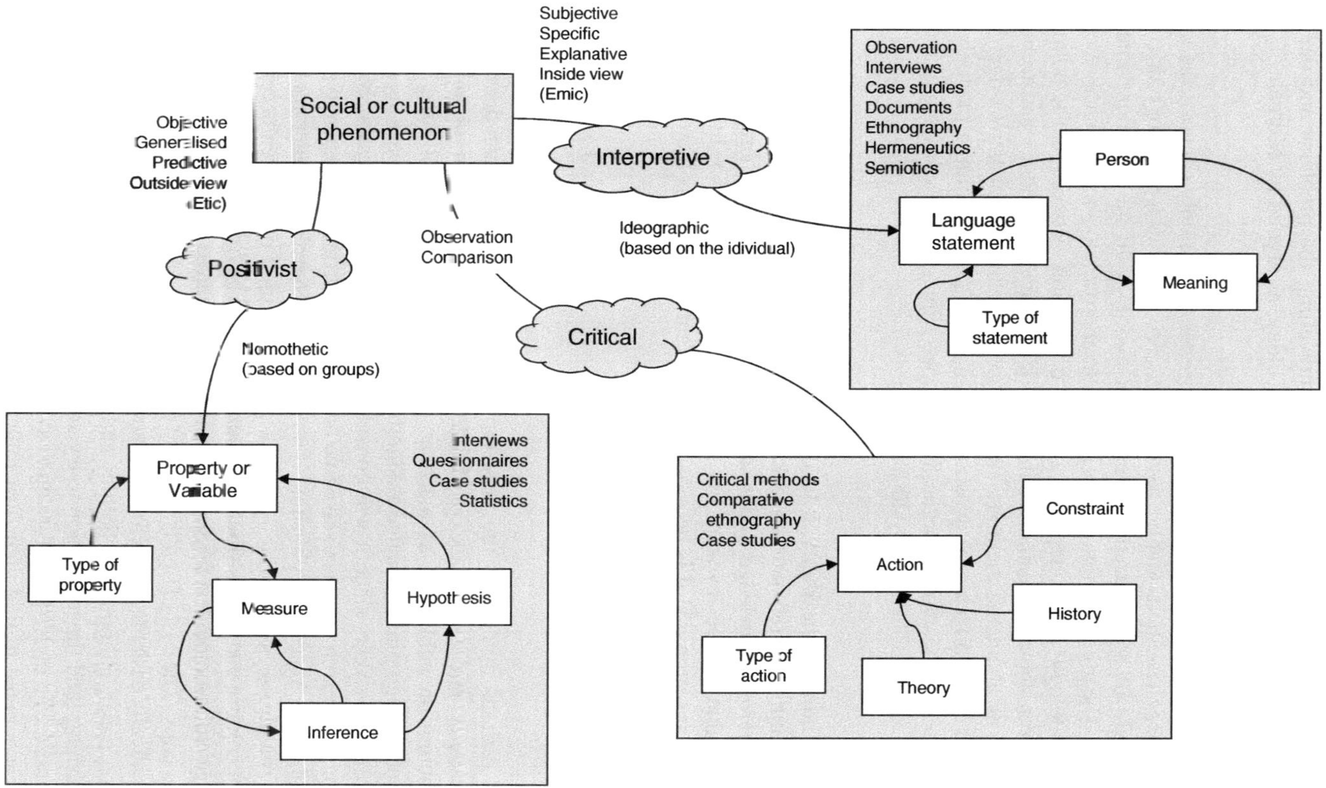

Fig. 10.1 A summary of research approaches, loosely based on Myers

the idea of "pragmatism" as a way of unravelling the problems and dangers of mixed methods research is a topical issue today, as argued by Morgan:

> "Fortunately, a pragmatic approach [to research] not only supports the kinds of research methods that we advocate but also provides a basis for reorienting the field of social science research methodology in the directions that we favor. The great strength of this pragmatic approach to social science research methodology is its emphasis on the connection between epistemological concerns about the nature of the knowledge that we produce and technical concerns about the methods that we use to generate that knowledge. This moves beyond technical questions about mixing or combining methods and puts us in a position to argue for a properly integrated methodology for the social sciences." (Morgan 2007: 74)

These ideas of *flexibility*, a focus on escaping the constraints of *technical concerns* about research and an acknowledgement that research is actually about *integration* of knowledge might suit many situations where there might be some theories that can be invoked, but where circumstances are so different from any previous research that it is necessary to maintain an openness that will permit new theories to emerge.

Final Thoughts

It is perhaps ironic that the very topic whose research we are discussing—the importance and consequences of information management in organisations—is impacting on publishing as much as anywhere else. The publishing of research outputs is beginning to change as significantly as is retailing, or banking, or travel. It is only a few years since it was considered normal and even reasonable for publication of research outputs to take two or three years, from submission to printing and distribution. Academic publishing is now being taken over by academics themselves, who—with varying success—are now managing their own "open access" journals that recognise that the distribution of content should be free and that it is reasonable to charge authors a modest fee for publication rather than to charge readers for their own paper copy. The cost of finalisation and distribution of academic outputs is, of course, dramatically easier using the Internet and the World Wide Web than it ever was using ink on paper, although the politics and squabbling associated with some academic publishing (and the temptation to try and cheat the system) go on as before.

Those who undertake information systems and information management research are encouraged to find their own routes for publication, including "working paper series" that are managed within their own institutions; also special interest groups and blogs, as well as the conventional routes through publishers, as appropriate.

Some Models and Frameworks Reviewed

11

The IMBOK could be seen as just another management framework; there are more than a few such frameworks around. This was not the first and it certainly will not be the last. Hence, it is important to examine how the IMBOK fits into the overall scheme of thinking.

The critical characteristic of the IMBOK is that it provides a picture of management concerns organised according to the *value* that is added, stage by stage, from the acquisition of information technology right through to the fulfilment of organisational strategy. Other frameworks are concerned with different things such as maturity, or layers rather than levels of management. But all are concerned in some way or another with the resulting *performance* of organisations that choose to use information technology and systems.

From the earliest days, it has been assumed that the performance of organisations depends on the quality of the work of the software developers who originate, integrate and support the program code that systems and therefore organisations; this belief is still held today (McLeod and MacDonell 2011). Elsewhere, it is argued that success depends on good strategic management (Ward and Peppard 2002). A review of these and other sources reveals that there is a trail of dependency from raw engineering practice through organisational change management to strategic thinking, that has all to be seen together in order to understand how information technology enables improved performance and strategic fulfilment.

Selected Models

Seven models or frameworks have been selected to provide an overview of how higher-level thinking has emerged since 1987 to more recent times. They are presented here chronologically, as seen this way they tell an interesting story about practitioner, management and academic thinking:

A. Bytheway, *Investing in Information*,
DOI 10.1007/978-3-319-11909-0_11

- Zachman (1987)
- ITIL (1989)
- Capability Maturity Model (CMM) (1992)
- Henderson and Venkatraman alignment model (1993)
- Jacobs' ladder (1995)
- COBIT (1996)
- Benefits dependency network (2005)

It is a fairly eclectic selection, including examples of academic, consulting and practitioner thinking.

Zachman Reveals Complexity (1987)

Based on a long career with IBM, the complexities of information technology management were revealed by John Zachman in a "Framework for information systems architecture" (Zachman 1987); Zachman took a broad view of the issues, but his ideas were necessarily detailed, and his frequently cited 6x6 matrix (see below), with layers of modelling and representation down the side and different perspectives on the business across the top, proved to be too complex for some managers to work with; 36 different points of concern (the intersection of the six rows and six columns of the matrix) were just too many to handle. After the initial publication of the first simpler framework, this extended version became the definitive view of what he had in mind (Fig. 11.1).

There have been many subsequent references to the Zachman framework (e.g. Frankel et al. 2003) and John Zachman himself still travels the world to talk about his ideas, but the framework seems to have failed to gain wide currency in the strategic or operational realms of management. Nevertheless, Zachman's seminal paper launched a number of important ideas: it promotes the idea of "architecture" as a way to deal with complexity (he started the paper using house building as a metaphor for systems development), thereby making clear the difference between the representation of a building (or system) in the architect's drawings (or the systems analyst's specifications) and the actual construction (or program coding). He draws an important distinction between the process and data perspectives of a system and the network that allows it to communicate. In his conclusions to the original 1987 paper, he writes:

> "When the question is asked, 'What is information systems architecture?' the answer is 'There is not an information systems architecture, but a set of them!' Architecture is relative. What you think architecture is depends on what you are doing" (Zachman 1987, p. 291)

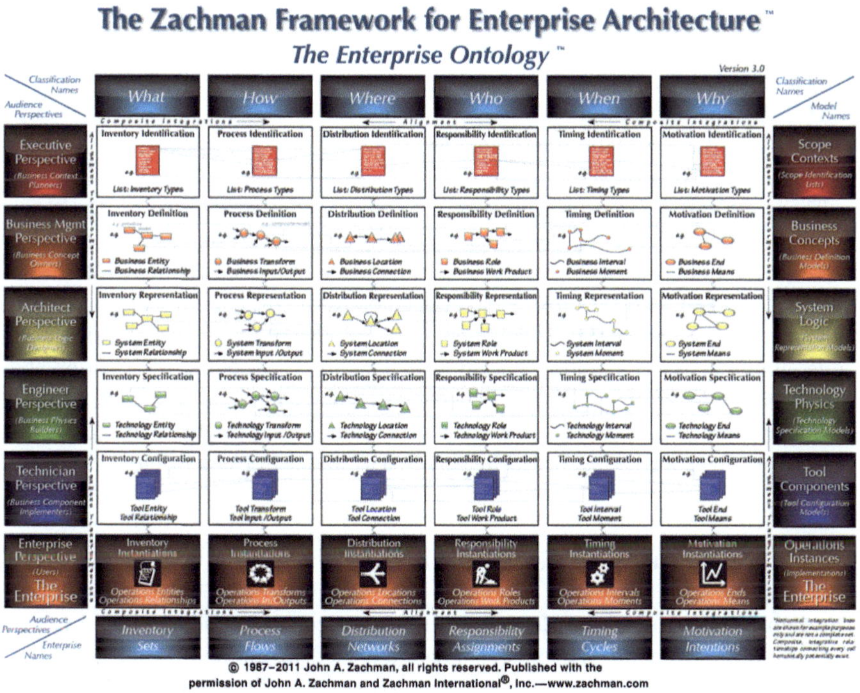

Fig. 11.1 The Zachman Framework ('Enterprise Architecture' version). © 1987–2011 John A. Zachman, all rights reserved. Published with the permission of John A. Zachman and Zachman International®, Inc.—www.zachman.com

In saying this, he reinforced the idea that the program coder had one view of what was to be produced and the database designer (and the network engineer) had another—this is not actually conducive to a mutual understanding of a single aim, unless all concerned can bring these viewpoints or perspectives together. It is not clear at first sight how Zachman expected the common understanding to be achieved, when each had their own view from a specific place in the framework.

ITIL (1989)

The IT Infrastructure Library was an initiative of the United Kingdom government to specify the services that were required in order to successfully deliver information technology benefits. It was migrated to the private sector so that it could be promulgated internationally without the constraints that might have arisen from government "ownership", and it was first published as such in 1989. In the 25-plus years that followed, it has been extended to become ever more holistic, and there are now volumes dealing with:

- ITIL Service Strategy
- ITIL Service Design
- ITIL Service Transition
- ITIL Service Operation
- ITIL Continual Service Improvement

These are just five out of a total of 21 volumes that are offered (at the time of writing). Interest in ITIL seems to have been sustained over the decades, and it has attracted the attention of academics and researchers. One study looked at the way that ITIL worked with ISO/IEC 15504 (a standard for software process assessment) in a small business context (Barafort et al. 2002). The official ITIL Website reveals quite vibrant activity, including surveys intended to garner better information about actual user experience (ITIL n.d.); there are copious references to ITIL in recent academic literature. This was a European initiative and, as might be expected, there were other ideas emerging in North America at about the same time.

Capability Maturity Model (CMM) (1992)

The Capability Maturity Model is an early and frequently cited example of good work coming from an academic source: the Software Engineering Institute at Carnegie Mellon University published the first edition of the model in 1993 (Paulk et al. 1993). A second edition became available in July 2009, still very focused on software engineering practice. The CMM now identifies five stages in achieving software engineering maturity:

- **Level 1: Initial**: chaotic, unstable, relying on the individual
- **Level 2: Repeatable**: basic standards and project management in place, QA Group at work
- **Level 3: Defined**: standard processes across the whole organisation; training and improvement processes in place
- **Level 4: Managed**: productivity and quality is measured; database of metrics in place to feed the improvement process
- **Level 5: Optimising**: continuous improvement, leading edge software engineering practices

In its early days, as the model was used to assess the performance of software engineers and systems developers around the world, people began to ask who had achieved the highest level (Level 5), and for some years, there were only two, Motorola in Bangalore and IBM in Florida (Stremlau 1996; Parthasarathy 2004).

What is perhaps most interesting about the CMM is that it stands as a very early example (if not the first?) of an idea that has become very widely adopted in other contexts. In personnel assessment, process management and supply chain management, as well as educational computing, many experts have chosen to focus on the emerging maturity and capability of organisations to do these different things well over time (Ginsberg and Quinn 1995; Curtis et al. 2002; Lockamy III and McCormack 2004). Meanwhile, parallel efforts to improve the return on information technology investments have continued and focused more carefully on the ways in which business and technology strategies can be more effectively aligned.

More recent empirical work by Luftman took an approach based on the maturity of strategic alignment, clearly based on the five levels of maturing in the earlier Capability Maturity Model (Luftman 2000). His descriptors for the five stages of maturity are as follows:

- Ad hoc process
- Committed process
- Established focused process
- Improved/managed process
- Optimised process

Luftman's recommendations are to evaluate maturity using an evaluation team and pre-defined terms, seemingly based on limited empirical work. Academics will ask whether this kind of approach can claim the rigour that comes from serious research. For example, Delone and McLean based their work (which has a simpler outcome) on their reading of more than 180 reports concerning "user satisfaction" (DeLone and McLean 1992, 2002), wherein there is yet another perspective on the issues of meeting users' needs by means of careful strategic management.

Henderson and Venkatraman Seek Simplicity (1993)

In the search for simpler but complete views of the problem, another frequently cited example is the Henderson and Venkatraman framework (Henderson and Venkatraman 1993). It relates business and IT issues at the internal and external levels using a two-by-two matrix. It suggests that there is a need for "functional integration" between the business and IT domains and that there is a need for "strategic fit" between the internal and external worlds. The four quadrants embodied in the framework are, in turn scope, competencies and governance in the external portion and processes, skills and infrastructure or architecture in the internal portion (Fig. 11.2).

Questions arise from a close examination of this model. It is interesting to see that competencies and skills are included, but why are they in different parts of the framework? As is made clear in the CMM, a skill can be seen as a low-level thing ("I can work this computer") but a competency is something else ("I can use this computer to reliably produce a useful econometric model"). The implication of "processes" being in both the internal business and internal IT quadrants is that business processes and IT processes must be functionally integrated, but how is that possible? A single IT process might contribute to a wide range of business processes; conversely, a typical business process might depend on many information

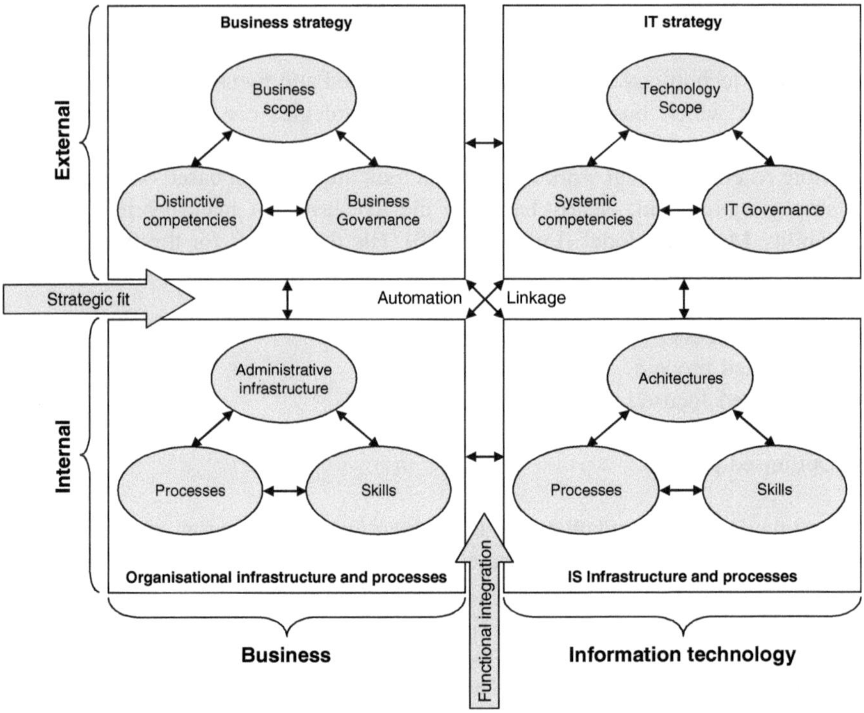

Fig. 11.2 The Henderson and Venkatraman alignment model (1993)

systems. Why do we have "administrative infrastructure" on the left, and "architectures" on the right?

The Henderson and Venkatraman model is simple at first sight, but it leads to a range of questions and lacks the sort of elegance and symmetry that makes these things memorable. It implies dependencies and relationships between its conceptual components, but these are not immediately evident on a first reading. However, their arguments do re-enforce the shifting nature of the problem:

> … the Strategic Alignment Model calls for a fundamental shift in the focus of the I/S function from an internal orientation toward one of strategic fit within the I/T domain, namely, recognition of the external I/T marketplace in terms of the scope of the technologies, the desired level of competencies, and the locus of governance. This shift is important if we consider that I/T has the potential to shape business competencies and actions in the product-market arena. (Henderson and Venkatraman 1993, p. 480)

In their conclusions, they note that it is necessary for others to work with their model and render it applicable, in specific situations, quoting contemporaneous work by (Luftman et al. 1993) that shows how to translate their model into …

> … management frameworks and action plans for the transformation of the enterprise. (Henderson and Venkatraman 1993, p. 482)

Later, as we have already seen, Luftman went further and adopted the CMM way of thinking—based on competency and maturity—in setting out an alternative approach to marrying need with capability in all kinds of organisations,[1] together with a survey (Luftman 2000).

Jacobs' Ladder (1995)

One might ask what senior business management were thinking in the 1990s, as technical managers and academics progressed in their own way? Persuasive, clear argument concerning the benefits and value to be derived from investments is what senior management want to hear.

Progressive organisations understood this and references to "information technology management" were supplanted by references to "information systems management" and then to just "information management", as in the case of BP Chemicals (Cross 1995), and "knowledge management", as in the case of Zeneca and others (Chase 1997).

At BP Chemicals, John Cross dubbed his idea "Jacob's ladder" he was seeking a management stairway to a strategic heaven, perhaps? The arrangement of the four steps in BP Chemical's "Jacob's ladder" is shown in the Fig. 11.3. At the bottom is the technology that comprises the infrastructure for systems and for business activity, and at the top, the business are the processes that serve the business strategy (Cross and Earl 1997). An important feature of the model is the insertion of "information" and "applications" between the two—it is this recognition that the management of information and applications (or more simply, the management of "systems"?) that begins to construct a chain of value from the infrastructure to the business process. Improved information and improved applications functionality is what begins to improve the quality and effectiveness of business processes (Fig. 11.3).

It is interesting that the creation of value is seen at the top, with in-house expertise; the realisation of value is seen at the bottom, based on the use of

[1] It has been noted that he found education to be a long way behind other kinds of organisation in achieving software and systems maturity (Grant 2011).

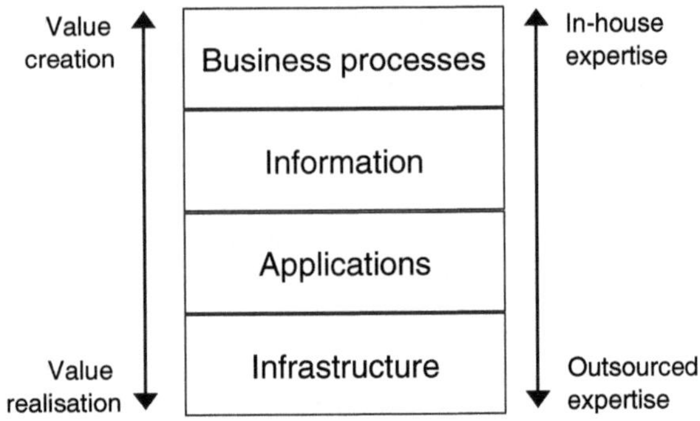

Fig. 11.3 "Jacob's ladder", as used in BP chemicals

outsourced expertise (IT outsourcing was one of the principal strategic outcomes for BP Chemicals at this time).

However, this notion of value generation is seen in other work. Zachman had already articulated his six "levels" and six "perspectives", from the representation of technology infrastructure (program code and data definitions), through technology, systems to the enterprise and its context (Zachman 1987); Venkatraman was promoting the idea that data, information, knowledge, action and result were all related in a similarly progressive way (Venkatraman 1996), and Ward has promoted the idea that benefits from IT investments are achieved at different levels (Ward and Peppard 2002). The significance of the BP story is that both the CEO and the CIO were absolutely committed to a programme of action to simplify and rationalise the operational costs of information technology and systems.

COBIT (1996)

No doubt prompted by the actions of progressive organisations like BP Chemicals, COBIT has migrated through at least six versions in its efforts to embrace more and more of "the problem":

- 1996: Audit of IT operations
- 1998: Control of IT and IS operations
- 2000: Management of IT and IS operations
- 2005: IT Governance
- 2007: Enterprise IT governance
- 2012: Consolidation of Risk and Security issues.

This extending scope of application reflects the general concern amongst IT management to reach further and further into the governance and strategic aspects of an organisation.

Lainhart provides an early introduction to COBIT and embellishes his description with quotations from practising audit and control managers; two typical comments are as follows:

> "COBIT provides tools to communicate with the managers of the business and bridge the gaps among technical issues, control needs, and business risks".
>
> "COBIT is excellent. It is the best benchmark document available in this country; and I recommend using it as a technology framework of policy".
> (Lainhart 2000, p. 24)

This positive move to link technology management to the strategic needs of an organisation is quite in line with the intentions of John Cross at BP Chemicals and has been well received. Like ITIL, COBIT continues to find support internationally (AbuMusa 2009) and in education (Khther and Othman 2013), where it is found to facilitate communications and reduce costs based on the analysis of three cases.

The latest version of COBIT, version 5, makes clear its intentions and objectives:

> "COBIT 5 provides a comprehensive framework that assists enterprises in achieving their objectives for the governance and management of enterprise IT. Simply stated, it helps enterprises create optimal value from IT by maintaining a balance between realising benefits and optimising risk levels and resource use. COBIT 5 enables IT to be governed and managed in a holistic manner for the entire enterprise, taking in the full end-to-end business and IT functional areas of responsibility, considering the IT-related interests of internal and external stakeholders. COBIT 5 is generic and useful for enterprises of all sizes, whether commercial, not-for-profit or in the public sector". (ISACA 2012, p. 13)

This feels like the beginnings of sound advice and, as with ITIL, there are copious references to COBIT in recent academic literature.

The Benefits Dependency Network (2005)

Work with senior business managers in Europe in the late 1990s led to a research project addressing the realisation of benefits—the results of this work are already incorporated here in the section dealing with business benefits (see Chap. 7). This work was consolidated and published (Ward and Daniel 2005), and the "benefits dependency network" stands as one of the most recent models for managers to work with. It parallels the IMBOK quite closely, as has been seen (Fig. 7.6) and so it needs no further explanation here.

The benefits dependency research led by John Ward led to a very high level of interest from working managers and has found wide support and usage.

Consolidation

These models all share the intention to separate technological, management and organisational issues. Whilst ITIL and COBIT embrace great detail and are all-encompassing, and CMM is principally concerned with a trajectory over time; nevertheless, it is possible to bring these disparate but related ideas together into a single table in order that they might be compared, and that is done below (Fig. 11.4).

Perusal of the table is revealing in that all perspectives align well, even though they see things from slightly different viewpoints and with different vocabularies. As can be seen, at the heart of the IMBOK is the idea of the business process and business information, both incorporated by Zachman in his enterprise model and seen by Ward and Daniel as the level where business change is to be found. The merit of the IMBOK is that it is strongly aligned to the generation of value from an investment in information technology, and it is entirely aimed at fulfilment of strategy as the ultimate objective.

There are some points of significant differences that need to be noted: first, Zachman‘s "representation of system" is really only of interest to technology management, but components of the other levels show strong empathy with the other viewpoints; second, surprising as it may seem, Cross *excluded* specific reference to benefits and business strategy in his "Jacob's ladder" model. Otherwise, one can argue that in all of these ideas, there are actually five levels at which management must operate (from the lowest to the highest):

- *information technology* must be acquired, configured, and used to provide the requisite infrastructure so that a business can store its data and operate its …
- *information systems*, some of which will necessitate changes to the way that the business operates its …
- *business processes*, wherein *business information* and knowledge are deployed in order to initiate the actions that are expected to deliver the desired …
- *business benefits*, that will in turn realise the organisation's …
- *business strategy*, that delivers stakeholder's expectations.

Hence, the arrangement of ideas in the IMBOK strongly reflects the historical thinking that is available. Other threads of research have also informed the development of the IMBOK, including a very extensive review of the literature that established the validity of many of the ideas within it, ideas from work at MIT, and at the Cranfield School of Management (Lambert and Peppard 1993; Venkatraman 1996; Ward and Daniel 2005); the guiding principle of value adding can be traced

	Zachman	ITIL	CMM / Luftman	Henderson & Venkatraman	Cross	COBIT	Ward 2005	IMBOK
	1987	1989	1992	1993	1995	1996	2005	
Highest	Context	ITIL Service Strategy	Optimized Process	Business		Enterprise IT governance	Strategic objective	Business strategy
	Enterprise model	ITIL Continual Service Improvement	Improved & Managed Process			Consolidation of Risk and Security issues.	Functional benefit	Business benefit
		ITIL Service Transition	Established & Defined Process	Strategic fit, functional integration	Business process	IT Governance	Business change	Business process
	System model	System model	Committed repeatable Process		Information, application	Management of IT and IS operations	Enabling change	Information system
	Technology	ITIL Service Operation	Ad Hoc Process		Infrastructure	Control of IT and IS operations	Technology	Information technology
Lowest	Representation of system			Information technology		Audit of IT operations		

Fig. 11.4 Consolidation of the frameworks

back to work by Edwards and Peppard (1997), and ideas about skills, competencies and capabilities were developed in conjunction with working business managers (Bytheway and Lambert 1998). The concept of value came strongly into focus (Peppard et al. 2001) and is evident in standard works dealing with IS/IT strategy (Ward and Peppard 2002). However, it was the research partnership in South Africa that melded all these ideas into a stable framework and then promoted it in the form of the IMBOK (HICTE 2003).

The IMBOK framework has proved to be useful because it allows assessment and analysis of the competencies that are needed to manage the successful delivery of benefits from information technology investments. From the preceding work, and in particular the review of a very wide range of literature that it accommodates, a set of 144 competencies have been identified organised into nine groups that correspond to the management domains in the IMBOK and the gaps between them (see Chap. 9, "Assessing information management capability", for details of this approach to competency assessment).

References

AbuMusa, A. (2009). Exploring the importance and implementation of COBIT processes in Saudi organizations: An empirical study. *Information Management and Computer Security, 17*(2), 73–95.

Angell, I. (2000). *The new barbarian manifesto: How to survive the information age.* London: Kogan Page.

Angell, I. (1997). Welcome to the "brave new world". *Information systems: An emerging discipline?* (pp. 363–383)., McGraw Hill Information Systems Series UK, McGraw Hill: Maidenhead.

Ansoff, I. (1957). Strategies for diversification. *Harvard Business Review, 35*(5), 113–124.

Barafort, B., Di Renzo, B. & Merlan, O. (2002). Benefits resulting from the combined use of ISO/IEC 15504 with the information technology infrastructure library (ITIL). *Product Focused Software Process Improvement* (pp.314–325). Heidelberg: Springer.

Beer, S. (1984). The viable system model: Its provenance, development, methodology and pathology. *Journal of the Operational Research Society, 35*, 7–25.

Bytheway, A. (1996). Strategic information modelling: some experiences with a new framework. *Journal of Applied Management Studies, 5*(1), 17–45.

Bytheway, A. & Lambert, R. (1998). Organisational competencies for harnessing IS/IT. Retrieved May 7, 2010, from http://www.imbok.org/docs/CompetenciesGoodPracticeGuide.pdf

Carr, N. (2003) IT doesn't matter. In: *Wringing real value from IT*, HBR OnPoint, pp 3–10

Chase, R. L. (1997). Knowledge management benchmarks. *Journal of Knowledge Management, 1*(1), 83–92.

Chatham, R., & Patching, K. (2000). *Corporate politics for IT managers: How to get streetwise.* Newton, MA, USA: Butterworth-Heinemann.

Chaudhry, A. S. (2013). Information management strategies of knowledge workers in the public sector in Kuwait. *Libri, 63*(2), 149–158. Retrieved June 29, 2014, from http://www.degruyter.com/view/j/libr.2013.63.issue-2/libri-2013-0012/libri-2013-0012.xml.

Cross, J. (1995). IT outsourcing : British Petroleum's competitive approach. *Harvard Business Review, 73*(3), 94.

Cross, J., & Earl, M. (1997). Transformation of the IT function at British Petroleum. *MIS Quarterly, 21*(4), 401–424.

Curtis, B., Hefley, W. E., Miller, S. A., Hefley, W. E. & Miller, S. (2002). The people capability maturity model: Guidelines for improving the workforce. Reading: Addison-Wesley.

Daft, R.L. (1983) Learning the craft of organizational research. *Academy of Management Review, 8*, 539–546.

Davis, F. (1989). Perceived usefulness, perceived ease of use, and user acceptance of information technology. *MIS Quarterly, 13*(3), 319–340.

DeLone, W. H. & McLean, E. R. (2002). Information systems success revisited. *HICSS. Proceedings of the 35th Annual Hawaii International Conference on System Sciences* (pp.2966–2976). Retrieved October 26, 2013, from http://ieeexplore.ieee.org/xpls/abs_all.jsp?arnumber=994345

A. Bytheway, *Investing in Information*,
DOI 10.1007/978-3-319-11909-0

DeLone, W. H., & McLean, E. R. (1992). Information systems success: The quest for the dependent variable. *Information Systems Research, 3*(1), 60–95.

DoD. (1979). *Military Handbook*. US Department of Defense.

Dragan, C. (2011). Information management in seaport clusters. *Scientific Journal of Maritime Research, 25*(2), 371–386.

Earl, M. J. (1993). Experiences in strategic information systems planning. *MIS Quarterly, 17*(1), 1–24.

Edwards, C., & Peppard, J. (1997). Operationalizing strategy through process. *Long Range Planning, 30*(5), 753–767.

Ginsberg, M. P., & Quinn, L. H. (1995). Process tailoring and the the software capability maturity model. Pittsburgh, PA: Software Engineering Institute.

Grant, K. (2011) Managing information technology in education (Conversation).

Henderson, J. C., & Venkatraman, N. (1993). Strategic alignment: Leveraging information technology for transforming organizations. *IBM Systems Journal, 32*(1), 4–16.

HICTE. (2003). *ICT in Higher Education*. Cape Town: University of the Western Cape.

ISACA. (2012). *Cobit 5: A business framework for the governance and management of enterprise IT*. Rolling Meadows. IL: Information Systems Audit and Control Association.

ITIL. (n.d.) *IT Infrastructure Library [Internet]*. Retrieved January 22, 2014, from http://www.itil-officialsite.com/.

Kaplan, R., & Norton, D. (1996). *The balanced scorecard—translating stragegy into action*. Boston, MA: Harvard University Press.

Khther, R. A., & Othman, M. (2013). COBIT framework as a guideline to effective IT governance in higher education. *International Journal of Information Technology Convergence and Services, 3*(1), 21–29.

Lacity, M. C., Solomon, S., Yan, A., & Willcocks, L. P. (2011). Business process outsourcing studies: A critical review and research directions. *Journal of Information Technology, 26*(4), 221–258.

Lainhart, J. W, I. V. (2000). COBIT : A methodology for managing and controlling information and information technology risks and vulnerabilities. *Journal of Information Systems, 14* (Supplement), 21–25.

Lambert, R., & Peppard, J. (1993). IT and new organizational forms: destination but no road map? *Journal of Strategic Information Systems,* 2(3), 180–206.

Larman, C., & Basili, V. R. (2003). Iterative and incremental developments. a brief history. *Computer, 36*(6), 47–56.

Lee, A. (1999). "Five challenges to the Information Systems Field", keynote address. *Proceedings BitWorld '99*. Cape Town, UWC. Retrieved August 22, 2004, from http://www.people.vcu.edu/~aslee/bitworld/Bitworld99-Keynote-Lee.htm

Lethbridge, J. (2012). Empty promises: The impact of outsourcing on NHS services. UNISON.

Lockamy, A, I. I. I., & McCormack, K. (2004). The development of a supply chain management process maturity model using the concepts of business process orientation. *Supply Chain Management: An International Journal, 9*(4), 272–278.

Luftman, J. (2000). Assessing business-IT alignment maturity. *Communications of the Association for Information Systems*, *4*(14), 1–51.

Luftman, J. N., Lewis, P. R., & Oldach, S. H. (1993). Transforming the enterprise: The alignment of business and information technology strategies. *IBM Systems Journal, 32*(1), 198–221.

McFarlan, F. W. (1984). Information technology changes the way you compete. *Harvard Business Review, 62*(3), 98–103.

McLeod, L., & MacDonell, S. G. (2011). Factors that affect software systems development project outcomes: A survey of research. *ACM Computing Surveys (CSUR), 43*(4), 24.

Myers, M., & Klein, H. (2011). A set of principles for conducting critical research in information systems. *MIS Quarterly, 35*(1), 17–36.

Orlikowski, W. J., & Baroudi, J. J. (1991). Studying information technology in organizations: Research approaches and assumptions. *Information Systems Research,* 2(1), 1–28.

Paetsch, F., Eberlein, A., & Maurer, F. (2003). Requirements engineering and agile software development. *2012 IEEE 21st International Workshop on Enabling Technologies: Infrastructure for Collaborative Enterprises* (pp. 308–308). New York: IEEE Computer Society.

Park, S. (2012). A New wave of government information management: The development of a function-based classification structure in a canadian government organization. *Journal of Library Metadata, 12*, 23–38.

Parthasarathy, B. (2004). India's Silicon Valley or Silicon Valley's India? Socially embedding the computer software industry in Bangalore. *International Journal of Urban and Regional Research, 28*(3), 664–685.

Patel, S. (1994). Doctoral thesis. Ashridge, UK: Ashridge Business School

Paulk, M. C., Curtis, B., Chrissis, M. B., & Weber, C. C. (1993). *Capability maturity model for software, Version 1.1*. Pittsburgh: Software Engineering Institute, Carnegie Mellon University (CMU/SEI-93-TR-024).

Pellegrinelli, S., & Bowman, C. (1994). Implementing strategy through projects. *Long Range Planning, 27*(4), 125–132.

Peppard, J., Lambert, R., & Edwards, C. (2001). Whose job is it anyway? *Information Systems Journal, 10*(4), 291–322.

Porter, M. (1985). *Competitive advantage: Creating and sustaining superior performance*. New York: Free Press.

Porter, M. E. & Millar, V. E. (1985, July-August). How information gives you competitive advantage. *Harvard Business Review, 85*(4), 149–153.

SEMTECHBIZ. (2012). *SEMTECHBIZ 2012: Semantic Technology and Business Conference [Internet]*. Retrieved August 4, 2013, from http://semtechbizuk2012.semanticweb.com/.

Sheriff, A., Bouchlaghem, D., El-Hamalawi, A., & Yeomans, S. (2012). Information management in UK-based architecture and engineering organizations: Drivers, constraining factors, and barriers. *Journal of Management in Engineering, 28*(2), 170–180.

Stremlau, J. (1996). Bangalore: India's Silicone city. *Monthly Labor Review, 50*, 119.

Varian, H. (2008). *Hal Varian Answers Your Questions [Internet]*. Retrieved April 6, 2014, from http://www.freakonomics.com/2008/02/25/hal-varian-answers-your-questions

Venkatraman (1996). Delivering IS success through service—A symposium.

Venkatraman, N. (1996) *Managing IT resources as a value center. Presentation material: IS Executive Seminar Series*, UK:Cranfield School of Management.

Ward, J., & Daniel, E. (2005). *Benefits management: Delivering value from IS and IT investments*. Chichester: Wiley.

Ward, J., & Peppard, J. (2002). *Strategic planning for information systems* (3rd ed.). Chichester: Wiley.

Zachman, J. A. (1987). A framework for information systems architecture. *IBM Systems Journal, 26*(3), 590–616.

Bibliography

Part 3 of the book (and some of what has gone before) draws on previously published work by the author and his colleagues. This short bibliography includes some of the background material that contributed to the IMBOK and to this book.

Bytheway, A. (2011). Assessing information management competencies in organisations.*The Electronic Journal Information Systems Evaluation,14*(2), 179–192.

Bytheway, A. (2003). Exploring information management.*UWC Working Paper, HictE Project.*

Bytheway, A. (2000). Jacob's ladder: One vision of information management. Retrieved May 7, 2010, from http://www.imbok.org

Bytheway, A. (1996). Strategic information modelling: some experiences with a new framework. *Journal of Applied Management Studies,5*(1), 17–45.

Bytheway, A. (1994). *Supply chain information management research project*. Cranfield School of Management: Cranfield UK.

Bytheway, A. (1997a). *Why are IS projects always so difficult?*. Cranfield School of Management: Cranfield UK.

Bytheway, A., & Braganza, A. (1997b). *Process based collaboration: strategies, tactics and benefits*. Cranfield School of Management: Cranfield UK.

Bytheway, A. J. (1997c). *Business Process thinking in Supply Chain and Information Management*. Cambridge MA: A seminar for the Center for Transportation Studies, MIT.

Bytheway, A., & Lambert, R. (1998) Organisational competencies for harnessing IS/IT. Retrieved May 7, 2010, from http://www.imbok.org/docs/CompetenciesGoodPracticeGuide.pdf.

Bytheway, A., & Strumpfer, C. (Eds.). (2005). *Proceedings CIDC 2006 Community Informatics for developing countries*. Cape Town: The Information Society Institute.

Bytheway, A., & Taswell, J. (2006). Information Management in the Property Industry: A Case Study of alignment of Business Needs and IT Opportunities. *CPUT Digital Knowledge*.

Bytheway, A. J. (1999). Guest Editor's Introduction: Successful software projects and how to achieve them. *IEEE Software, 16*(3), 0015–0017.

Bytheway, A. J., & Hearn, G. (1999) *Academic CS/IS infrastructure in South Africa: An exploratory stakeholder perspective*. Cape Town, University of the Western Cape. Retrieved May 5, 2013, from http://www.uwc.ac.za.

Edwards, C., Ward, J., & Bytheway, A. (1995). *The essence of information systems* (2nd ed.). Hemel Hempstead: Prentice Hall.

Mitrovic, Z., & Bytheway, A. J. (2011). Servicing adequacy in e-Government: small business development services in Cape Town. *The African journal of Information and Communication* (11), 40–54.

A. Bytheway, *Investing in Information*,
DOI 10.1007/978-3-319-11909-0

Index

A. Bytheway, *Investing in Information*,
DOI 10.1007/978-3-319-11909-0

MIX
Papier aus verantwortungsvollen Quellen
Paper from responsible sources
FSC® C105338

If you have any concerns about our products,
you can contact us on
ProductSafety@springernature.com

In case Publisher is established outside the EU,
the EU authorized representative is:
Springer Nature Customer Service Center GmbH
Europaplatz 3, 69115 Heidelberg, Germany

Printed by Libri Plureos GmbH
in Hamburg, Germany